Batsford Chess Library

Essential Chess Openings

Jon Speelman and Raymond Keene

An Owl Book
Henry Holt and Company
New York

Library of Congress Catalog Card Number: 92-54269

ISBN 0-8050-2430-1 (An Owl Book: pbk.)

Henry Holt books are available at special discounts for
bulk purchases for sales promotions, premiums,
fund-raising, or educational use. Special editions or
book excerpts can also be created to specification.

For details contact: Special Sales Director,
Henry Holt and Company, Inc., 115 West 18th Street,
New York, New York 10011.

First American Edition—1992

Printed in the United Kingdom
Recognizing the importance of preserving the written
word, Henry Holt and Company, Inc., by policy, prints
all of its first editions on acid-free paper. ∞

10   9   8   7   6   5   4   3   2   1

Advisor: R. D. Keene GM, OBE
Technical Editor: Andrew Kinsman

Contents

Symbols

+	Check
++	Double check
!	Good move
!!	Excellent move
?	Bad move
??	Blunder
!?	Interesting move
?!	Dubious move
±	Small advantage for White
∓	Small advantage for Black
±	Clear advantage for White
∓	Clear advantage for Black
+−	Winning advantage for White
−+	Winning advantage for Black
=	The position is equal
∞	The position is unclear
⧜	With counterplay
△	With the idea of
1−0	White wins
0−1	Black wins
½−½	Draw
Ch	Championship
(ol)	Olympiad
corr	Correspondence
(ct)	Candidates
(izt)	Interzonal
(zt)	Zonal
(m)	Match

How to Use This Book

This book has been specifically designed for the school, club, county or tournament player, and those who wish to upgrade their opening skills against a chess computer. It is especially valuable for players who wish to progress up to the level of obtaining a World Chess Federation (FIDE) rating. FIDE publishes its twice a year rating list starting at the rating of 2000 (175 on the British Chess Federation equivalent), so any dedicated enthusiast now has a published world ranking within his or her grasp. This book aims to help the reader to reach that level.

Follow these steps:

i) Play through the main line in bold print running from left to right across the top of each page.

ii) From this point on the vertical columns running from the top of the page downwards show the main alternative branches. These are time-honoured main lines which will always be valid and have been very carefully selected to give the best play on both sides. For any vertical column which has blank spaces in it the reader should assume that the blank spaces correspond to the moves in the vertical column cited on the immediate left.

iii) If you wish to gain further insight into the different possibilities and nuances of the main branches, sub-variations are indicated at the appropriate places by lower case lettering such as *(a)*, *(b)* etc.

The book is easily portable, no variation strays from the main page and it is written in easy to understand algebraic notation, a full explanation of which is given overleaf. Particularly important positions are illustrated by a diagram, indicated by [Dia] in the text.

Algebraic Notation

The moves contained in this book are given in what is known as 'Figurine Algebraic Notation'. This somewhat complicated-sounding term actually describes a very simple way of writing down the moves. Readers familiar with the system can jump ahead to the games themselves, but those who are comparatively new to the game or who have only learned the older English Descriptive notation will find what follows helpful. It is assumed that the reader already knows how to *play* chess.

Each piece is represented by a symbol, called a 'Figurine', as follows:

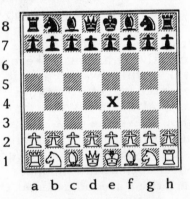

Pawn	♙
Knight	♘
Bishop	♗
Rook	♖
Queen	♕
King	♔

The squares on the chessboard are described by co-ordinates, consisting of a letter followed by a number (see diagram). For instance the square marked with a cross is called 'e4'. This follows exactly the same principle as reading off a reference on an A–Z street guide or road map. Everybody can pick this up in a matter of minutes. There is no mystery to it at all!

CENTRE GAME and DANISH GAMBIT

1 e4 e5 2 d4 exd4

	(1)	(2)	(3)	(4)
3	Qxd4 (a)		c3	
	Nc6		dxc3 (g)	
4	Qe3		Bc4 (h)	
	Nf6		cxb2	
5	Nc3	e5	Bxb2	
	Bb4	Ng4	Nf6 (i)	d5!
6	Bd2	Qe4 (d)	e5	Bxd5
	0-0	d5	d5	Bb4+ (j)
7	0-0-0	exd6+	exf6	Nc3 (k)
	Re8	Be6	dxc4	Bxc3+
8	Bc4	Ba6!? (e)	Qxd8+	Bxc3
	Na5 (b)	Qxd6	Kxd8	Nf6
9	Bd3	Bxb7	fxg7	Qf3
	d5	Qb4+	Bb4+	Nxd5
10	Qg3	Qxb4	Nc3	exd5∓
	dxe4 (c)	Nxb4 (f)	Rg8=	

(a) 3 Nf3 Bc5 4 Nxd4 Nf6 5 Nc3 d5! 6 exd5 0-0 7 Be2 Nxd5 8 Ne4=.

(b) 8 ... d6.

(c) 11 Nxe4 Nxe4 12 Bxe4 Bxd2+ 13 Rxd2 Qe7∓.

(d) 6 Qe2 d6 7 f3 (7 exd6+ Be6∓/∓; 7 h3 Ngxe5! 8 f4 Qh4+ 9 Kd1 Qd4 10 Qe4 Qf2∓) 7 ... Nh6! 8 Bxh6 Qh4+∓.

(e) 8 dxc7 Qd1+! 9 Kxd1 Nxf2+∓.

(f) 11 Na3 Rb8∓ Mieses – Burn, Breslau 1912.

(g) 3 ... d5 4 exd5 Nf6 5 Bb5+ c6 6 dxc6 bxc6 7 Bc4 Bc5 8 Qe2+ Qe7 9 Qxe7+ Kxe7 10 cxd4 Bxd4 11 Nf3±; 3 ... d3 4 Bxd3 Bc5 5 Nf3 d6 6 Qc2=; 3 ... Qe7!? 4 cxd4 Qxe4+ 5 Be3 Bb4+ 6 Nc3 Nf6 7 Nf3 Nd5∞/∓.

(h) 4 Nxc3 Nc6 5 Nf3 - Scotch Gambit Accepted cols 1-2.

(i) 5 ... Bb4+ 6 Kf1! Nf6 7 e5 d5 8 Bb5+ c6 9 exf6 cxb5 10 fxg7 Rg8 11 Qc2±; 5 ... d6 6 f4 Be6 7 Bxe6 fxe6 8 Qb3 Qc8 9 Nf3∞.

(j) 6 ... Nf6 7 Bxf7+ Kxf7 8 Qxd8 Bb4+ 9 Qd2 Bxd2+ 10 Nxd2=.

(k) 7 Kf1 Nf6! 8 Qa4+ Nc6 9 Bxc6+ bxc6 10 Qxb4 Rb8∓.

BISHOP'S OPENING

1 e4 e5 2 Bc4

	(1)	*(2)*	*(3)*	*(4)*
2	Nf6			Bc5 *(f)*
3	d4	d3	f4	c3 *(g)*
	exd4	c6 *(d)*	Nxe4	Nf6
4	Nf3	Nf3	d3	d4
	Nxe4 *(a)*	d5	Nd6	exd4
5	Qxd4	exd5 *(e)*	Bb3	e5
	Nf6! *(b)*	cxd5	e4	d5
6	Bg5	Bb3	dxe4	exf6
	Be7	Bb4+	Nxe4	dxc4
7	Nc3	c3	Bxf7+	Qh5
	Nc6 *(c)*	Bd6	Kxf7	0-0!
8	Qh4	Bg5	Qd5+	Qxc5
	d5	Be6	Ke8	Re8+
9	0-0-0	d4	Qxe4+	Ne2
	Be6∞	e4=	Qe7∓	d3 *(h)*

(a) 4 ... d5 5 exd5 Bb4+ 6 c3 Qe7+ 7 Kf1?! dxc3 8 Nxc3 0-0 9 Bg5 h6 10 Bh4 Bf5=

(b) 5 ... Nc5 6 Bg5! f6 7 Be3 c6 8 Nc3 d5 9 0-0-0 Be7 10 Qh4±.

(c) 7 ... c6 8 0-0-0 d5 9 Rhe1 Be6 10 Bd3 Nbd7∞.

(d) (1) 3 ... d5? 4 exd5 Nxd5 5 Nf3 Nc6 6 0-0 Be7 7 Re1 Bg4!? (7 ... f6 8 d4±) 8 h3 Bxf3 9 Qxf3 Nd4 10 Qg4! 0-0 11 Rxe5 Nf6 12 Qd1+- Larsen - Berger, Amsterdam (izt) 1964.

(2) 3 ... Nc6 4 Nc3 Bb4 5 Nf3 d6 6 0-0 Bxc3 7 bxc3 Bg4 8 h3 Bh5 9 Bb3 Nd7 10 Be3 Qe7 11 Rb1 Nd8 12 Kh2 f6 13 Qd2 Bf7 14 Nh4 g6 15 f4± Larsen - Davies, London (Watson, Farley & Williams) 1989.

(e) 5 Bb3 Bd6 (5 ... dxe4?! 6 Ng5) 6 Nc3 Be6 7 Bg5 Qa5 8 0-0 Nbd7 9 exd5 cxd5 10 Re1± Nunn - Murey, Lucerne (ol) 1982.

(f) 2 ... f5?! 3 d3! Nf6 4 f4 d6 5 Nf3 fxe4 6 dxe4 Bg4 7 fxe5 Bxf3 8 Qxf3 dxe5 9 Qb3±; 2 ... c6 3 d4 d5 4 exd5 cxd5 5 Bb5+ Bd7 6 Bxd7+ Nxd7 7 dxe5 Nxe5±.

(g) 3 Nf3 Nc6 - Giuoco Piano; 3 b4 Bxb4 4 f4 d5! 5 exd5 e4=.

(h) 10 Be3 dxe2=.

VIENNA GAME

1 e4 e5 2 ♘c3

	(1)	(2)	(3)	(4)
2	♘f6			♘c6 (j)
3	♗c4		f4	f4!? (k)
	♘xe4	♘c6	d5	exf4
4	♕h5	d3	fxe5	♘f3 (l)
	♘d6	♗c5 (e)	♘xe4	g5
5	♗b3 (a)	♗g5	♘f3 (g)	d4
	♘c6 (b)	h6	♗e7 (h)	g4!
6	♘b5 (c)	♗h4	d4	♗c4
	g4	d6	0-0	gxf3
7	♕f3	♘a4	♗d3	0-0
	f5	♗b6	f5	d5!
8	♕d5	♘xb6	exf6	exd5
	♕e7	axb6	♗xf6	♗g4
9	♘xc7+	f3!?	0-0	♕e1+
	♔d8	♗e6	♘c6	♗e7
10	♘xa8	♘e2	♘xe4	♗xf4
	b6∞ (d)	d5 (f)	dxe4 (i)	♘xd4∓

(a) 5 ♕xe5+ ♕e7=.

(b) 5 ... ♗e7 6 ♘f3 ♘c6! (6 ... 0-0? 7 h4±) 7 ♘xe5 0-0 8 ♘d5 ♘d4 9 0-0 ♘xb3 10 axb3 ♘e8=.

(c) 6 d4 ♘xd4 7 ♕d5 ♘e6 8 ♕xe5 c6 9 ♘c3 ♕f6∓.

(d) e.g: 11 d3 (11 ♘xb6) 11 ... ♗b7 12 h4 f4 13 ♕f3 ♗h6!∞.

(e) 4 ... ♘a5 5 ♘ge2 ♘xc4 6 dxc4±.

(f) 11 ♗xf6 gxf6 12 exd5 ♗xd5 13 ♘c3! ♗e6 14 ♗xe6 fxe6=/± Larsen - Spassky, Tilburg 1978.

(g) 5 d3 ♗b4!? (5 ... ♘xc3; 5 ... ♕h4+; 6 g3 ♘xg3 7 ♘f3±) 6 dxe4 ♕h4+ 7 ♔e2 ♗xc3 8 bxc3 ♗g4+ 9 ♘f3 dxe4 10 ♕d4 ♗h5 11 ♔e3 ♗xf3 12 gxf3 ♕e1+ 13 ♔f4 ♕h4+ =.

(h) 5 ... ♗b4 6 ♕e2 ♗xc3 7 bxc3 0-0 8 ♕e3 ♘c6 9 ♗d3±.

(i) 11 ♗xe4 ♘xd4 12 ♘g5 ♗f5 13 c3 ♗xg5 14 ♗xg5 ♕xg5 15 ♕xd4 ♗xe4 16 ♕xe4= Spielmann - Reti, Vienna 1922.

(j) 2 ... ♗c5 3 ♗c4 ♘f6 4 d3 d6 5 f4 ♗e6 6 ♗xe6 fxe6 7 ♘f3± Short - Speelman, London (m) 1991.

(k) 3 g3 ♗c5 4 ♗g2 d6 5 ♘ge2 ♘f6 6 0-0!? h5!? Augustin - Nunn, Moscow 1977; 3 ♗c4 ♗c5? 4 ♕g4! g6±.

(l) 4 d4 ♕h4+ 5 ♔e2 d6! 6 ♘f3 ♗g4 7 ♗xf4 f5 8 ♕d2∓.

KING'S GAMBIT ACCEPTED

1 e4 e5 2 f4 exf4 3 ♘f3

	(1)	(2)	(3)	(4)
3	d5		♗e7	
4	exd5		♗c4	♘c3
	♘f6		♘f6 (g)	♘f6 (j)
5	♗b5+ (a)		e5 (h)	e5 (k)
	c6 (b)		♘g4	♘g4
6	dxc6		♘c3	d4
	bxc6	♘xc6	♗h4+ (i)	♘e3
7	♗c4	d4	♔f1	♗xe3
	♘d5 (c)	♗d6	0-0	fxe3
8	♘c3!	0-0 (e)	♕e2	♗c4
	♗e7	0-0	d6	d6
9	0-0	♘bd2	e6	0-0
	0-0	♗g4	♘h6	0-0
10	d4	♘c4	g3	♕d3
	♘b6	♗c7	♗f6−	♘c6
11	♗d3 (d)	c3 (f)		exd6=

(a) (1) 5 c4 c6 6 d4 ♗b4+ 7 ♘c3 cxd5 8 ♗xf4 0-0 9 ♗e2 dxc4 10 ♗xc4 ♘d5! 11 ♗d2 ♘b6∓/∓.
  (2) 5 ♘c3 ♘xd5 6 ♘xd5 ♕xd5 7 d4 ♗e7 8 c4 ♕e4+=.

(b) 5 ... ♗d7 6 ♗c4 ♕e7+ 7 ♗e2 ♘xd5 8 0-0 ♘c6 9 c4 ♘b6 10 d4 g5 11 ♘c3±.

(c) 7 ... ♗d6 8 ♕e2+! ♔f8∞/±.

(d) 11 ... g5 12 ♘e2 ♗e6 13 b3 ♘8d7 14 c4±.

(e) 8 ♕e2+ ♗e6 9 ♘g5!?/?! 0-0 10 ♘xe6 fxe6⯰/±.

(f) 11 ... ♘d5 12 ♕d3± △ 13 ♗xc6 14 ♘ce5.

(g) 4 ... ♗h4+ 5 ♔f1 (5 g3?! fxg3 6 0-0 gxh2+ 7 ♔h1 d5!) 5 ... d5! 6 ♗xd5 ♘f6 7 ♘c3 ♘xd5 8 ♘xd5 f5 9 ♘xh4 ♕xh4 10 ♘xc7+ ♔d8 11 ♘xa8 fxe4 12 ♕e1 ♕h5! 13 ♕xe4 ♖e8 14 ♕f3 ♕e5 15 ♔f2 ♕c5+ 16 ♔f1 ♕e5! 17 ♔f2=; 17 ♕f2 f3!∞.

(h) 5 ♘c3? ♘xe4! 6 ♘e5 ♘g5! 7 d4 d6 8 ♘d3 f3∓/-+.

(i) 6 ... d6 7 d4 dxe5 8 dxe5 ♕xd1+ 9 ♘xd1 ♗e6 10 ♗xe6 fxe6 11 h3± Bronstein - Holmov, Moscow 1961.

(j) 4 ... ♗h4+!? 5 ♔e2 d6 (5 ... d5) 6 d4 ♗g4 7 ♗xf4 ♘c6 Euwe, e.g. 8 ♕d3 ♗g5 9 ♗g3∞/±.

(k) 5 d4 d5 6 ♗d3 dxe4 7 ♘xe4 ♘c6 8 ♗xf4 0-0 9 c3 ♘xe4 10 ♗xe4 ♗h4+!? 11 ♔f1∞/± ♗g4? 12 ♕d3±.

KING'S GAMBIT ACCEPTED

1 e4 e5 2 f4 exf4 3 ♘f3 g5

	(5)	(6)	(7)	(8)
4	h4		Bc4	
	g4		Bg7	g4
5	♘e5	♘g5?!	d4 (h)	0-0
	♘f6 (a)	h6!	h6	gxf3
6	d4 (b)	♘xf7	0-0	♕xf3
	d6	Kxf7	d6	♕f6
7	♘d3	Bc4+ (f)	c3 (i)	e5
	♘xe4	d5	♘c6	♕xe5
8	Bxf4	Bxd5+	g3	Bxf7+!?
	Bg7 (c)	Kg7	g4 (j)	Kxf7
9	c3! (d)	d4	♘h4	d4
	0-0	f3!	f3	♕xd4+
10	♘d2	gxf3	♘d2	Be3
	Re8	♘f6!	♘f6!	♕f6
11	♘xe4 (e)	♘c3 (g)	♘f5∓	Bxf4∞

(a) (1) 5 ... Bg7 6 d4 d6 7 ♘xg4 Bxg4 8 ♕xd4 Bxd4 9 c3 Be5 10 Bxf4 ♘f6 11 ♕f3 ♘bd7 12 g3 ♕e7 13 ♘d2 0-0-0=.

(2) 5 ... d6 6 ♘xg4 ♘f6 7 ♘xf6+ (7 ♘f2?! Planinc - Korchnoi, Moscow 1975) 7 ... ♕xf6 8 ♘c3 c3 9 Be2! Rg8 10 f3± Korchnoi.

(b) 6 ♘xg4 ♕xe4! 7 ♕e2 ♕e7 8 ♘c3 ♘g3 9 ♕xe7+ Bxe7∓.

(c) 8 ... ♕e7 9 ♕e2 Bg7 10 c3 h5 11 ♘d2 ♘xd2 12 Kxd2 ♕xe2+=.

(d) 9 ♘c3 ♘xc3 10 bxc3 c5 11 Be2 cxd4 12 0-0 ♘c6 13 Bxg4 0-0 14 Bxc8 Rxc8 15 ♕g4 Spassky - Fischer, Mar del Plata 1960 15 ... Kh8!∓.

(e) 11 ... Rxe4+ 12 Kf2 ♕f6 13 g3 Bh6 14 ♕d2!∞.

(f) 7 d4 f3! 8 Bc4+ Kg7 - column.

(g) 11 ... Bb4 12 Bc4 gxf3 13 Rg1+ ♘g4 14 ♕xf3 ♕xh4+ 15 Rg3 Rf8 16 Bf4 Be7!∓ △ 17 0-0-0? Rxf4!

(h) 5 h4?! h6 6 d4 d6 7 c3 ♘c6 8 ♕b3 ♕e7 9 0-0 ♘f6 10 hxg5 hxg5 11 ♘xg5 ♘xd4! 12 Bxf7+ Kd8 13 cxd4 ♘xe4∓.

(i) 7 ♘c3 Be6! 8 Bxe6 fxe6 9 e5 ♘c6! Levenfish.

(j) 8 ... Bh3!? 9 gxf4 Bxf1 10 ♕xf1∞.

(k) 10 ♕b3 ♕d7! 11 ♘d2 ♘a5 12 ♕c2 ♘xc4 13 ♘xc4 ♘e7∓ Kaplan - Karpov, Stockholm (World Junior Ch) 1969.

KING'S GAMBIT ACCEPTED

1 e4 e5 2 f4 exf4

	(9)	(10)	(11)	(12)
3	♘f3		♗c4 (e)	♘c3!?
	d6	♘f6	♕f6!	♕h4+
4	d4 (a)	e5	♘c3	♔e2
	g5	♘h5	c6	d5!
5	h4	♗e2! (c)	♗b3 (f)	♘xd5
	g4	d6 (d)	d5	♗g4+
6	♘g1!	0-0	exd5	♘f3
	♗h6 (b)	dxe5	cxd5!	♗d6! (h)
7	♘c3	♘xe5	d4	d4
	c6	♕d4+	♗d6	♘c6
8	♘ge2	♔h1	♘ge2	e5
	♕f6	♘f6	0-0	0-0-0
9	g3	♘d3	0-0	♗xf4
	f3	♗d6	g5	♘ge7
10	♘f4∞	c3±/±	♘xd5 (g)	c4 (i)

(a) 4 ♗c4 h6 5 d4 (5 b3!?) 5 ... g5 6 0-0 - col 7; 4 d3!? g5 5 h4 g4 6 ♘g1! ♗h6 7 ♗d2 ♘d6 8 ♘c3 ♗e6 9 ♘xe2!∞.

(b) (1) 6 ... ♕f6 7 ♘c3 c6 8 e5 dxe5 9 ♘e4 ♕e7 10 dxe5 ♕xe5 11 ♕e2∞.

(2) 6 ... f3!? 7 gxf3 ♗e7 8 ♗e3 ♗xh4+ 9 ♔d2∞.

(c) (1) 5 g4?! fxg3 6 d4 d5 7 ♘g5 g6∓/-+ e.g: 8 ♕f3 f6 9 e6 ♕e7!

(2) 5 ♕e2 ♗e7 6 d4 0-0 7 g4!?/?! fxg3 8 ♕g2 d6 9 hxg3 ♗g4 10 ♘h2 ♘xg3!∓.

(3) 5 ♘c3 d6 6 ♗c4 ♘c6 7 ♕e2 ♗e6! 8 ♗xe6 fxe6=.

(4) 5 d4 d6 6 ♕e2!? d5 7 c4 ♗e6 8 cxd5 ♗xd5 9 ♘c3 ♘c6 10 ♗d2!∞/±.

(d) 5 ... g5!?/?! 6 0-0 ♖g8 7 d4 d5 8 ♕d3 ♖g6 9 ♘h4! ♖h6 10 ♗xh5 ♖xh5 11 ♘f5±.

(e) 3 ♗e2 d5 4 exd5 ♘f6 5 ♘f3 ♗e7 6 0-0 0-0 7 ♘c3 ♘xd5 8 ♘xd5 ♕xd5 9 d4 g5=/±.

(f) 5 ♕f3 d5! 6 exd5 ♗d6 7 d3 ♗g4 8 ♕f2 0-0 9 ♗xf4 ♖e8+ 10 ♔f1 ♗xf4 11 ♕xf4∓; 5 ♕e2 d5! 6 exd5+ ♗e7∓.

(g) 10 ... ♘c6 11 h4! h6 12 hxg5 hxg5 13 ♘ec3= Tartakower.

(h) 6 ... ♘c6!? 7 ♘xc7+ ♔d8! 8 ♘xa8∞.

(i) 10 ... ♗b4! 11 ♗g3 ♕h5 12 ♘xe7+ ♗xe7∓.

KING'S GAMBIT DECLINED

1 e4 e5 2 f4

Falkbeer Counter-Gambit		King's Gambit Declined	
(13)	*(14)*	*(15)*	*(16)*
2 d5		♗c5	
3 exd5 *(a)*		♘f3	
e4 *(b)*		d6	
4 d3		♘c3	c3
♘f6		♘f6	♘f6!
5 ♕e2?! *(c)*	dxe4!	♗c4	fxe5
♗g4	♘xe4	♘c6	dxe5
6 ♘f3 *(d)*	♘f3!	d3	♘xe5
♕xd5	♗c5	♗g4	♕e7
7 ♘bd2	♕e2!	♘a4!	d4
♘c6!	♗f5 *(e)*	♘d4	♗d6
8 dxe4	♘c3	♘xc5	♘f3
♕h5	♕e7	dxc5	♘xe4
9 ♕b5	♗e3	c3!	♗e2
0-0-0	♗xe3	♘xf3+	0-0
10 ♕xh5	♕xe3	gxf3	0-0
♘xh5∓	♘xc3±	♗h5±	c5=

(a) 3 ♘f3 dxe4 4 ♘xe5 ♘d7 5 d4 exd3 6 ♘xd3 ♘gf6 7 ♘c3 ♘b6=.

(b) 3 ... c6!? (Nimzowitsch) 4 ♘c3 exf4 5 ♘f3 ♘f6 6 d4 ♗d6 7 ♕e2+ ♕e7 (7 ... ♔f8 8 ♘e5 cxd5 9 ♗xf4±) 8 ♕xe7+ ♔xe7 9 ♘e5 ♘xd5 10 ♘xd5+ cxd5 11 ♗xf4 f6 12 ♘d3 ♘c6± Tetenbaum - Estrin, Moscow 1959.

(c) (1) 5 ♘d2?! exd3! 6 ♗xd3 ♘xd5 7 ♕e2+ ♕e7! 8 ♘e4 ♘b4 9 ♗b5+ ♘8c6 10 c3 ♗f5!∓.
(2) 5 ♘c3 ♗b4 6 ♗d2 e3 7 ♗xe3 0-0 8 ♗d2 ♗xc3 9 bxc3 ♖e8+ 10 ♗e2 ♗g4 11 ♔f2! (11 c4?? c6 12 dxc6 ♘xc6 13 ♔f1 ♖xe2-+ Schulten - Morphy, New York 1857) 11 ... ♗xe2 12 ♘xe2 ♕xd5∞.

(d) 6 ♕e3 ♘xd5 7 ♕xe4+ ♗e7 8 f5 ♘f6 9 ♕xb7 ♘bd7∞/∓/∓?

(e) 7 ... ♗f2+? 8 ♔d1 ♕xd5+ 9 ♘3d2! f5 10 ♖c3 ♕d4 11 ♘xe4 fxe4 12 c3 ♕e3 13 ♕h5+ (13 ♘xe4±/+-) 13 ... ♔f8 14 ♗c4 ♕xf4 15 ♕d5+- Reti - Breyer, Ressburg 1920; 7 ... f5 8 ♗e3 ♕xd5 9 ♗xc5 ♕xc5 10 ♘c3±.

LATVIAN GAMBIT et al

1 e4 e5 2 ♘f3

	Latvian Gambit (1)	Latvian Gambit (2)	QP Counter Gambit (3)	Philidor Gambit (4)
2	f5!?		d5?!	d6
3	♘xe5	♗c4!? (c)	exd5	d4
	♕f6	fxe4	e4	f5!?
4	♘c4 (a)	♘xe5	♕e2	♗c4 (g)
	dxe4	♕g5?! (d)	♘f6	exd4!
5	♘c3	d4	♘c3	♘g5
	♕g6 (b)	♕xg2	♗e7	♘h6
6	d3	♕h5+	♘xe4	0-0! (h)
	♗b4	g6	♘xd5	♘c6
7	♗d2	♗f7+	d3	exf5
	♗xc3	♔d8	0-0	♗xf5
8	♗xc3	♗xg6	♕d1!	♖e1+
	♘f6	♕xh1+	♖e8	♔d7
9	♗xf6	♔e2	♗e2±	c3
	gxf6	c6 (e)		♕f6
10	dxe4	♘c3		♕b3
	♕xe4+	♘f6		♗e7
11	♘e3±	♕h4! (f)		♘e6 (i)

(a) 4 d4 d6 5 ♘c4 fxe4 6 ♘e3 ♘c6 7 d5 ♘e5 8 ♗e2±.

(b) 5 ... ♕e6 6 ♘e3±/±; 6 d3 exd3+ 7 ♘e3 dxc2 8 ♕xc2±.

(c) 3 exf5 e4 4 ♘e5 ♘f6 5 ♗e2 d6 6 ♗h5+ ♔e7 7 ♘f7 ♕e8 8 ♘c3 ♘xh5 9 ♘d5+ ♔xf7! 10 ♕xh5+ g6 11 fxg6+ ♔g7±; 3 d4 fxe4 4 ♘xe5 ♘f6 5 ♗e2! (TN) d6 6 ♘g4 ♘xg4?! 7 ♗xg4 ♘d7 8 ♘c3 ♘f6 9 ♗xc8 ♕xc8 10 0-0 ♗e7 11 ♗g5!± (Romanishin).

(d) 4 ... d5 5 ♕h5+ g6 6 ♘xg6 hxg6 (6 ... ♘f6 7 ♕e5+ ♗e7 8 ♗b5+ c6 9 ♘xe7 ♕xe7 10 ♕xe7+±) 7 ♕xg6+! ♔d7 8 ♗xd5 ♘f6 9 ♘c3 ♕e7 10 b3! ♘a6? (10 ... ♖h6! 11 ♕f7±) 11 ♗a3!±.

(e) 9 ... ♕xc1 10 ♘f7+ ♔e8 11 ♘xh8+ hxg6 12 ♕xg6+ ♔d8 13 ♘f7+! ♔e7 14 ♘c3 ♕xc2+ 15 ♔e1 d6 16 ♘d5+±.

(f) 11 .. ♗e7 12 ♗g5 ♕xa1 13 ♗xf6 ♗xf6 14 ♕xf6+±.

(g) 4 ♘c3!?; 4 dxe5!? fxe4 5 ♘g5 d5 6 e6 ♗b4+ 7 c3 ♗c5 8 ♘xe4 ♗e7 9 ♘g5± Sax – Kosten, Hastings 1990/91.

(h) 6 ♘xh7? ♘g4!∓.

(i) 11 ... ♖ab8∞/±/± Adorjan – Mestel, Moscow 1977.

PHILIDOR'S DEFENCE

1 e4 e5 2 ♘f3 d6 3 d4

	(1)	(2)	(3)	(4)
3	♘f6			♘d7 (h)
4	♘c3		dxe5	♗c4
	♘bd7	exd4	♘xe4	c6 (i)
5	♗c4	♘xd4 (c)	♘bd2 (f)	0-0
	♗e7	♗e7 (d)	♘c5!? (g)	♗e7
6	0-0 (a)	♗e2 (e)	♘c4	dxe5
	0-0	0-0	d5	dxe5
7	♕e2	0-0	♗g5	♘g5!
	c6	♘c6	♕d7	♗xg5 (j)
8	a4	♘xc6	♘e3	♕h5
	♕c7 (b)	bxc6	c6	g6
9	h3	b3	♘d4	♕xg5
	b6	♘d7	♘e6	♕xg5
10	♖d1±	♗b2=	♗h4±	♗xg5±

(a) 6 ♘g5 0-0 7 ♗xf7+ ♖xf7 8 ♘e6 ♕e8 9 ♘xc7 ♕d8 10 ♘xa8 b5 11 ♘xb5 ♕a5+ 12 ♘c3 ♘xe4 13 0-0 ♘xc3∓ Sozin; 6 dxe5 dxe5 7 ♗xf7+ ♔xf7 8 ♘g5+ ♔g8 (8 ... ♔g6!?) 9 ♘e6 ♕e8 10 ♘xc7 ♕g6 11 ♘xa8 ♕xg2 12 ♖f1 ♘c5 13 ♕e2 ♗h3∞/= 14 ♗e3 ♕xf1+ 15 ♕xf1 ♗xf1 16 ♔xf1 ♔f7 17 ♘c7 ♘fxe4!

(b) 8 ... ♕e8!? △ ... ♗d8-b6.

(c) 5 ♕xd4 ♗e7 6 ♗g5 0-0 7 0-0-0 ♘c6 8 ♕d2 h6=.

(d) 5 ... g6!? 6 ♗f4 (6 g3; 6 ♗e2) 6 ... ♗g7 7 ♕d2 0-0 8 0-0-0∞/±/=.

(e) (1) 6 ♗f4 0-0 7 ♕d2 d5 8 e5?! (8 ♘db5) 8 ... ♘h5 9 ♗g3 c5 10 ♘b3 d4 11 ♘e4 ♕d5∓ Jurtaev - Antoshin, Frunze 1979.
(2) 6 g3 d5 7 e5 ♘g4 8 ♘f3 (8 e6 ♘f6 9 ♗h3 ♘c6!∓ Speelman - Georgadze, Hastings 1979/80) 8 ... ♗c5 9 ♕xd5∞/±(?).

(f) 5 ♗c4 c6 6 exd6 ♘xd6! 7 ♗b3 ♗e7=; 5 ♕d5 ♘c5 6 ♗g5 ♗e7 7 exd6 ♕xd6 8 ♘c3 h6 9 ♗e3 c6 10 ♕xd6 ♗xd6±.

(g) 5 ... ♘xd2 6 ♗xd2 ♗e7 7 ♗d3 ♘c6 8 ♕e2 ♗e6=.

(h) 3 ... exd4 4 ♘xd4 g6 5 ♘c3 cf. note *(d)*.

(i) 4 ... ♘gf6?? 5 dxe5! ♘xe5 (5 ... dxe5 6 ♘g5!+-) 6 ♘xe5 dxe5 7 ♗xf7+ ♔xf7 7 ♕xd8 ♗b4+ 9 ♕d2+-.

(j) 7 ... ♘h6? 8 ♘e6! fxe6 9 ♗xh6 gxh6 10 ♕h5+ ♔f8 11 ♗xe6 ♕e8 12 ♕xh6#.

PETROFF'S DEFENCE

1 e4 e5 2 ♘f3 ♘f6

	(1)	(2)	(3)	(4)
3	d4		♘xe5 (f)	
	exd4	♘xe4	d6 (g)	
4	e5 (a)	♗d3	♘f3	
	♘e4	d5	♘xe4	
5	♕xd4	♘xe5	d4 (h)	
	d5	♗e7 (d)	d5	
6	exd6	0-0	♗d3	
	♘xd6	♘d7! (e)	♕e7	♗d6
7	♘c3 (b)	c4	0-0	0-0
	♘c6	♘xe5	♘c6	0-0
8	♕f4	dxe5	♖e1	c4
	g6!	c6	♗g4	♘f6 (j)
9	♗d3 (c)	cxd5	c4	♘c3
	♗g7	♕xd5	♘f6	dxc4
10	♗e3	♕e2	cxd5	♗xc4
	♗e6	♘c5	♘xd5	♗g4
11	0-0-0	♗c2	♘c3	h3
	♕f6±	♗e6±	0-0 (i)	♗h5±

(a) 4 ♗c4 – Bishop's Opening col 1.

(b) 7 ♗d3 ♘c6 8 ♕f4 g6 9 ♘c3 – column; 7 ♗g5 ♘c6! 8 ♕e3+ ♗e7 9 ♘c3 ♘f5 10 ♗xe7 ♘cxe7=; 7 ... f6!?

(c) 9 ♗d2 ♕e7+! 10 ♗e2 ♗e6 11 0-0-0 ♗g7 12 h4 h6 13 ♖he1 ♕f6=.

(d) 5 ... ♗d6 6 0-0 0-0 7 c4±/± e.g. 7 ... ♘c6 8 cxd5 ♘xd4 9 ♗xe4 ♗xe5 10 ♘c3 ♗f5 11 ♗e3 ♗xe4 12 ♘xe4.

(e) 6 ... 0-0 7 c4 ♘f6 8 ♗g5 ♘bd7 9 ♘c4 dxc4 10 ♗xc4 ♘b6 11 ♗b3±/±.

(f) 3 ♗c4 ♘xe4 4 ♘c3 ♘c6!=; 4 ... ♘xc3 5 dxc3∞/∓.

(g) 3 ... ♘xe4?! 4 ♕e2 ♕e7 5 ♕xe4 d6 6 d4±.

(h) 5 ♕e2 ♕e7 6 d3 ♘f6 7 ♗g5 ♕xe2+ 8 ♗xe2 ♗e7 9 ♘c3=.

(i) 12 ♗e4 ♘f6 13 d5 ♘b4 14 a3 ♘xe4 15 ♖xe4 ♗xf3 16 ♕xf3±.

(j) 8 ... c6 9 cxd5 cxd5 10 ♘c3 ♘xc3 11 bxc3 ♗g4 12 ♖b1 ♘d7 13 h3 ♗h5 14 ♖b5 ♘b6 15 c4 ♗xf3 16 ♕xf3 dxc4 17 ♗c2 ♕d7 18 a4 ♗c7 19 ♖c5 ♗d6 Timman – Anand, Tilburg 1991 20 a5!±.

PONZIANI and SCOTCH GAMBIT DECLINED

1 e4 e5 2 ♘f3 ♘c6

	Ponziani		Scotch Gambit Declined	
	(1)	(2)	(3)	(4)
3	c3 (a)		d4	
	d5	♘f6	cxd4	
4	♕a4!	d4	c3	
	dxe4 (b)	♘xe4	d5	♘f6 (f)
5	♘xe5	d5	exd5	e5
	♕d5	♘e7 (c)	♕xd5	♘e4
6	♘xc6	♘xe5	cxd4	♕e2
	bxc6	♘g6	♘f6 (e)	f5!
7	♗c4	♗d3	♘c3	exf6
	♕d7	♘xe5!	♗b4	d5
8	0-0	♗xe4	♗e2	♘xd4
	♘f6	♗c5	♘e4	♘xd4
9	d3	♕h5	♗d2	cxd4
	exd3	d6	♗xc3	♔f7
10	♗xd3	♗g5	bxc3	fxg7
	♗b7	♗g4	♘xd2	♗b4+
11	♕c2±	♕h4 (d)	♕xd2∓	♔d1 (g)

(a) 3 ♗e2 ♘f6 4 d3 d5 5 ♘bd2 ♗e7=.

(b) 4 ... ♘f6 5 ♘xe5 ♗d6 6 ♘xc6 bxc6 7 d3 0-0 8 ♗e2! ♕e8 9 ♘d2 ♖b8 10 0-0 c5∞/±.

(c) (1) 5 ... ♘b8 6 ♗d3 (6 ♘xe5!? ♗c5 7 ♕g4 0-0∞) 6 ... ♘c5 7 ♘xe5 ♘xd3+ 8 ♘xd3 d6=.

(2) 5 ... ♗c5?! 6 dxc6 ♗xf2+ 7 ♔e2 bxc6? (7 ... d5) 8 ♕a4 f5 9 ♘bd2 0-0 10 ♘xe4 fxe4 11 ♕xe4 ♗b6±.

(d) = Kuijf - Anand, Wijk aan Zee 1990.

(e) 6 ... ♗g4 7 ♗e2 0-0-0 8 ♗e3 ♗b4+ 9 ♘c3 ♘ge7 10 0-0 ♕d7 11 ♖c1=.

(f) 4 ... d3 5 ♗xd3 d6 6 h3 g6 (6 ... ♗c5) 7 ♗g5 ♘f6! 8 ♘bd2 ♗g7= Raaste - Westerinen, Helsinki 1979.

(g) 11 ... ♖e8∞ Levy - Boey, Siegen (ol) 1970.

SCOTCH GAMBIT ACCEPTED and SCOTCH GAME

1 e4 e5 2 Nf3 Nc6 3 d4 exd4

	Scotch Gambit		Scotch Game	
	(1)	(2)	(3)	(4)
4	c3		Nxd4	
	dxc3?! (a)		Nf6	
5	Bc4 (b)		Nxc6 (h)	Bc5
	d6	Nf6 (e)	bxc6	Be3
6	Nxc3	Nxc3	e5 (i)	Qf6
	Nf6 (c)	Bb4	Qe7	c3
7	Qb3	0-0 (f)	Qe2	Nge7
	Qd7	Bxc3	Nd5	Bc4
8	Ng5	bxc3	c4	b6 (l)
	Ne5	d6	Ba6 (j)	0-0
9	Bb5	e5	Nd2 (k)	Bb7
	c6	Nxe5	Nb4!	b4!?
10	f4	Nxe5	Nf3	Nxd4
	Neg4 (d)	dxe5 (g)	c5=	cxd4∞

(a) 4 ... d5; 4 ... Nf6; 4 ... d3 cols 3-4.

(b) 5 Nxc3 Bb4 6 Bc4 Nf6 col 2; 6 ... d6 7 Qb3?! Bxc3+ 8 bxc3 Qd7∓ △ 9 ... Na5.

(c) 6 ... Be6 7 Bxe6 fxe6 8 Qb3 Qc8 9 Ng5 Nd8 10 f4! Be7 11 f5 Bxg5 12 Bxg5 Nf7 13 fxe6 Nxg5 15 Qb5+±.

(d) 11 h3 cxb5 12 hxg4 h6 13 Nxb5 d5! 14 Be3 Nxg4 15 Bd4±.

(e) 5 ... cxb2?! 6 Bxb2 Bb4+ 7 Nc3 Nf6 8 Qc2 d6 9 0-0-0 0-0 10 e5 Ng4 11 Nd5 Bc5 12 exd6 cxd6 13 h4 h6 14 Ng5!

(f) 7 e5 d5 8 Bb3 Ne4 9 0-0 Bxc3 10 Bxd5 Bf5 11 bxc3 Nxc3 12 Bxc6+ bxc6 13 Qe1∞ Keres.

g) 11 Qb3 Qe7 12 Ba3 c5 13 Bb5+∞ Kf8!?; 13 ... Bd7 14 Bxd7+ Qxd7 15 Bxc5 Qc6 △ ... 0-0-0.

(h) 5 Nc3 - Four Knights.

(i) 6 Bd3 d5 7 Qe2 Be7 8 0-0 0-0 9 Bf4 Rb8=.

(j) 8 ... Nb6 9 Nd2 Qe6 10 b3 a5 11 Bb2 Bb4 12 a3 Bxd2+ 13 Qxd2± Kasparov - Karpov, World Ch (16), Lyons 1990.

(k) 9 b3 0-0-0 10 g3 Re8 11 Bb2 f6 12 Bg2 fxe5 13 0-0∞ Kasparov - Karpov, World Ch (14), Lyons 1990.

(l) 7 ... 0-0 8 0-0 Bb6 9 Nc2!± Kasparov - Short, Linares 1992.

SCOTCH FOUR KNIGHTS and FOUR KNIGHTS GAME

1 e4 e5 2 Nf3 Nc6 3 Nc3 Nf6

Scotch Four Knights		Four Knights Game	
(1)	(2)	(3)	(4)
4 d4		Bb5	
exd4		Bb4	Nd4 (g)
5 Nd5 (a)	Nxd4	0-0	Nxd4 (h)
Qe7 (b)	Bb4	0-0	exd4
6 Bf4 (c)	Nxc6	d3	e5
d6	bxc6	d6	dxc3
7 Nxd4	Bd3	Bg5	exf6
Nxd5	d5	Bxc3	Qxf6!
8 exd5	exd5	bxc3	dxc3
Nxd4	cxd5	Qe7	Qe5+
9 Qxd4	0-0	Re1	Qe2
Bf6–	0-0	Nd8	Qxe2+
10	Bg5	d4	Bxe2–
	c6 (d)	Ne6	
11	Qf3	Bc1	
	Bd6– (e)	c5 (f)	

(a) Belgrade Gambit

(b) 5 ... Nxe4!? 6 Qe2 f5 7 Ng5 d3 8 cxd3 Nd4 9 Qh5+ g6 10 Qh4 c6 11 dxe4 cxd5 12 exd5 Qa5+ =.

(c) 6 Bc4 0-0 7 0-0 d6 8 Nxd4 Nxd4 9 Qxd4 Nxd5 10 Bxd5 Bf6 11 Qd3 a5 13 a4 c6=.

(d) 10 ... Be6= e.g. 11 Nb5 c5 12 c3 Ba5 13 Qa4 Bb6 14 Qh4 h6 15 Bxh6 gxh6 16 Qxh6 c4 17 Qg5+ – draw.

(e) 11 ... Be7 12 Rae1 h6 13 Bxh6 gxh6 14 Qe3 d4 15 Qxh6 Qd6 16 Qg5+ Kh8 17 Rxe7 Qxe7 18 Qh6+ – draw; 11 ... Bd6 12 Bxf6; 12 Rae1!? Rb8 13 Nd1 Bd7 (13 ... Rb4!?) 14 b3 Re8=.

(f) 12 Bf1=/± Nc7!? △ 13 d5?! b5!; 12 ... Rd8 13 d5 Nc7!? (13 ... Nf8 Trifunovic – van Scheltinga, Amsterdam 1950).

(g) 4 ... Bc5?! 5 0-0 0-0? (5 ... d6) 6 Nxe5! Nxe5 7 d4 Bd6 8 f4 Nc6 9 e5±.

(h) (1) 5 Nxe5?! Qe7 6 Nf3 (6 f4 Nxb5 7 Nxb5 d6 8 Nf3 Qxe4+ 9 Kf2 Ng4+ 10 Kg3 Qg6 11 Nh4 Qh5 12 h3 Qxb5 13 hxg4 g5!∓) 6 ... Nxb5 7 Nxb5 Qxe4+∓;

(2) 5 Ba4 Bc5 6 Nxe5 0-0 7 Nd3 Bb6 8 e5 Ne8 9 Nd5 d6 10 Ne3 Qg5!∞ Short – Timman, Linares 1992.

GIUOCO PIANO, EVANS GAMBIT, HUNGARIAN DEFENCE

1 e4 e5 2 Nf3 Nc6 3 Bc4

	Giuoco Piano (1)	Evans Gambit (2)	(3)	Hungarian (4)
3	Bc5			Be7
4	d3	b4!?		d4
	Nf6	Bxb4 (d)		d6
5	c3	c3		d5
	d6	Ba5	Bc5 (g)	Nb8
6	b4	d4	d4	Bd3
	Bb6	d6 (e)	exd4	Nf6
7	a4	Qb3	0-0	c4
	a6 (a)	Qd7	d6	0-0
8	0-0	dxe5	cxd4	h3
	0-0	Bb6!	Bb6	Nbd7
9	Bg5 (b)	0-0	Nc3 (h)	Nc3
	Bg4	Na5	Bg4	Ne8
10	Nbd2	Qb4	Bb5	0-0
	h6 (c)	Nxc4 (f)	Kf8 (i)	g6±

(a) 7 ... a5!? 8 b5 Ne7 9 Nbd2 Ng6 10 0-0 0-0 11 Bb3 d5 12 Ba3± Ljubojevic - Korchnoi, Brussels 1987.

(b) 9 Ra2!? △ Bb3, Nbd2 (Na3)-c4.

(c) 11 Bh4 g5 12 Bg3 Nh5 13 Ba2 Qf6 14 Nc4 Ba7 15 Ne3 Miles - Keogh, Amsterdam (zt) 1978 15 ... Bxf3! 16 Qxf3 Qxf3 17 gxf3 Ne7∞; 11 Bxf6± Miles.

(d) 4 ... Bb6 5 a4! a6 6 Nc3 Nf6 7 Nd5 Nxd5 8 exd5 e4 9 dxc6 0-0 10 Bb2! exf3 11 Qxf3 Qe7+(!)∞/±.

(e) 6 ... exd4 7 0-0 Nge7! 8 cxd4 (8 Ng5 d5 9 exd5 Ne5) 8 ... d5 9 exd5 Nxd5 10 Ba3 Be6 11 Bb5 Bb4 12 Bxc6 bxc6 13 Bxb4 Nxb4 14 Qa4 Qd6= Pachman.

(f) 11 Qxc4 dxe5 12 Nxe5 Qe6∓ Keres.

(g) 5 ... Be7 6 d4 Na5 7 Nxe5 (7 Bxf7+!? Kxf7 8 Nxe5+ Kf8 9 Qf3+ Nf6 10 g4 d6 11 g5 dxe5 12 gxf6 Bxf6 13 dxe5 Nc6 14 exf6 Qxf6 15 Qg3 Qe5= Inkiov - Minev, Bulgaria 1977) 7 ... Nxc4 8 Nxc4 d5 9 exd5 Qxd5 10 Ne3 Qd8 11 0-0=.

(h) 9 d5!? Na5 10 Bb2 Ne7 11 Bd3 0-0 12 Nc3 Ng6 13 Ne2 c5 14 Qd2 f6∓/∞!?; 9 h3 Nf6 10 Re1 h6 11 Ba3 0-0∞.

(i) 11 Be3 Nge7 12 a4 a5 13 Bc4 Bh5 14 Rb1 Nb4 15 d5=.

GIUOCO PIANO

1 e4 e5 2 ♘f3 ♘c6 3 ♗c4 ♗c5

	(1)	(2)	(3)	(4)
4	c3			d3
	♘f6		♕e7	♘f6
5	d4		d4	♘c3
	exd4		♗b6 (e)	d6
6	cxd4		0-0	♗g5
	♗b4+		d6	h6 (h)
7	♘c3	♗d2	a4	♗xf6
	♘xe4	♗xd2+ (c)	a6	♕xf6
8	0-0	♘bxd2	h3	♘d5
	♗xc3! (a)	d5	♘f6	♕d8
9	d5	exd5	♖e1	c3
	♗f6!	♘xd5	0-0 (f)	♘e7
10	♖e1	♕b3	b4	♘e3
	♘e7∓/∓ (b)	♘ce7 (d)	♔h8 (g)	0-0-/± (i)

(a) 8 ... ♘xc3 9 bxc3 d5! 10 cxb4 dxc4 11 ♖e1+ ♘e7 12 ♗g5 f6 13 ♕e2 ♗g4 (13 ... fxg5 14 ♕xc4) 14 ♗f4 ♔f7± Keres; 9 ... ♗xc3? 10 ♗a3! d5 11 ♗b5 ♗xa1 12 ♖e1+ ♗e6 13 ♕a4 ♖b8 14 ♘e5+- Corte - Bolbochan, Panama 1946.

(b) 11 ♖xe4 d6 12 ♗g5 ♗xg5 13 ♘xg5 0-0 14 ♘xh7 - draw; 13 ... h6! 14 ♗b5+ (14 ♕e2 hxg5 15 ♖ae1 ♗e6! 16 dxe6 f6∓; 14 ♕h5 0-0 15 ♖ae1 ♘f5∓) 14 ... ♗d7 15 ♕e2 ♗xb5 16 ♕xb5+ ♕d7 17 ♕e2 ♔f8! 18 ♘xf7!? ♔xf7 19 ♖e1 ♘g8! 20 ♖e6 ♔f8! 21 f4 ♘f6 22 ♖e7 ♖e8!-+ Barczay - Portisch, Budapest 1969.

(c) 7 ... ♘xe4!? 8 ♗xb4 ♘xb4 9 ♗xf7+ ♔xf7 10 ♕b3+ d5 11 ♘e5+ ♔e6! 12 ♕xb4 c5 13 ♕a3! cxd4 14 ♘f3± Keres.

(d) 11 0-0 0-0 12 ♖fel c6 13 a4 ♕b6! 14 a5 ♕xb3 15 ♘xb3 ♖d8 16 ♘c5 ♖b8 17 ♘e5 ♔f8=.

(e) 5 ... exd4? 6 0-0! d3 7 e5!±.

(f) 9 ... h6!? 10 ♗e3 g5!?

(g) 11 ♖a2!? ♘g8± △ ... f6; 11 ... exd4? 12 a5 ♗a7 (12 ... ♗e6!) 13 cxd4 ♘xb4 14 ♖ae2±.

(h) 6 ... ♘a5!? 7 ♗b3! ♘xb3 8 axb3 ♗e6 9 ♘a4! (9 0-0 ♗b6=) 9 ... h6 (9 ... ♗b6 10 ♗xf6!±) 10 ♗h4 ♗g4 11 ♘xc5 dxc5 12 h3 ♗xf3 13 ♕xf3 ♕d6 14 ♗xf6 ♕xf6 15 ♕xf6 gxf6 16 ♖a5!± Hug - Barle, Paris 1975.

(i) 10 ... c6?! 11 d4 cxd4 12 ♘xd4±.

TWO KNIGHTS DEFENCE

1 e4 e5 2 ♘f3 ♘c6 3 ♗c4 ♘f6

	(1)	*(2)*	*(3)*	*(4)*
4	♘g5			0-0!?
	d5		♗c5	♘xe4
5	exd5		♗xf7+! *(h)*	♘c3
	♘a5	♘d4	♔e7	♘xc3!?
6	♗b5+ *(a)*	c3	♗d5	dxc3
	c6	b5	♖f8 *(i)*	f6
7	dxc6	♗f1!	♘f3	♘h4
	bxc6	♘xd5	d6	g6
8	♗e2 *(b)*	♘e4 *(f)*	c3	f4
	h6	♘e6 *(g)*	♗g4	f5
9	♘f3 *(c)*	♗xb5+	♗xc6	♘f3
	e4	♗d7	bxc6	e4
10	♘e5	♗xd7+	d4	♘g5
	♗d6 *(d)*	♕xd7±	♗d6±	♗c5+ *(j)*

(a) 6 d3 h6 7 ♘f3 e4 8 dxe4?! ♘xc4 9 ♕d4 ♘d6 10 ♘c3 ♘fxe4! 11 ♘xe4 ♕e7 12 0-0 ♘xe4 13 ♖e1 f5 14 ♘d2 ♕c5!∓.

(b) 8 ♕f3?! ♖b8! 9 ♗xc6+?! (9 ♗d3 h6∓) 9 ... ♘xc6 10 ♕xc6+ ♗d7 11 ♘f3 0-0∓.

(c) 9 ♘h3!? (Steinitz) 9... ♗c5 10 0-0 0-0 11 d3 ♘b7∞.

(d) (1) 11 f4 exf3 12 ♘xf3 0-0 13 d4 ♖e8 14 0-0 c5 15 0-0 cxd4 16 ♔h1 ♗c5 17 c3 dxc3 18 ♘xc3=; 11 ... ♕c7 12 0-0 0-0 13 ♘c3 ♗f5!? (13 ... ♗xe5±) 14 a3 ♘d5! 15 b4 ♘b7 △ ... ♖ae8∞.

(2) 11 d4 exd3 12 ♘xd3 ♕c7 13 b3 0-0 14 ♗b2 ♘d5 15 h3 ♗f5∞/=; 11 ... ♕c7!? 12 f4 0-0 13 c3 c5 14 ♘a3 ♖d8 15 ♘b5 ♕b6 16 ♘xd6 ♖xd6∞/±.

(e) 5 ... ♘xd5? 6 d4! (6 ♘xf7!? - 'Fried Liver') 6 ... ♗b4+ 7 c3 ♗e7 8 ♘xf7 ♔xf7 9 ♕f3+ ♔e6 10 ♕e4!±; 5 ... b5 6 ♗f1! ♘xd5 7 ♗xb5 ♗d7 8 d4±.

(f) 8 cxd4∞.

(g) 8 ... ♕h4 9 ♘g3 ♗g4 10 f3 e4 11 fxg4 ♗d6 12 ♗xb5+ ♔d8 13 0-0 exf3 14 ♖xf3 ♖b8 15 a4!±.

(h) 5 ♘xf7 ♗xf2+!∞.

(i) 6 ... ♕e8 7 d3 d6 8 ♗xc6 bxc6 9 ♗e3 ♕g6 10 ♘f3 ♗xe3 11 fxe3 ♕xg2 12 ♖g1 ♕h3 13 ♖xg7+ ♔d8 14 ♖g3± Anand - Beliavsky, Linares 1991.

(j) 11 ♔h1 ♕f6 12 b4!? ♗b6∞; 12 ♕d5!?; 12 ♗f7+?!/?

TWO KNIGHTS DEFENCE

1 e4 e5 2 Nf3 Nc6 3 Bc4 Nf6

	(5)	(6)	(7)	(8)
4	d4			d3
	exd4			Be7
5	0-0		e5	0-0
	Bc5	Nxe4	d5 (f)	0-0
6	e5	Re1	Bb5	Nbd2
	d5!? (a)	d5	Ne4	d6
7	exf6	Bxd5	Nxd4	c3
	dxc4	Qxd5	Bc5 (g)	Na5
8	Re1+	Nc3	0-0 (h)	Bb5
	Be6	Qa5	0-0	a6
9	Ng5	Nxe4	Bxc6	Ba4
	Qd5 (b)	Be6	bxc6	b5
10	Nc3	Neg5 (d)	Be3	Bc2
	Qf5	0-0-0	Bd7	c5
11	Nce4	Nxe6	f3	a4±
	0-0-0	fxe6	Ng5	
12	g4 (c)	Rxe6 (e)	f4 (i)	

(a) 6 ... Ng4 7 Bf4 0-0 8 h3 Nh6 9 Bg5 Be7 10 Bxh6 gxh6 11 Bd5 d6 12 Bxc6 bxc6 13 Nxd4 dxe5 14 Nxc6 Qd6!= Bernstein - Llorens, Barcelona 1945.

(b) 9 ... Qxf6? 10 Nxe6 fxe6 11 Qh5++-.

(c) 12 ... Qe5 13 Nxe6 fxe6 14 Bg5 (14 fxg7 Rhg8 15 Bh6 d3 16 c3 d2!? 17 Re2 Rd3! 18 Nxc5 Qxc5 19 Rxd2 Ne5∞) 14 ... g6! 15 f7 Be7 16 f4 Qg7 17 Bxe7 Nxe7 18 Ng5 d3 19 Nxe6 Qxf7 20 Nxd8 Rxd8∞ Keres.

(d) 10 Bd2 Bb4 11 Nxd4 Nxd4 12 c3 Be7 13 cxd4 Qd5 14 Bb4 Bxb4 15 Qa4+ Qc6 16 Qxb4 0-0-0 17 Nc3 Qb6 18 Qxb6 axb6=.

(e) 12 ... Bd6 13 Bg5 Rdf8 14 Bh4 (14 Qe2 Kd7! 15 Bh4 Re8 16 Re1 Qxe1+ 17 Nxe1 Rxe6=) 14 ... Qh5 15 Bg3=.

(f) 5 ... Ng4!? 6 Qe2 (6 0-0 d6! 7 exd6 Bxd6 8 Re1+ Kf8∓) 6 ... Qe7 7 Bf4 f6 8 exf6 Nxf6 9 Nbd2 d6=.

(g) 7 ... Bd7 8 Bxc6 bxc6 9 0-0 Be7 10 f3 Nc5∞/±.

(h) 8 Nxc6?! Bxf2+ 9 Kf1 Qh4 10 Nd4+ c6 11 Nf3 Ng3+ 12 Kxf2 Ne4++!∓.

(i) 12 ... Ne4 13 Nd2±.

RUY LOPEZ

1 e4 e5 2 Nf3 Nc6 3 Bb5

	Old Steinitz Defence (1)	Bird's Defence (2)	Cordel's Defence (3)	(4)
3	d6	Nd4 (d)	Bc5	
4	d4	Nxd4	c3!? (f)	f5
	Bd7	exd4	Nf6	d4
5	Nc3	0-0	d4	fxe4
	Nf6 (a)	c6	exd4	Bxc6
6	Bxc6!	Ba4	e5 (g)	dxc6
	Bxc6	Nf6	Ne4	Nfd2
7	Qd3!	Re1 (e)	0-0	Bd6 (j)
	exd4 (b)	d6	d5	dxe5
8	Nxd4	d3	exd6 (h)	e3
	Bd7	Be7	0-0	fxe3 (k)
9	Bg5	c3	dxc7	Bc5
	Be7	dxc3	Qf6!	Qh5+
10	0-0-0	Nxc3±	Bxc6	g6 (l)
	0-0 (c)		bxc6 (i)	

(a) 5 ... exd4 6 Nxd4 Nf6 (6 ... g6) 7 Bxc6 bxc6 8 Qd3 Be7 9 Bg5 0-0 10 0-0-0±

(b) 7 ... Nd7(!) 8 Be3 exd4 9 Bxd4 f6 10 Nh4±/±.

(c) 11 f4 Ne8 12 Bxe7 Qxe7 13 Nd5 Qd8 14 g4!±.

(d) (1) 3 ... Nge7!? Cozio 4 0-0 Ng6 5 d4 exd4 6 Nxd4 Bc5 7 Nb3 Bb6± Dzindzihashvili - Larsen, Tilburg 1978; 5 c3 d6 6 d4 Bd7 7 Ng5!?± Zukertort - Anderssen, 1867.

(2) 3 ... g6 4 c3 d6 5 d4 Bd7 6 0-0 Bg7 7 dxe5!?±.

(e) 7 d3; 7 c3!?

(f) 4 0-0 Nd4 (4 ... Nf6!? col 8 note [k]) 5 Nxd4 Bxd4 6 c3 Bb6 7 d4 c6 8 Ba4! d6 9 Na3 Nf6 10 Bg5 h6 11 Bxf6±.

(g) 6 0-0 Nxe4 7 cxd4 Bb6 8 Qc2 Nd6 9 Re1+ Ne7 △ ... h6!∞.

(h) 8 Nxd4!? 0-0 9 f3 Ng5 10 Be3 f6!?; 10 ... Ne6±.

(i) 11 cxd4 Bb6! 12 Re1 Bf5 13 Nc3 Rfe8 14 Nxe4 Bxe4 15 Bg5 Qd6 16 Bd8 Bxc7 17 Bxc7 Qxc7± Euwe.

(j) 7 ... Qg5? 8 dxc5 Qxg2 9 Qh5+ Kd8 10 Rf1 Bh3 11 Qxe5±.

(k) 9 Ne4!?

(l) 11 Qf3 Qh4+ 12 g3 Qh3 13 Ne4 Bg4 14 Qf1±.

RUY LOPEZ
Berlin Defence

1 e4 e5 2 Nf3 Nc6 3 Bb5 Nf6 4 0-0

	(5)	*(6)*	*(7)*	*(8)*
4	Nxe4			d6 *(k)*
5	d4		Re1	d4
	Nd6	Be7	Nd6	Bd7
6	dxe5 *(a)*	dxe5 *(f)*	Nxe5	Nc3
	Nxb5	0-0 *(g)*	Be7	exd4 *(l)*
7	a4(!) *(b)*	Be3	Bd3	Nxd4
	d6!	a6	0-0	Be7
8	e6!?/!	Bc4	Nc3	Bf4
	fxe6! *(c)*	d6	Nxe5	Nxd4
9	axb5	Bd5	Rxe5	Qxd4
	Ne7	Qf5	Bf6!	0-0
10	Nc3	Nd4	Re3	Rad1
	Nf5!? *(d)*	Nxd4	g6 *(i)*	Bxb5
11	Nd4!	Qxd4	b3	Nxb5
	Qf6?!	dxe5	Bd4!	a6
12	b6!!± *(e)*	Qxe5 *(h)*	Re2 *(j)*	Nc3±/±

(a) 6 Bxc6 dxc6 7 dxe5 Nf5 8 Qxd8+ Kxd8 9 Nc3 h6! 10 Ne2 g5 11 h3 Bg7 12 Rd1+ Bd7 13 g4 Ne7 14 Ng3±.

(b) 7 c4 d6! 8 e6 fxe6 9 cxb5 Ne7 10 Re1 Nf5 11 Ng5 Be7=.

(c) 8 ... Bxe6? 9 axb5 Ne5 10 Nd4± △ 11 f4.

(d) 10 ... Ng6 11 Ng5±; 10 ... e5!?

(e) 12 b6!! cxb6 (12 ... Nxd4? 13 Rxa7+-) 13 Nb5 Qd8 14 Ne4±.

(f) 6 Qe2 Nd6 7 Bxc6 bxc6 8 dxe5 Nb7 (8 ... Nf5!? 9 Qe4±) 9 Re1 0-0 10 Nc3±.

(g) 6 ... d5 7 Nc3!? (7 Nd4) 7 ... Nxc3 8 bxc3 0-0 9 Re1 Bg4? (9 ... Na5) 10 h3 Bh5 11 Rb1±.

(h) 12 ... Nd6 13 Nc3! Bxc2 14 Rac1 Bg6 15 Rfd1⩲/±.

(i) 10 ...Ne8? 11 Bxh7+ Kxh7 12 Qh5+ Kg8 13 Rh3+-.

(j) 12 ... b6= Sherwin – Bisguier, USA Ch 1962/3.

(k) 4 ... Bc5!? 5 Nxe5 Nxe4 6 Qe2 Nxe5 7 d4 Be7 8 dxe5 Nc5 9 Rd1! 0-0 10 Bc4±.

(l) 6 ... Be7 7 Re1 exd4! (7 ... 0-0 8 Bxc6 △ 9 dxe5±/+-) 8 Nxd4 0-0=; 6 ... Be7 7 dxe5 Nxe5 (7 ... dxe5 8 Re1 Bd6 9 Bg5±) 8 Bxd7+ Nexd7 9 Nd4 0-0 10 Nf5 Re8 11 Qf3 Bf8±.

Schliemann Defence and Schliemann Deferred

1 e4 e5 2 Nf3 Nc6 3 Bb5

	(9)	(10)	(11)	(12)
3	f5!?			a6
4	Nc3!?		d3	Ba4
	fxe4	Nd4 (d)	fxe4 (g)	f5?!
5	Nxe4	Ba4 (e)	dxe4	d4
	d5!? (a)	Nf6	Nf6	exd4 (h)
6	Nxe5	exf5	0-0	e5!?
	fxe4	Bc5	d6	Bc5
7	Nxc6	0-0	Nc3	0-0
	Qd5!? (b)	0-0	Be7	Nge7
8	c4	Nxe5	Qd3	Bb3!
	Qd6	d5	Bg4	d5
9	Nxa7+	Ne2	h3	exd6
	Bd7	Qe7	Bxf3	Qxd6
10	Bxd7+ (c)	Nxd4 (f)	Qxf3±	Re1 (i)

(a) 5 ... Nf6 6 Qe2!? (6 Nxf6+ Qxf6 7 Qe2 Be7 8 Bxc6
bxc6 9 Qxe5 Qf7 10 d3 d6 11 Qf4∞/±) 6 ... d5! 7 Nxf6+ gxf6
8 d4 Bg7 9 dxe5 0-0 10 Bxc6 bxc6 11 e6 Re8 12 0-0 Rxe6∞.

(b) (1) 7 ... bxc6? 8 Bxc6+ Bd7 9 Qh5+ Ke7 10 Qe5+ Be6 11
f4 exf3 12 0-0 Rb8 13 d4 Nf6 14 d5±.

   (2) 7 ... Qg5?! 8 Qe2 Nf6 9 f4 Qh4+ (9 ... Qxf4 10
Ne5+ c6 11 d4 Qh4+ 12 g3 Qh3 13 Bc4 Be6 14 Bg5 0-0-0 15
0-0-0 Bd6=) 10 g3 Qh3 11 Ne5+ c6 12 Bc4 Bc5 13 d3 Ng4 14
Nf7 Bf2+ 15 Kd1 e3 16 Qf3 Nh6 (16 ... Nf6 17 f5! Nd5!∞
Tseitlin) 17 Qe4+ Kf8 18 Bxe3! Bxe3! 19 Qxe3 Nxf7 20 Re1
Qd7! Tseitlin.

   (c) 10 ... Qxd7 11 Qh5+ g6 (11 ... Kd8 12 Nb5 Nf6 13 Qe2
Bc5 14 0-0 Rf8 15 d4!±) 12 Qe5+ Kf7 13 Nb5! c6 14 Qd4!

   (d) 4 ... Nf6 5 exf5 Bc5 6 0-0 0-0 7 Nxe5 △ d4±.

   (e) 5 Bc4; 5 exf5!?

   (f) 10 ... Qxe5 11 Nf3 Qxf5 12 d4±.

   (g) 4 ... Nf6 5 exf5 Bc5 6 0-0 0-0 7 Nxe5 △ d4±.

   (h) 5 ... fxe4?!/? 6 Nxe5 Qh4 7 0-0 Bd6?!/? (7 ... Nf6±)
8 f4 exf3 9 Nxf3 Qh5 10 c3 Nf6 11 Qe1+ Ne7 12 Bb3±.

   (i) 10 ... h6 11 Nbd2 b5 12 a4 Bb7?! 13 axb5 axb5 14 Rxa8+
Bxa8 15 Re6 Qd7 16 Qe1!± Taimanov.

RUY LOPEZ
Exchange Variation

1 e4 e5 2 Nf3 Nc6 3 Bb5 a6 4 Bxc6 dxc6 (a)

	(13)	(14)	(15)	(16)
5	0-0			d4
	f6		Bg4 (f)	exd4
6	d4		h3	Qxd4
	exd4	Bg4	h5 (g)	Qxd4
7	Nxd4	dxe5 (c)	d3 (h)	Nxd4
	c5	Qxd1	Qf6	Bd6
8	Nb3 (b)	Rxd1	Nbd2!? (i)	Nc3
	Qxd1	fxe5	Ne7	Ne7
9	Rxd1	Rd3	Re1	Be3
	Bg4!?	Bd6! (d)	Ng6	f6
10	f3	Nbd2	d4	0-0
	Bd7	Nf6	Bd6	Bd7
11	Nc3	Nc4	hxg4	Rad1
	0-0-0	0-0	hxg4	c5
12	Be3±	Nfxe5 (e)	Nh2 (j)	Nde2=

(a) 4 ... bxc6?! 5 0-0 d6 (5 ... Qf6!?) 6 d4 f6 7 c4±.

(b) 8 Ne2 Qxd1 9 Rxd1 Bd7 10 Rbc3 0-0-0 11 Bf4 Ne7 12 Bg3 Nc6 13 Nd5 Ne5=.

(c) 7 c3!? exd4 8 cxd4 Qd7 9 Be3 0-0-0 10 Nbd2±.

(d) 9 ... Bxf3 10 gxf3! Nf6 11 Nbd2 b5 12 a4 Bd6 13 Nb3± Adorjan - Tringov, Varna 1972.

(e) 12 ... Be2 13 Re3 Bxc4 14 Nxc4 Bc5 15 Rf3 Nxe4 16 Be3 Rxf3 17 gxf3 Nd6= ½-½ Kasparov - Tal, USSR Ch 1978.

(f) (1) 5 ... Qd6!? 6 d3 f6 7 Be3 Be6 8 Nbd2±.

(2) 5 ... Bd6 6 d4 exd4 7 Qxd4 f6 8 Be3 (8 e5!) 8 ... Ne7 9 Nbd2 Be6 10 Rad1 0-0= Hort - Westerinen, BRD 1979.

(3) 5 ... Ne7!? 6 d4 exd4 7 Nxd4 g6 8 Nb3! Qxd1 9 Rxd1± Hort - Nunn, Hastings 1977/78.

(g) 6 ... Bxf3 7 Qxf3±/±.

(h) 7 c3 Qd3 8 hxg4 (8 Re1!? Bxf3 9 Qxf3 Qxf3 10 gxf3∞/=) 8 ... hxg4 9 Nxe5 Bd6! 10 Nxd3 Bh2+=.

(i) 8 Be3!? Bxf3 9 Qxf3 Qxf3 10 gxf3 Bd6 11 Kg2 Ne7 12 Rg1 f6 13 Kf1 g5 14 Nd2 Kf7=.

(j) 12 ... Rxh2 13 Qxg4(!) Qh4 14 Qxh4 Rxh4 15 Nf3 Rh5 16 c3!± Pinter - Perenyi, Budapest 1972.

RUY LOPEZ
Steinitz Defence Deferred

1 e4 e5 2 Nf3 Nc6 3 Bb5 a6 4 Ba4 d6 5 c3

	(17)	(18)	Siesta Variation (19)	(20)
5	Bd7		f5!?	
6	d4		exf5	
	Nge7	g6	Bxf5	
7	Bb3 (a)	0-0 (e)	0-0	d4
	h6	Bg7	Bd3	e4
8	Nbd2 (b)	dxe5 (f)	Re1	Ng5
	Ng6	dxe5	Be7	d5
9	Nc4	Be3	Re3 (h)	f3
	Be7	Nf6	e4	e3 (l)
10	Ne3	Nbd2	Ne1	f4
	Bg5	0-0 (g)	Bg5	Nf6
11	Nxg5! (c)	Bc5	Rh3 (i)	0-0
	hxg5	Re8	Nf6 (j)	Bd6
12	g3!± (d)	Bc2±	Nxd3∞ (k)	Bxe3 (m)

(a) 7 Be3 Ng6 8 h4 Bg4 9 Bxc6+ bxc6 10 Nbd2 Be7=.

(b) (1) 8 Nh4 exd4 9 cxd4 Nxd4! 10 Qxd4 Nc6 11 Qd5=.

(2) 8 Be3 g5!? (8 ... Ng6) 9 Bxg5 hxg5 10 Nxg5 Nd5! 11 Nxf7∞.

(c) 11 0-0 Bxe3=; 11 Nd5 Bxc1 12 Rxc1 0-0=.

(d) 12 ... Nce7 (12 ... Bh3? 13 Qf3! △ 13 ... Qf6? 14 Qxf6 gxf6 15 Nd5+-) 13 Bd2 f6±.

(e) 7 dxe5 dxe5 8 Bg5 Be7=; 7 Be3.

(f) 8 d5 Nb8 9 c4±.

(g) 10 ... Qe7 11 b4 b6 12 Bb3 0-0 13 Qc2±.

(h) 9 Bc2! Bxc2 10 Qxc2 Nf6 11 d4±; 9 Qb3!? Rb8∞/=.

(i) 11 Nxd3? Bxe3 12 Nb4 Bxf2+-+ Adams - Piket, Wijk aan Zee 1991.

(j) 11 ... Nh6!? 12 Nxd3 exd3 12 Qe1+!? (13 Rxd3 0-0∞) 13 ... Kd7 14 Rxd3 Qe8 15 Qf1∞/±.

(k) 12 ... exd3 13 Rxd3 0-0 14 Rh3 Qe7 15 Na3 Rae8 16 Nc2∞/=.

(l) 9 ... h6!? 10 fxe4 hxg5 11 exf5 Bd6∞.

(m) 12 ... 0-0 13 Nf3 Ng4 14 Bc1 Na5 15 h3 Nf6 16 Bc2 Bxc2 17 Qxc2 c5∞ Mihaljlov - Vitolins, corr 1977.

RUY LOPEZ
Steinitz Defence Deferred

1 e4 e5 2 ♘f3 ♘c6 3 ♗b5 a6 4 ♗a4 d6

	(21)	(22)	(23)	(24)
5	0-0	d4!?	♗xc6	c4
	♗g4 (a)	b5	bxc6	♗g4
6	h3	♗b3	d4	♘c3
	h5 (b)	♘xd4 (f)	f6	♘f6 (l)
7	d4 (c)	♘xd4	♗e3	h3
	b5	exd4	♘e7 (j)	♗xf3
8	♗b3	c3 (g)	♘c3	♕xf3
	♘xd4	dxc3 (h)	♘g6	♗e7
9	hxg4	♘xc3!? (i)	♕d3	d3
	hxg4	♘f6	♗e7	♘d7
10	♘g5	0-0	h4	0-0
	♘h6	♗e7	h5	♘c5
11	g3!? (d)	♖e1	0-0-0 (k)	♗xc6+
	c6 (e)	0-0∞		bxc6=

(a) 5 ... ♗d7 6 c3 g6 7 d4 - col 18; 5 ... ♗d7 6 d4!?

(b) 6 ... ♗h5 7 c3 ♘f6 8 ♖e1±.

(c) 7 d3; 7 ♗xc6+ bxc6 8 d4 ♕f6 9 ♘bd2 ♗e6!?; 9 ... ♗d7!?=.

(d) 11 c3 ♘xb3 12 axb3 ♗e7 13 ♕d5 ♖c8 14 ♖xa6 ♗xg5 15 ♕c6+∞; 11 f4 d5! 12 ♗xd5 ♗c5 13 ♗e3 ♕d6 14 b4 ♗b6 15 c4∞.

(e) 11 ... ♕d7 12 ♗d5 c6 13 c3±; 11 ... c6 12 f4 ♗e7 13 ♗e3 ♘xb3 14 cxb3! (14 axb3 d5±) 14 ... d5 15 ♕c2 ♖c8 16 ♗c5!∞/±/± Kapengut - Vorotnikov, Vilnius 1977.

(f) 6 ... exd4? 7 ♗d5 ♗b7 8 ♘xd4±/±.

(g) 8 ♗d5 ♖b8 9 ♗c6+ ♗d7 10 ♗xd7+ ♕xd7 11 ♕xd4=; 8 ♕xd4?? c5 9 ♕d5 ♗e6 10 ♕c6+ ♗d7 11 ♕d5 c4-+.

(h) 8 ... ♗b7 9 cxd4 ♘f6 10 f3 ♗e7 11 0-0 0-0±.

(i) 9 ♕d5 ♗e6 10 ♕c6+ ♗d7 11 ♕d5=.

(j) 7 ... ♖b8 8 b3 g6 9 ♕d2±; 7 ... g6 8 ♕d2±.

(k) (1) 11 ... ♗e6 12 d5!? cxd5 13 ♘xd5 ♕c8?! 14 ♘d2 ♗d8 15 ♘c4 ♘e7 16 ♘db6! ♗xc4 17 ♘xc4±.

(2) 11 ... ♗d7 12 ♕c4 ♕c8 13 dxe5 fxe5 14 ♘g5 ♗xg5 15 hxg5±.

(3) 11 ... a5!?

(l) 6 ... g6!? 7 d3 ♗g7 8 ♘d5 h6 9 b4 ♔f8=.

RUY LOPEZ

1 e4 e5 2 ♘f3 ♘c6 3 ♗b5 a6 4 ♗a4 ♘f6 (a)

Archangel Variation

	(25)	(26)	(27)	(28)
5	0-0		d3	♗xc6 (g)
	b5		d6	dxc6
6	♗b3		c3	d3 (h)
	♗b7 (b)		g6	♗d6
7	d4 (c)	♖e1	♘bd2	♘bd2
	♘xd4	♗c5	♗g7	c5
8	♘xd4 (d)	c3	♘f1	♘c4
	exd4	0-0	0-0	♘d7
9	e5	d4	♘g3	a4!?
	♘e4	♗b6	h6	b6
10	c3!	♗g5	0-0	0-0
	d3	d6	0-0	0-0=
11	♗e3!? (e)	a4 (f)	♗c2=	

(a) 4 ... b5 5 ♗b3 ♘a5 6 0-0 d6 7 d4 exd4 8 ♘xd4 ♗b7 (8 ... c5? 9 ♗d5±) 9 ♘d2 c5 10 ♕e1 ♘xb3 11 ♘xb3±.

(b) 6 ... ♗e7 7 a4 b4 8 ♕e2 0-0 9 a5! d6 10 c3 h6±.

(c) (1) 7 d3 ♗d6!? 8 c3 0-0 9 ♘bd2∞ Watson – Hellers, Oslo 1991.

(2) 7 c3 ♘xe4 8 d4 ♘a5 9 ♗c2 exd4 10 b4 ♘c4 11 ♗xe4 ♗xe4 12 ♖e1 d5 13 ♘xd4 c5! 14 bxc5 ♗xc5 15 f3 0-0 16 fxe4 dxe4∞ Nunn – Beliavsky, Amsterdam 1990.

(d) 8 ♗xf7+!? ♔xf7 9 ♘xe5+ ♔g8 10 ♕xd4 c5=/∓.

(e) 11 ♕xd3 ♘c5=; 11 ♕f3 ♕e7=; 11 ♗e3!? c5 12 c4 d5 13 ♕xd3! dxc4 14 ♕xd8+ ♖xd8 15 ♗c2 ♗e7 16 a4! b4 17 ♗d1 ♖d5 18 f3 ♖d3 19 ♗c1 ♘g5 20 ♗e2±.

(f) 11 ... h6 12 ♗h4 g5!? (12 ... exd4 13 axb5 axb5 14 ♖xa8 ♗xa8 15 cxd4 ♖e8 16 ♘c3 g5 17 ♕d2!!∞) 13 ♗g3 (13 ♘xg5 hxg5 14 ♗xg5∞ Diaz – Rodriguez, Cienfuegos 1983) 13 ... ♖e8 14 h4 ♘a5 15 hxg5! ♘xb3 16 gxf6 ♘xa1 17 ♗h4!∞/= Mestel – Beliavsky, Mexico 1978.

(g) (1) 5 ♘c3 b5 6 ♗b3 ♗e7 7 ♗d5? (7 0-0 col. 39) 7 ... b4 8 ♗xc6 dxc6 9 ♘e2 ♘xe4 10 ♘xe5 ♗d6 11 ♘c4 0-0 ∓.

(2) 5 ♕e2 b5 6 ♗b3 ♗e7 cols 41–42; 5 ♕e2 ♗e7!? 6 c3 d6 7 0-0 0-0 8 d4±/=.

(h) 6 ♘c3 ♗g4 7 h3 ♗h5 8 d3 ♘d7 9 ♗e3 ♗b4=.

RUY LOPEZ
Open Variation

**1 e4 e5 2 ♘f3 ♘c6 3 ♗b5 a6 4 ♗a4 ♘f6 5 0-0 ♘xe4
6 d4 b5 7 ♗b3 d5 8 dxe5 ♗e6 9 c3**

	(29)	(30)	(31)	(32)
9	♗c5		♗e7	
10	♘bd2		♘bd2	♗e3
	0-0		0-0	0-0
11	♗c2		♗c2	♘bd2
	♗f5	f5!?/?! (d)	f5 (h)	♗g4
12	♘b3	♘b3	♘b3	♘xe4
	♗g6 (a)	♗g4	♕d7	dxe4
13	♘fd4	♘fd4	♘fd4	♕d5!
	♗xd4	♘xd4	♘xd4	exf3
14	cxd4 (b)	♘xd4	cxd4	♕xc6
	a5	♗xd4 (e)	a5	fxg2
15	♗e3	♕xd4! (f)	f3!	♕xg2
	a4 (c)	c5 (g)	a4 (i)	♕d7 (j)

(a) 12 ... ♗g4 13 h3 ♗h5 14 g4! ♗g6 15 ♗xe4 dxe4 16 ♘xc5 exf3 17 ♕f4± Karpov - Korchnoi, World Ch (14) 1978.

(b) 14 ♘xd4 ♕d7 15 ♘xc6 ♕xc6 16 ♗e3 ♖fe8 17 f3? ♘xc3!∓ Speelman - Timman, London (6) 1989.

(c) 16 ♘c1 a3 17 b3 f6 18 exf6 ♕xf6 19 ♘e2 ♕e7!? 20 ♖c1 ♘b4∞ Speelman - Timman, London (4) 1989.

(d) 11 ... ♘xf2 12 ♖xf2 f6 13 exf6 ♗xf2+ 14 ♔xf2 ♕xf6 15 ♘f1 ♘e5 16 ♗e3 ♖ae8 17 ♗c5 ♘xf3 18 gxf3 ♖f7∞ Ivanchuk - Yusupov, Linares 1990.

(e) 14 ... ♕d7 15 f3 ♘c5±.

(f) 15 cxd4 f4 16 f3 ♘g3 17 hxg3 fxg3 18 ♕d3 ♗f5 19 ♕xf5 ♗xf5 20 ♗xf5 ♕h4 21 ♗h3 ♕xd4+ 22 ♔h1∞/=.

(g) 16 ♕d1 ♘g5!?±/±; 16 ... f4 17 f3 ♘g5 (17 ... ♘g3? 18 hxg3 fxg3 19 ♕d3 ♗f5 20 ♕xf5+-) 18 a4±.

(h) 11 ... ♘xd2 12 ♕xd2 f6 13 exf6 ♗xf6 14 ♘g5 ♗xg5 15 ♕xg5 ♕xg5 16 ♗xg5±.

(i) 16 fxe4 axb3 17 ♗xb3 fxe4 18 ♗e3±/= Grünfeld - Tal, Riga (izt) 1979.

(j) 16 ♗h6! gxh6 17 f3 ♗c5+ 18 ♔h1 ♖ae8±.

RUY LOPEZ
Open Variation

1 e4 e5 2 ♘f3 ♘c6 3 ♗b5 a6 4 ♗a4 ♘f6 5 O-O ♘xe4 6 d4 *(a)*

	(33)	(34)	(35)	(36)
6	b5			♗e7 *(k)*
7	♗b3			♕e2
	d5			f5
8	dxe5			dxe5
	♗e6			O-O
9	♕e2 [Dia]		♘bd2	♖d1
	♗e7! *(b)*		♘c5	♕e8
10	♖d1		c3	♗b3+
	O-O *(c)*		d4 [Dia]	♔h8
11	c4		♘g5!? *(g)*	♘bd2
	bxc4		♕xg5 *(h)*	♘c5
12	♗xc4	♗c5	♕f3	♘c4
	♕d7 *(d)*	♗e3	O-O-O! *(i)*	♕h5
13	♘c3	♗xe3	♕xc6 *(j)*	♖e1
	♘xc3	♕xe3	♕xe5	f4
14	bxc3	♕b8	♘f3	♗d2
	f6	♗b3	♕d5!!	♕g6±
15	exf6	♕b6 *(f)*	♗xd5	
	♗xf6 *(e)*		♗xd5–	

(Column 1)

(Column 3)

(a) 6 Rel Nc5 7 Nxe5 Be7 8 Bxc6 dxc6 9 d4 Ne6 10 Be3 0-0=.

(b) (1) 9 ... Na5 10 Rd1 Bc5 11 Be3 Bxe3 12 Qxe3 c5 13 c3 0-0 14 Ne1! c4 15 Bc2 f5 16 exf6 Qxf6 17 f3 Nd6±;

(2) 9 ... Bc5 10 Be3 Qe7 11 Rd1 Rd8 12 Nbd2 Bxe3 13 Qxe3 Nc5 14 c3±;

(3) 9 ... Nc5 10 Rd1 Nxb3 11 axb3 Qc8 12 c4! Nb4 13 cxb5 axb5 14 Rxa8 Qxa8 15 Bd2!±.

(c) 10 ... Nc5 11 Be3 0-0 12 c4 bxc4 13 Bxc4 Na5 14 Bxd5! Bxd5 15 Nc3 Bxf3 16 Qxf3 Qe8 17 b4±/±.

(d) 11 ... dxc4?! 12 Rxd8 Rfxd8 13 Nc3 Nxc3 14 bxc3 h6!±.

(e) 16 Bg5 (16 Ng5!?) 16 ... Kh8! 17 Bxf6 Rxf6 18 Ng5±/=.

(f) 16 Qe2 (16 Qe1!?) 16 ... Rad8 17 Nc3 Nxc3 18 bxc3±.

(g) 11 Bxe6 Nxe6 12 cxd4 Ncxd4 13 Ne4 Be7 14 Be3 Nf5 15 Qc2 0-0 16 Rad1 Nxe3 17 fxe3 Qc8 18 Nd4 Nxd4 19 exd4 Qe6= Short – Yusupov, Montpellier 1985.

(h) 11 ... dxc3 12 Nxe6 fxe6 13 bxc3 Qd3 14 Nf3 Qxd1 15 Bxd1±/± Karpov – Korchnoi, World Ch (10) 1978.

(i) (1) 12 ... Kd7 13 Bd5 Bxd5 14 Qxd5+ Bd6! 15 Nc4 Qf5 16 Nb6+!!±.

(2) 12 ... Bd7 13 Bxf7+ Ke7 14 Bd5 Nxe5 15 Qe2 d3 16 Qe1 c6 17 f4 Qh6 18 Bf3!± P Wolff – Flear, London 1990.

(j) 13 Bxe6+ fxe6 14 Qxc6 Qxe5 15 b4!± Timman – Smyslov, Germany 1979.

(k) (1) 6 ... exd4!? 7 Rel d5 8 Nxd4 Bd6 9 Nxc6 Bxh2+ 10 Kh1! Qh4 11 Rxe4+ dxe4 12 Qd8+ Qxd8 13 Nxd8+ Kxd8 14 Kxh2±.

(2) 6 ... b5 7 Bb3 Be7 8 Nxe5 Nxe5 9 dxe5 Bb7 10 Qg4 0-0 11 f3 Ng5=.

1 e4 e5 2 ♘f3 ♘c6 3 ♗b5 a6 4 ♗a4 ♘f6 5 0-0 ♗e7

	(37)	*(38)*	*(39)*	*(40)*
6	d4		♘c3	d3
	exd4		b5	b5!? *(g)*
7	e5	♖e1	♗b3	♗b3
	♘e4	0-0 *(b)*	d6	d6
8	♘xd4 *(a)*	e5	♘d5 *(d)*	a4
	0-0	♘e8	♘xe4 *(e)*	♘a5
9	♘f5!?	♗f4 *(c)*	d4	axb5
	d5	b5	♗b7	♘xb3
10	♗xc6	♗b3	♖e1	cxb3
	bxc6	d5	♘a5	0-0
11	♘xe7+	c3	dxe5	♘c3
	♕xe7	♗f5	♘xb3	♗b7
12	♖e1	♘xd4	axb3	bxa6
	♖e8	♘xd4	dxe5	♗xa6
13	f3	cxd4	♖xe4	♕c2
	♘d6!	c6	♗xd5	c6∞
14	♗f4=/∓	♘c3±	♖xe5 *(f)*	

(a) 8 b4?!/? 0-0 9 a3 b5 10 ♗b3 d5 11 h3?! ♗b7 12 ♗b2 a5!∓ Lein - Vasyukov, Tirachiapallis 1978.

(b) 7 ... b5 8 e5 ♘xe5 9 ♖xe5 d6 10 ♖e1 bxa4 11 ♘xd4 ♗d7 12 ♕f3 0-0 13 ♘c6 ♗xc6 14 ♕xc6=.

(c) 9 c3!? dxc3 10 ♘xc3 d6 11 ♘d5?! (11 exd6=) 11 ... ♘xe5 12 ♘xe5 dxe5 13 ♖xe5 ♗d6 14 ♗g5 f6∓ Zapata - Karpov, Brussels 1986.

(d) 8 d3 ♘a5 9 ♘e2 0-0=; 8 a4 b4 9 ♘d5 ♘a5 10 ♗a2 ♘xd5 11 ♗xd5 c6 12 ♗a2 c5=.

(e) 8 ... ♗b7 9 ♘xe7 ♕xe7 10 d3 ♘a5 11 ♘h4 g6 12 f4 ♘xb3 13 axb3 ♘xe4 14 ♘f3 ♘c5 15 fxe5 dxe5 16 d4! ♘e4 17 dxe5 ♕c5 18 ♕d4± Keres — Smejkal, Tallinn 1971 - 17 ... 0-0= Keres △ ... f6.

(f) 14 ... ♗xf3 15 ♕xf3 0-0=.

(g) 6 ... d6=.

RUY LOPEZ

1 e4 e5 2 Nf3 Nc6 3 Bb5 a6 4 Ba4 Nf6 5 0-0 Be7

	Worral Attack		Delayed Exchange Deferred	
	(41)	*(42)*	*(43)*	*(44)*
6	Qe2		Bxc6	
	b5		dxc6	
7	Bb3		Nc3	d3 *(g)*
	0-0		Bg4!? *(e)*	Nd7
8	c3		h3	Nbd2
	d5!		Bh5	0-0
9	exd5!?	d3(!)	g4	Nc4
	Bg4	Re8	Bg6 *(f)*	f6
10	dxc6 *(a)*	Re1	Nxe5	Nh4
	e4	Bb7	Nxe4	Nc5
11	d4	Nbd2	Re1	Qf3 *(h)*
	exf3	Qd7 *(b)*	Nxc3	Ne6
12	gxf3	Nf1	bxc3	Nf5
	Bh5	Rad8	0-0	Nd4
13	Bf4	Bg5 *(c)*	Rb1±	Nxe7+
	Re8∞	Na5 *(d)*		Qxe7 *(i)*

(a) 10 h3 Bxf3 11 Qxf3 e4 12 Qe2 Na5 13 Bc2 Qxd5∓.

(b) 11 ... Bf8 12 a3 Na5 13 Ba2 c5 14 b4 Short - Hübner, Manila (izt) 1990 14 ... cxb4! 15 cxb4 Nc6 16 Bb2 a5!=.

(c) 13 Ng3!?

(d) 14 Bc2 dxe4 15 dxe4 Nc4 16 Ne3 Nxe3! (16 ... Nxb2? 17 Nxe5 Qe6 18 Nxf7± Keres - Geller, Budapest 1952) 17 Qxe3 Ng4=.

(e) 7 ... Nd7 8 d4 exd4 (8 ... f6) 9 Qxd4 0-0 10 Rd1±/±.

(f) 9 ... Nxg4!?

(g) 7 Qe1 Nd7 8 d4 exd4 9 Nxd4 Nc5! 10 Qe3 0-0=.

(h) 11 Nf5 Bxf5 12 exf5 Qd5 13 Qg4 Rad8 14 Re1 Rfe8 15 Nd2 Qf7∞ Tal - Dorfman, Lvov 1984.

(i) 14 Qd1 Be6 15 Ne3=(/±) Mestel - Lein, Hastings 1979/80.

RUY LOPEZ
Marshall Attack

1 e4 e5 2 ♘f3 ♘c6 3 ♗b5 a6 4 ♗a4 ♘f6 5 O-O ♗e7
6 ♖e1 b5 7 ♗b3 O-O 8 c3 d5 9 exd5

	(45)	(46)	(47)	(48)
9	♘xd5			e4?!
10	♘xe5			dxc6
	♘xe5			exf3
11	♖xe5		♘f6?! (d)	d4!
	c6!		d4	fxg2 (g)
12	d4		♗d6	♕f3
	♗d6 [Dia]		♖e1	♗e6
13	♖e1 (a)		♘g4	♗f4
	♕h4		h3	♗d5
14	g3		♕h4	♗xd5
	♕h3		♕f3 [Dia]	♘xd5
15	♗e3		♘xf2? (e)	♗g3±
	♗g4		♗d2!	
16	♕d3	f5?	♗b7	
	♖ae8!	f4	♕xb7	
17	♘d2	♖ae8 (c)	♘d3 (f)	
	♖e6 (b)			

(column 1)

(column 3)

(a) 13 ♖e2 ♗g4 14 f3 ♗h5 15 ♗xd5 cxd5 16 ♘d2 f5 17 ♕b3 ♗f7 18 ♘f1 f4 19 ♗d2 ♕d7 20 ♖ae1 a5 21 a3 a4 22 ♕d1 ♗g6 23 ♗c1 ♖f7 24 h3 ♗f5 25 ♘h2 h5 26 ♖f2 ♖af8∞ Kamsky - Ivanchuk, Linares 1991.

(b) 17 ... ♕h5 18 ♘f1 ♖e6 19 ♗d1 f5 20 ♗xg4 ♕xg4 21 ♗d2 ♖g6 22 ♔g2 f4 23 f3 ♕h5 24 g4 ♕h4 25 ♖e2 ♖xg4+∓ Ivanchuk - Adams, Terrassa 1991; 17 ... ♖e6:

(1) 18 a4 f5! 19 ♕f1 ♕h5 20 f4 bxa4 21 ♖xa4 ♖b8 (21 ... g5?!/?) 22 ♗f2! (22 ♗xd5+ cxd5 23 ♕g2 ♕e8 24 ♕xd5 ♔h8 25 ♔f2 g5∞) 22 ... ♖xe1 23 ♕xe1 ♖e8 24 ♕f1 ♖e2 25 ♖xa6! ♗h3 26 ♕d1 ♗g4 27 ♕f1 ♗h3 (Rohde - Beliavsky, Alicante 1978) 28 ♖xc6!?; 28 ♕d1=.

(2) 18 c4!? ♗f4!; ((i) 19 ♕f1!? ♘xe3 20 ♕xh3 ♗xh3 21 cxb5 ♘c2! 22 ♗xe6 fxe6 23 gxf4 ♘xa1 24 ♖xa1 ♖xf4= (Plachetk(a); (ii) 19 cxd5? ♖h6 20 ♕e4 ♕xh2+ 21 ♔f1 f5! 22 d6+ ♔h8 23 ♕xc6 ♖xd6! 24 ♕b7 ♗xe3 25 ♖xe3 f4!-+; (iii) 19 ♗xf4 ♘xf4 20 ♕f1 ♘e2+ 21 ♔h1 ♕h6∞/∓.

(3) 18 ♕f1 ♕h5 19 ♕g2?! (19 a4!∞) 19 ... ♖fe8 20 ♘f1 f5 21 ♗d2 ♗f3 22 ♗d1 ♖e2!∓ Kuzmin - Beliavsky, USSR (zt) Lvov 1978.

(c) 18 ♘d2 g5 19 ♕f1 ♕h5 20 ♕g2! gxf4 21 ♗xd5+ ♔h8 22 ♗xf4 ♗xf4 23 ♗xc6! ♗e3+ 24 ♔h1 ♗h3 (24 ... ♖e6 25 ♗f3!+- Fischer) 25 ♕e2! ♗g4 26 ♗xe8 ♖xe8 27 ♕xe3± (Boleslavsky).

(d) (1) 11 ... ♘f4 12 d4 ♘g6 13 ♖h5! ♗b7 14 ♕g4! ♖e8 15 ♗e3±.

(2) 11 ... ♘b6!? 12 d4 ♗d6 13 ♗g5 ♕d7 14 ♖e1 ♗b7 15 ♘d2±.

(e) 15 ... h5 16 ♗e3±.

(f) 18 ♖e2 ♖ae8 19 ♕f3 ♖xe2 20 ♕xe2 ♕g3 21 ♕f3! ♕h2+ 22 ♔f1 ♕h1+ 23 ♔e2+-.

(g) 11 ... ♗g4 12 gxf3! ♗h5 13 ♗f4 ♗d6 14 ♗e5±; 11 ... ♗d6 12 ♕xf3 ♖e8 13 ♗d2 ♗g4 14 ♕d3±.

RUY LOPEZ

**1 e4 e5 2 Nf3 Nc6 3 Bb5 a6 4 Ba4 Nf6 5 O-O Be7
6 Re1 b5 7 Bb3 O-O**

	(49)	(50)	(51)	(52)
8	d4			a4
	d6		Nxd4!?	Bb7
9	c3		Bxf7+ (f)	d3
	Bg4		Rxf7	d6
10	d5	Be3	Nxe5	Bd2 (h)
	Na5	exd4	Rf8!	b4
11	Bc2	cxd4	Qxd4	c3
	c6 (a)	Na5 (d)	Bb7	bxc3
12	h3	Bc2	Nc3	Nxc3
	Bxf3!? (b)	Nc4	Qe8!?	Na5
13	Qxf3	Bc1	Bg5 (g)	d4
	cxd5	c5	b4!	Nxb3
14	exd5	b3	Ne2!	Qxb3
	Nc4	Nb6	Nxe4	Rb8
15	Nd2	Nbd2	Bxe7	Qc2
	Nb6	Rc8	Qxe7	d5
16	Nf1 (c)	Bb2 (e)	Ng3±	exd5 (i)

(a) 11 ... Qc8(!) 12 Nbd2 c6 13 dxc6 Qxc6 14 h3 Be6=; 12 h3 Bd7 13 Nbd2 c6 14 dxc6 Qxc6 15 Nf1=/±.

(b) (1) 12 ... Bh5? 13 dxc6 Qc7 14 Nbd2 Nxc6 15 Nf1 Rac8?! 16 Ng3±.

(2) 12 ... Bd7 13 Nxe5 dxe5 14 d6 Be6 15 dxe7 Qxe7 16 Qf3±.

(3) 12 ... Bc8 13 dxc6 Qc7 14 Nbd2 Qxc6 15 Nf1 Nc4=.

(c) (1) 16 ... Nbxd5 17 Ng3 Nc7 18 a4 bxa4 19 Bxa4±.

(2) 16 ... Ne8 17 a4 bxa4 18 Bxa4 Nxa4 19 Rxa4 f5 20 c4 Qc8±.

(3) 16 ... Qc7!? 17 Ng3 g6 18 Bh6 Rfc8 19 Rad1 Nfd7 20 Nf5 Bf8 21 Re4 Qd8! 22 Rg4 Rc4!∓.

(d) 11 ... d5!? 12 e5 Ne4 13 Nc3 Nxc3 14 bxc3 Na5 15 Bc2=.

(e) 16 ... cxd4 17 h3 Bh5 18 Bxd4=.

(f) 9 Nxd4 exd4 10 e5 Ne8 11 c3 dxc3 12 Nxc3∞.

(g) 13 Nd3(!)± △ Bf4.

(h) 10 Nc3 Na5 11 Ba2 b4 12 Ne2 c5 13 Ng3 Rb8=.

(i) 16 ... exd4 17 Nxd4 Nxd5 18 Nf5 Bf6=.

RUY LOPEZ
Closed Variation

**1 e4 e5 2 Nf3 Nc6 3 Bb5 a6 4 Ba4 Nf6 5 0-0 Be7
6 Re1 b5 7 Bb3 d6 8 c3 0-0 9 h3**

	(53)	*(54)*	*(55)*	*(56)*
9	h6		Bb7	Nd7 *(f)*
10	d4		d4	d4
	Re8		Re8	Bf6 *(g)*
11	Nbd2		Nbd2 *(d)*	a4
	Bf8		Bf8	Na5 *(h)*
12	Nf1		a4	Bc2
	Bd7	Bb7	h6	Nb6
13	Ng3	Ng3	Bc2	axb5
	Na5	Na5	exd4	axb5
14	Bc2	Bc2	cxd4	Nbd2
	Nc4	Nc4	Nb4	c5
15	Nh2!?	b3	Bb1	dxc5
	c5	Nb6	c5	dxc5
16	b3	a4	d5	Qe2
	Nb6	d5 *(b)*	Nd7	c4
17	f4	Nxe5	Ra3	Nh2!?
	cxd4	dxe4	f5	Qc7
18	cxd4	Nxe4!?	Nh2	Ng4
	Qc8! *(a)*	Nxe4 *(c)*	Nf6 *(e)*	Bxg4=

(a) 18 ... Qe7 19 Nf3±; 18 ... Qc8 19 Qe2 (19 Nf3 Bxh3!) 19 ... Qc3 20 Be3 exd4 21 Bf2 Rac8= Tal - Geller, USSR Ch 1977.

(b) 16 ... c5 17 d5 c4 18 b4 Bc8 19 Be3 Bd7 20 a5± Fischer - Gligoric, Rovinj - Zagreb 1970.

(c) 19 Bxe4 Bxe4 20 Rxe4 f6 21 Nc6 Qd5 22 Rxe8 Rxe8 23 axb5 axb5± Gligoric.

(d) 11 Ng5 Rf8 12 Nf3!=; 12 f4? exf4 13 Bxf4 Na5 14 Bc2 Nd5!∓.

(e) 19 Rf3 Re5 20 Rxf5 Rxf5 21 exf5 Bxd5 Khalifman - Karpov, Reggio Emilia 1991/92; 22 Ng4!±.

(f) 9 ... Be6 10 d4 Bxb3 11 axb3 Re8 12 d5 Nb8 13 c4±.

(g) 10 ... Nb6 11 Nbd2 exd4 12 cxd4 d5=/±.

(h) 11 ... Bb7 12 Na3 exd4 13 cxd4 Nb6 14 Bf4± Kasparov - Karpov, World Ch (10), New York 1990.

RUY LOPEZ

1 e4 e5 2 ♘f3 ♘c6 3 ♗b5 a6 4 ♗a4 ♘f6 5 0-0 ♗e7
6 ♖e1 b5 7 ♗b3 d6 8 c3 0-0 9 h3

	Chigorin		Breyer	
	(57)	(58)	(59)	(60)
9	♘a5		♘b8	
10	♗c2		d4	d3 (h)
	c5		♘bd7	♘bd7
11	d4		♘bd2	♘bd2
	♕c7 (a)		♗b7	♗b7
12	♘bd2		♗c2	♘f1
	♘c6	cxd4 (b)	♖e8	♘c5
13	dxc5	cxd4	♘f1 (f)	♗c2
	dxc5	♗b7 (c)	♗f8	♖e8
14	♘f1	♘f1	♘g3	♘g3
	♗e6	♖ac8	g6	♗f8
15	♘e3	♖e2!	a4	b4
	♖ad8	d5	c5	♘cd7
16	♕e2	dxe5	d5	d4
	c4	♘xe4	♘b6	g6
17	♘f5	♘g3	♕e2	a4
	♗xf5	f5 (d)	♘xa4	♗g7
18	exf5±	exf6 (e)	♗xa4 (g)	♗d3 (i)

(a) (1) 11 ... ♘c6 12 ♘bd2 cxd4 13 cxd4 exd4?! 14 ♘b3 d3 15 ♗xd3 ♗b7 16 ♗d2 ♖e8 17 a4 ♗f8=.

(2) 11 ... ♘d7 12 ♘bd2 cxd4 13 cxd4 ♘c6 14 ♘b3 a5 15 ♗e3 a4 16 ♘c1 exd4 17 ♘xd4 ♘xd4 18 ♗xd4±.

(3) 11 ... ♗b7 12 d5 ♘c4!? 13 a4 ♘b6 14 a5 ♘bd7∞/= Beliavsky – Romanishin, Reggio Emilia 1990/91.

(b) 12 ... ♗d7 13 ♘f1 ♘c4 14 ♗d3 ♘b6 15 ♘g3±.

(c) 13 ... ♘c6 14 ♘b3 a5 15 ♗e3 a4 16 ♘bd2 ♘b4 17 ♗b1 ♗d7 18 a3 ♘c6 19 ♗a2±.

(d) 17 ... ♘xg3 18 fxg3±.

(e) 18 ... ♗xf6 19 ♗xe4 dxe4 20 ♘xe4 ♗xe4 21 ♖xe4 ♕c2 22 ♕d5+! ♔h8 23 ♘e1±.

(f) 13 b4!? ♗f8 14 a4 a5 15 bxa5 ♖xa5 16 ♖b1 ♗a6±.

(g) 18 ... bxa4 19 ♖xa4 ♗c8±.

(h) 10 a4 ♗b7 11 d3 ♘bd7 12 axb5 axb5 13 ♖xa8 ♗xa8=.

(i) 18 ... bxa4 19 dxe5 ♘xe5 20 ♘xe5 ♖xe5=.

SICILIAN DEFENCE

1 e4 c5

Wing Gambit

	(1)	(2)	(3)	(4)
2	b3	b4?!	g3	♘e2
	e6!? (a)	cxb4	d5!?	♘c6
3	♗b2	♗b2 (d)	exd5	♘bc3
	♘f6	♘f6	♕xd5	♘f6
4	e5	e5	♘f3	g3 (h)
	♘d5	♘d5	♗g4	d5!
5	♘f3	♘f3	♗g2	exd5
	♗e7	e6	♕e6+!	♘d4!
6	c4	d4	♔f1	♗g2 (i)
	♘c7 (b)	b6	♗h3 (e)	♗g4
7	♘c3	a3	b4!? (f)	0-0
	f6	♗b7	cxb4	♘xd5= (j)
8	♘e4	axb4	a3	
	fxe5	♗xb4+	b3!?	
9	♘xe5	c3	♘c3	
	0-0	♗e7∓	♘f6	
10	d4! (c)		♖b1 (g)	

(a) 2 ... d6 3 ♗b2 ♘f6 4 ♗b5+ ♗d7 5 ♗xd7+ ♕xd7 6 ♗xf6!? gxf6 7 ♘c3 f5= Spassky – Hübner, Buenos Aires (ol) 1978.

(b) 6 ... ♘b4!?; 6 ... ♘f4!?

(c) 10 ... cxd4 11 ♕xd4 ♗b4+ 12 ♘c3! ♘c6 13 ♘xc6 ♗xc3+ 14 ♕xc3 bxc6±; 12 ♔d1? d6!∓ Westerinen – Tal, Tallinn 1973.

(d) 3 a3 d5! 4 exd5 ♕xd5 5 ♘f3 e5 6 axb4 ♗xb4∓.

(e) 6 ... ♘c6 7 h3 ♗h5 8 ♘c3 ♘f6 9 d3 ♕d7 10 a4∞ Short – Hjartarson, Solingen v Reykjavik 1990.

(f) 7 d4 cxd4 8 ♘xd4 ♕d7 9 ♘c3 ♘c6 10 ♘xc6 ♕xc6 11 ♕d5=.

(g) 10 ... g6 11 ♖xb3 b6±/∞.

(h) 4 d4 cxd4 5 ♘xd4.

(i) 6 ♘xd4? cxd4 7 ♘b5 e5!

(j) Keres.

SICILIAN DEFENCE

1 e4 c5

	Grand Prix (5)		Morra Gambit (6)	(7)	Closed (8)
2	f4		d4!?		♘c3
	e6 (a)		cxd4		♘c6
3	♘f3		c3		g3
	♘c6 (b)		dxc3		g6
4	♗b5		♘xc3		♗g2
	♘ge7		♘c6		♗g7
5	0-0		♘f3		d3
	a6		e6		d6
6	♗e2		♗c4		f4 (g)
	g6		d6		♘f6 (h)
7	d3		0-0		♘f3
	♗g7		♘f6	♘ge7	0-0
8	c3		♕e2	♗g5	0-0
	0-0		♗e7	a6! (e)	♖b8
9	♗e3		♖d1	♕e2	h3
	d6 (c)		e5 (d)	h6 (f)	b5 (i)

(a) (1) 2 ... d5 3 exd5 ♕xd5 (3 ... ♘f6!? 4 ♗b5+ ♗d7 5 ♗xd7+ ♕xd7 6 c4 e6 7 ♕e2 ♗d6 8 d3 0-0∞) 4 ♘c3 ♕d8 5 ♘f3 ♘f6 6 ♘e5!±.

(2) 2 ... ♘c6 3 ♘c3 d6 4 ♗c4 g6 5 0-0 ♗g7 6 d3± Short – Gelfand, Linares 1992.

(b) 3 ... d5!? 4 exd5 exd5 5 ♗b5+ ♗d7 (5 ... ♘c6!?) =/±.

(c) 10 d4 cxd4 11 ♘xd4 ♘xd4 12 ♗xd4 e5! 13 fxe5 Larsen – Kavalek, Las Palmas 1974 13 ... ♘c6!=.

(d) 10 h3 0-0 11 ♗e3 ♗e6 12 ♗xe6 fxe6 13 ♖ac1 ♖ac8 14 b4! a6 15 b5=.

(e) 8 ... h6?? 9 ♘b5 d5 10 exd5 hxg5 11 dxe6!+-.

(f) 10 ♗e3 (10 ♗h4 g5!?/!) 10 ... ♘g6∞.

(g) 6 ♘f3; 6 ♘ge2; 6 ♘h3!?.

(h) (1) 6 ... e5 7 ♘h3! ♘ge7 8 0-0 ♘d4 9 f5 gxf5 10 ♕h5!± Spassky – Hort, Bugojno 1978.

(2) 6 ... e6 7 ♘f3 ♘ge7 8 0-0 0-0=.

(3) 6 ... f5!? 7 ♘f3 ♘f6 8 0-0 0-0 9 ♔h1=/±.

(i) 10 a3 a5 11 ♗e3 b4 12 axb4 axb4 13 ♘e2 ♗b7 14 b3 ♖a8 15 ♖c1± Spassky – Geller (m) 1968.

SICILIAN DEFENCE

1 e4 c5

	Closed (ctd) (9)	Nimzowitsch (10)	(11)	O'Kelly (12)
2	♘c3	♘f3		
	♘c6	♘f6		a6
3	g3	e5	♘c3	c4 *(i)*
	g6	♘d5	♘c6 *(f)*	♘c6
4	♗g2	♘c3!? *(c)*	d4	d4
	♗g7	e6	d5	cxd4
5	d3	♘xd5!?	exd5	♘xd4
	d6	exd5	♘xd5	♘f6
6	♗e3	d4	♘xd5	♘c3
	e5 *(a)*	♘c6	♕xd5	e5?! *(j)*
7	♕d2	dxc5	♗e3	♘f5!
	♘ge7	♗xc5	cxd4	d5
8	f4	♕xd5	♘xd4	cxd5
	♘d4	♕b6 *(d)*	♗d7!? *(g)*	♗xf5
9	♘f3	♗c4	♘b5!? *(h)*	exf5
	0-0 *(b)*	♗xf2+ *(e)*		♘d4±/± *(k)*

(a) (1) 6 ... ♘f6 7 h3 0-0 8 ♕d2 ♘d4=/±.

(2) 6 ... e6!? 7 ♕d2 ♘d4 (7 ... ♘ge7 8 ♗h6 0-0 9 h4∞) 8 ♘d1 e5 9 c3 ♘e6 10 ♘e2±.

(b) 10 0-0 exf4 (10 ... f5) 11 ♗xf4 ♘xf3+ 12 ♖xf3 ♗e6 13 ♗h6 ♘c6 14 ♗xg7 ♔xg7 15 ♖af1 ♕e7=.

(c) 4 d4! cxd4 5 ♕xd4 e6 6 ♗c4 ♘c6 7 ♕e4 d6 8 exd6±.

(d) 8 ... d6 9 exd6 ♕b6∞.

(e) 10 ♔e2 0-0 11 ♖f1 ♗c5 12 ♘g5 ♘d4+ 13 ♔d1 ♘e6 14 c3 d6 15 b4 ♗xb4 16 ♖b1∞/±.

(f) 3 ... d5 4 exd5 ♘xd5 5 ♗b5+ ♗d7 6 ♘e5 ♘f6 (6 ... ♗xb5? 7 ♕f3!) 7 ♘d7±.

(g) 8 ... ♕a5+ 9 c3 ♘xd4 10 b4! ♕e5 11 ♕xd4±.

(h) 9 c3 ♘xd4 10 ♕xd4 ♕xd4 11 ♗xd4± Speelman - Wedberg, Skara 1980; 9 ♘b5 ♕e5! 10 ♕d5!?±; 10 c3!?

(i) (1) 3 d4?! cxd4 4 ♘xd4 ♘f6 5 ♘c3 e5=.

(2) 3 c3 d5 4 exd5 ♕xd5 5 d4±.

(3) 3 b4!?

(j) 6 ... d6 7 ♗e2 e6 8 0-0 ♗e7±.

(k) 10 ♗d3 ♘xd5 (10 ... ♗e7!?) 11 0-0 ♗b4 12 ♗e4!±.

SICILIAN DEFENCE

1 e4 c5 2 c3

	(13)	(14)	(15)	(16)
2	♘f6		d5 *(f)*	
3	e5		exd5	
	♘d5		♛xd5	
4	d4		d4	
	cxd4		e6	
5	cxd4 *(a)*		♘f3	
	d6	e6	♘f6	
6	♘f3	♘f3	♗d3 *(g)*	
	♘c6	b6!?	cxd4	♗e7!?
7	♗c4	♗d3 *(e)*	cxd4	0-0
	♘b6 *(b)*	♗b4+	♘c6	0-0
8	♗b5	♗d2	0-0	c4!? *(j)*
	dxe5	♗xd2+	♗e7	♛d8
9	♘xe5 *(c)*	♛xd2	♘c3	dxc5
	♗d7	♗a6	♛d6	♘a6
10	♗xc6	♘c3	♗e3 *(h)*	♛e2
	♗xc6	♗xc3	0-0	♘xc5
11	♘xc6 *(d)*	bxc3±	♖c1 *(i)*	♗c2=

(a) 5 ♛xd4 e6 6 ♘f3 (6 ♗c4 ♘c6 7 ♛e4 d6=) 6 ... ♘c6 7 ♛e4 d6 8 ♘bd2 dxe5 9 ♘xe5 ♘xe5 10 ♛xe5 ♛d6=.

(b) 7 ... e6!? 8 0-0 ♗e7 9 ♛e2 0-0 10 ♘c3 dxe5 11 dxe5 ♘xc3 12 bxc3 ♛c7!?±/=; 12 ... b6 13 ♛e4 ♗b7 14 ♗d3±.

(c) 9 ♗xc6+ bxc6 10 ♘xe5 ♗a6 11 ♘c3 e6=/∓.

(d) 11 ... bxc6 12 0-0 g6 13 ♖e1 ♗g7 14 ♗g5 0-0! 15 ♗xe7 ♛xd4 16 ♘c3 ♛xd1 17 ♖axd1 ♖fe8=.

(e) 7 a3!?

(f) (1) 2 ... e6 3 d4 d5 4 exd5 (4 e5 French cols 33–34) 4 ... exd5 (4 ... ♛xd5) 5 ♘f3 ♘c6 6 ♗b5 ♗d6!? 7 ♗e3 cxd4 8 ♗xd4±.

   (2) 2 ... b6!? 3 d4 ♗b7 4 ♗d3± cf col 14.

(g) 6 ♘a3 ♘c6 (6 ... cxd4?! 7 ♘b5! ♛d8 8 ♘bxd4±) 7 ♗e2 ♛d8!=.

(h) 10 ♛e2 0-0 11 ♖d1 ♘d5!=.

(i) 11 ... ♗d7 12 a3 ♖fc8= Nunn - Zilber, Hastings 1979/80; 11 ... b6? 12 ♘e4!±; 11 ... ♖d8!?; 11 ... ♘b4!?.

(j) 8 ♛e2 ♘c6 9 dxc5 ♖d8 10 ♖d1 ♛xc5 11 ♗g5 ♗d7=.

SICILIAN DEFENCE

1 e4 c5 2 Nf3 Nc6 3 Bb5

	(17)	(18)	(19)	(20)
3	g6		e6	Nf6 (j)
4	0-0		0-0	Nc3
	Bg7		Nge7	Nd4!? (k)
5	Re1	c3	Re1 (g)	e5
	e5(!)	Nf6 (c)	a6	Nxb5
6	Bxc6 (a)	Re1 (d)	Bf1 (h)	Nxb5
	dxc6! (b)	0-0	d5!? (i)	Nd5
7	d3	d4 (e)	exd5	0-0
	Qe7	cxd4	Qxd5	a6
8	a4	cxd4	Na3	c4!
	Nh6!?	d5	Qd8	Nb6
9	Nbd2	e5	Nc4	Nc3
	f6	Ne4	Nf5	d5
10	Nc4=/±	Nc3 (f)	a4±	d4± (l)

(a) (1) 6 b4!? cxb4 (6 ... Nxb4) 7 a3 Nge7! 8 axb4 0-0 9 Bb2 d6 10 Bxc6 Nxc6 11 b5 Qb6 12 Na3 Na5=.

(2) 6 c3 Nge7 7 d4?! cxd4 8 cxd4 exd4 9 Bf4 a6! 10 Bc4 d6!∓.

(b) 6 ... bxc6? 7 c3 △ 8 d4±/±.

(c) 5 ... e5 6 d4!? cxd4 7 cxd4 exd4 8 Bf4 a6 9 Ba4 b5 10 Bb3 d6 11 a4!↻/±.

(d) (1) 6 e5 Nd5 7 d4 cxd4 8 cxd4 0-0 9 Nc3 Nc7=.

(2) 6 d4!? cxd4 7 cxd4 Nxe4 8 d5 Nd6 9 Na3 a6↻.

(e) 7 h3!? e5!?=.

(f) 10 Nc3 Nxc3 11 bxc3=/±; 10 Bxc6!? bxc6 11 Nbd2 c5 12 dxc5 Nxc5 13 Nb3 Nxb3 14 Qxb3 d4∞.

(g) 5 b3 a6 6 Bxc6 Nxc6 7 Bb2 b6(!)± Plaskett – Speelman, London 1978; 5 c3 a6 6 Ba4±.

(h) 6 Bxc6 Nxc6 7 d4 cxd4 8 Nxd4 d6± (8 ... Be7!? 9 Nxc6 bxc6 10 Qg4).

(i) 6 ... Ng6(!) 7 c3 Be7 8 d4 cxd4 9 cxd4 d5=.

(j) 3 ... Qb6!? 4 Nc3 (4 a4) 4 ... e6 5 0-0 Nge7 6 Re1 Nd4 7 a4!? a6 8 Bc4 Ng6 9 d3±; 3 ... Qc7!!?

(k) 4 ... a6 5 Bxc6 dxc6 6 0-0±.

(l) 10 ... e6 11 Bg5 Qd7 12 cxd5 Nxd5 13 Nxd5 Qxd5 14 dxc5± Sax – Sveshnikov, Hastings 1977/78.

SICILIAN DEFENCE

1 e4 c5 2 ♘f3 ♘c6 3 d4 cxd4 4 ♘xd4

	Lowenthal		Four Knights	
	(21)	*(22)*	*(23)*	*(24)*
4	e5!?		♘f6	
5	♘b5		♘c3	
	a6 *(a)*		e6 [Dia]	
6	♘d6+		♘db5	♗e2 *(j)*
	♗xd6		♗b4 *(g)*	♗b4
7	♕xd6		a3	0-0
	♕f6 [Dia]		♗xc3+	♗xc3
8	♕d1!	♕a3 *(d)*	♘xc3	bxc3
	♕g6	♘ge7 *(e)*	d5	♘xe4
9	♘c3	♘c3	exd5	♗d3
	♘ge7	♖b8!	exd5 *(h)*	d5
10	h4	♗e3	♗d3	♗a3
	h5	b5	0-0	♘xd4
11	♗g5 *(b)*	♘d5	0-0	cxd4
	d5	♘xd5	d4!?	♕a5
12	exd5!	exd5	♘e2 *(i)*	♕c1
	♘b4	b4	♗g4	♗d7
13	♗xe7! *(c)*	♕d3 *(f)*	f3±	♖b1∓ *(k)*

(column 1)

(column 3)

(a) 5 ... d6? 6 c4±; 6 Bc4±.

(b) 11 Rh3?! d5! 12 Rg3 Bg4!

(c) 13 ... Kxe7 14 Nd3 Nxd3+ 15 Qxd3 Qxd3 16 cxd3±; 14 d6+!? Kd8! 15 Nd3 Nxd3+ 16 Qxd3 Qxd3 17 cxd3 Bf5 18 0-0-0±/±.

(d) (1) 8 Qd2?! Nge7 9 Nc3 d6! 10 Qg5 Nb4 11 Nd3 Be6=/∓;

(2) 8 Qd3?! Nge7 9 Nc3 d5! 10 Nxd5 Nxd5 11 Qxd5 (11 exd5 Bf5 12 Qd2 Nd4∞) 11 ... Be6 12 Qd1 Rd8 13 Nd2 Qg6!∞.

(3) 8 Qxf6 Nxf6 9 Nc3 Nb4! (9 ... d5 10 Bg5!) 10 Nd3 Nxd3+ 11 cxd3 h6=;

(4) 8 Qc7!? Nge7 9 Nc3 Nb4 10 Nd3 d5 11 0-0 d4 12 Ne2 0-0 13 Bd2! Nxd3 14 cxd3±.

(e) 8 ... Qg6 9 Be3! Qxe4 10 Nc3 Qb4 11 Qxb4 Nxb4±.

(f) 13 ... Ne7 14 d6 Nf5 15 0-0-0 Bb7 16 Bc5 0-0=.

(g) 6 ... d6 7 Bf4 e5 8 Bg5 - Pelikan cols 28-36.

(h) 9 ... Nxd5 10 Bd2±/±.

(i) 12 Ne4 Bf5! 13 Bg5 Bxe4 14 Bxe4 h6 15 Bh4± Kir. Georgiev - Chandler, Leningrad 1987.

(j) (1) 6 Be3?! Bb4 7 Bd3 d5 8 Nxc6 bxc6 9 e5 Nd7 10 Qg4 Bf8!=/∓.

(2) 6 g3!? d5 7 Bg2 Bb4 8 exd5 Nxd5 9 0-0 Nxc3 10 bxc3 Bxc3 11 Nxc6 Qxd1 12 Rxd1 Bd7 13 Rb1 Bxc6 14 Bxc6+ bxc6∞.

(3) 6 Nxc6!? bxc6 7 e5 Nd5 8 Ne4 Qc7 (8 ... f5) 9 f4 Qb6 10 c4! Ne3 11 Qd3! Nf5 12 g4 Nd4 13 Bg2 h5 14 g5 Bb7 15 Be3 Nc2+ 16 Kf2 Nxe3 17 Qxe3 Qxb2+ 18 Kg3 Ba6 19 Rab1 h4+ 20 Kh3± Kasparov - Illescas, Linares 1992.

(k) 13 ... Bc6 14 Nb4 Qc7 15 Qa3 a5 16 Bxe4 dxe4 17 c4 f6 18 Nd6= Geller - Hasin, USSR Ch 1958.

SICILIAN DEFENCE
Pelikan/Sveshnikov

1 e4 c5 2 Nf3 Nc6 3 d4 cxd4 4 Nxd4 Nf6 5 Nc3 e5

	(25)	(26)	(27)	(28)
6	Nde2 (a)	Ndb5		
	Bc5 (b)	d6		
7	Ng3	a4	Nd5 (f)	Bg5
	d6	Nb4!? (c)	Nxd5	Be6
8	Be2	Na3 (d)	exd5	Nd5!?
	Be6	Be7	Ne7 (g)	Rc8
9	0-0	Bb5+	c4 (h)	Bxf6
	a6	Nd7	Nf5 (i)	gxf6
10	Bg5	Nc4	Bd3	c3
	h6	0-0	Be7	a6
11	Bxf6	0-0 (e)	0-0	Na3
	Qxf6	Nf6	a6	b5!? (k)
12	Nd5	Ne3	Nc3	Nc2
	Qd8	Be6	0-0	f5
13	c3=	Qe2=	b4 (j)	exf5±

(a) (1) 6 Nxc6?! bxc6 7 Bc4 Bb4 8 Bg5 Bxc3+ 9 bxc3 Qa5∓.

(2) 6 Nf5 d5 7 exd5 Bxf5 8 dxc6 bxc6=.

(3) 6 Nf3?! Bb4 7 Bc4 Nxe4 8 Bxf7+? (8 Qd5 Nd6 9 Bb3 Qa5!; 8 0-0! Nxc3 9 bxc3 Be7 10 Qd5=/∓) 8 ... Kxf7 9 Qd5+ Ke8 10 Qxe4 d5∓.

(4) 6 Nb3?! Bb4 7 Bd3 d5 8 exd5 Nxd5 9 Bd2 Bxc3! 10 bxc3 0-0 11 0-0 f5∓.

(b) 6 ... Bb4!?=.

(c) 7 ... h6 8 Nd5!?±; 7 ... a6; 7 ... Be6.

(d) 8 Bg5 Be6 9 Bxf6!? gxf6=.

(e) 11 Nxd6?? Bxd6 12 Qxd6 Nxc2+.

(f) 7 Be3 - col 47.

(g) 8 ... Nb8 9 c4 Be7 10 Bd3 0-0 11 0-0 a6 12 Nc3 Nd7 13 Qc2 g6=/±.

(h) 9 c3!? Nf5!=; 9 ... Ng6? 10 Qa4! Bd7 11 Qc4! Rc8 12 Qb4 Bxb5 13 Qxb5+±/±.

(i) 9 ... Ng6=; 9 ... a6?? 10 Qa4+-.

(j) 13 ... a5! 14 Ba3 axb4 15 Bxb4 Nd4=/∓

(k) 11 ... f5.

SICILIAN DEFENCE
Pelikan/Sveshnikov

1 e4 c5 2 ♘f3 ♘c6 3 d4 cxd4 4 ♘xd4 ♘f6 5 ♘c3 e5
6 ♘db5 d6 7 ♗g5 a6 8 ♘a3 *(a)* b5 *(b)*

	(29)	(30)	(31)	(32)
9	♘d5 *(c)*		♗xf6	
	♗e7 *(d)*		gxf6	
10	♗xf6	♘xe7	♘d5	
	♗xf6	♘xe7 *(f)*	f5	
11	c3 *(e)*	♗xf6	♗xb5?! *(j)*	♕d3
	0-0	gxf6	axb5	f4!?
12	♘c2	c4!? *(g)*	♘xb5	g3
	♗g5	♗b7	♖a4!	♗g7
13	a4	cxb5!? *(h)*	♘bc7+	♕c3!?
	bxa4	♗xe4	♔d7	♗b7
14	♖xa4	♕a4	0-0	gxf4
	a5	d5	♖xe4	♔f8
15	♗c4	bxa6+	♕h5	♔f8
	♖b8	♔f8	♘e7	♖g1
16	b3	♕b4	♕xf7	0-0-0
	♔h8±/=	♖g8 *(i)*	♔c6∞	♗xd5=

(a) 8 ♗xf6 gxf6 9 ♘a3 d5!?; 9 ... f5!?

(b) 9 ... ♗e6!? cf. col 28; 9 ... d5? 10 ♘xd5 ♗xa3 11 bxa3 ♕a5+ 12 ♕d2 ♕xd2+ 13 ♗xd2 ♘xd5 14 exd5± Sax - Velimirovic, Rio (izt) 1979.

(c) 9 ♘ab1 ♗e7 10 ♗xf6 ♗xf6 11 a4 b4 12 ♘d5 ♗g5=.

(d) 9 ... ♕a5+!? 10 ♗d2 ♕d8 11 c4!? (11 ♗g5=; 11 ♘xf6+) 11 ... ♘xd5 (11 ... b4? 12 ♕a4±) 12 exd5∞.

(e) 11 c4 b4 12 ♘c2 (12 ♕a4!?) 12 ... a5 13 ♗e2 0-0=.

(f) 10 ... ♕xe7 11 ♗d3 0-0 12 0-0 h6=.

(g) 13 ♕f3 f5 14 exf5 ♗xf5 15 ♗d3±/=.

(h) 13 ♗d3 bxc4 14 ♘xc4 d5= Ljubojevic - Tseshkovsky, Riga (izt) round 12!

(i) Ljubojevic - Adorjan, Riga (izt) round 3! ∞/∓.

(j) 11 ♘xb5!? axb5 12 ♗xb5 ♗d7 (12 ... ♗b7! 13 exf5 ♖a5!?∞ - Sveshnikov) 13 exf5 ♗g7 14 a4 ♘d4! 15 ♗xd7+ ♕xd7 16 c3 ♕b7 17 ♘e3 ♗h6 18 cxd4 ♗xe3 19 fxe3 ♕xg2 20 ♖f1 ♕xb2 ½-½ Nunn - Adorjan, Skara 1980.

SICILIAN DEFENCE
Pelikan/Sveshnikov

1 e4 c5 2 Nf3 Nc6 3 d4 cxd4 4 Nxd4 Nf6 5 Nc3 e5
6 Ndb5 d6 7 Bg5 a6 8 Na3 b5 9 Bxf6 gxf6 10 Nd5 f5 (a)

	(33)	(34)	(35)	(36)
11	Bd3!			exf5
	Be6			Bxf5
12	Qh5		c4!?	c3!
	Bg7		Qa5+	Bg7
13	c3	0-0(!)	Kf1!	Nc2
	0-0	f4	fxe4	0-0 (f)
14	exf5	c4 (c)	Bxe4	Nce3
	Bxd5	bxc4	Bg7	Qe6!?
15	f6	Bxc4	Rc1	g4!?
	e4	0-0	Rc8	Qh4!?
16	fxg7	Rac1	cxb5	Bg2
	Re8	Rb8	axb5	e4!?
17	Be2	b3	Nf6+	Bxe4
	Re5	Qd7 (d)	Ke7!	Rae8
18	Qh6	h3	Nh5	Rg1
	Rg5 (b)	Kh8	Bh6	f5
19	Nc2	Rfd1	Rxc6	gxf5
	Ne5=/±	Nd4 (e)	Rxc6=	Bxf5∞

(a) 10 ... Bg7 11 Bd3 Ne7 12 Nxe7 Qxe7 13 0-0 0-0 14 c4 f5 15 Re1 fxe4 16 Bxe4 Rb8 17 cxb5 axb5 18 Qd3 f5 19 Bd5+ Kh8∞ Kosten - Chandler, Hastings 1990/91.

(b) (1) 18 ... Qg5 19 Qxg5 Rxg5 20 Nc2! Bc4 21 Ne3 d5 22 a4 Bxe2 23 h4!± (Nunn);

(2) 18 ... b4!?/! 19 Nc4 Bxc4 20 Bxc4 bxc3 21 bxc3 d5!∞/∓?;

(3) 18 .. Re6? 19 Qd2! Re5±/±.

(c) (1) 14 Kh1!? Rb8 15 Nb1 h6 16 Nd2 0-0 17 g4±.

(2) 14 c3 0-0 15 Nc2=.

(d) 17 ... Bxd5?! 18 Bxd5 Nb4? (18 ... Nd4) 19 Rfd1± Stean - Sax, Las Palmas 1978.

(e) 20 Nc2 Nxc2 21 Rxc2 f5∞/= Tukmakov - Sveshnikov, USSR Ch 1978.

(f) 13 ... Be6 14 Nce3 Ne7 15 g3 Nxd5 16 Nxd5 0-0 17 Bg2 a5 18 0-0∞/± Geller - Fedorowicz, New York 1990.

SICILIAN DEFENCE
Accelerated Dragon

1 e4 c5 2 ♘f3 ♘c6 (a) 3 d4 cxd4 4 ♘xd4 g6

	(37)	(38)	(39)	(40)
5	c4!			♘c3
	♗g7		♘f6	♗g7 (g)
6	♗e3	♘c2	♘c3	♗e3
	♘f6	♘f6	♘xd4	♘f6!?
7	♘c3	♘c3	♕xd4	♘xc6!? (h)
	♘g4	d6	d6	bxc6
8	♕xg4	♗e2	♗e2	e5
	♘xd4	♘d7	♗g7	♘d5!? (i)
9	♕d1	♗d2	♗g5	♘xd5
	♘e6 (b)	0-0	h6	cxd5
10	♖c1	0-0	♗e3	♕xd5
	b6	♘c5	0-0	♖b8
11	b4!	b3 (c)	♕d2	♗xa7
	♗b7	a5 (d)	♔h7	♖xb2
12	♗d3±	♔h1=/± (e)	0-0 (f)	♗d4 (j)

(a) 2 ... g6 (Hyper-accelerated Dragon) 3 d4∓:

(1) 3 ... cxd4!? 4 ♕xd4 ♘f6 5 ♗b5! ♘c6 6 ♗xc6 bxc6 (6 ... dxc6 7 ♕xd8+±)7 e5 ♘d5 8 0-0 ♗g7 9 ♕h4 0-0 10 ♗h6±.

(2) 3 ... ♗g7!? 4 dxc5!? (4 c4! cxd4 - 4 ... ♕a5+!? - 5 ♘xd4 ♘c6 cols 37-39; 4 c3±) 4 ... ♕a5+ 5 ♘fd2 ♕xc5 6 c4±.

(b) 9 ... e5? 10 ♘b5! 0-0 11 ♕d2 ♕h4 12 ♗d3 d5 (12 ... ♘xb5 13 cxb5±) 13 cxd5 ♘xb5 14 ♗xb5 ♕xe4 15 0-0±.

(c) 11 b4!? ♘e6 (11 ... ♗xc3) 12 ♖c1 a5 13 a3 axb4 14 axb4 ♘ed4 15 ♘xd4 ♘xd4 16 ♗e3 ♘xe2+ 17 ♕xe2 ♗e6=/± Speelman - de Silva, London 1978.

(d) 11 ... ♗xc3!?

(e) Timman - Miles, Wijk aan Zee 1978.

(f) 12 ... ♗e6 13 f4±.

(g) 5 ... ♘f6 6 ♘xc6!? bxc6 7 e5 ♘g8! (7 ... ♘d5? 8 ♘xd5 cxd5 9 ♕xd5 ♖b8 10 e6!±/+-) 8 ♗c4!? ♗g7 9 ♕f3 f5 10 ♗f4 ♖b8 11 0-0±.

(h) 7 ♗c4 ♕a5 (7 ... 0-0 8 ♗b3±; 8 f3? ♕b6!∓) 8 0-0 0-0 9 ♘b3 ♕c7 10 f4 d6 11 ♗e2± cf. col 66-67.

(i) 8 ... ♘g8 9 f4±.

(j) 12 ... ♖xc2 13 ♗d3 e6 14 ♕a8 ♖c6 15 ♕a4 ♕c7∞.

1 e4 c5 2 ♘f3 d6

	(41)	(42)	(43)	(44)
3	♗b5+			d4
	♗d7		♘d7!? (e)	cxd4 (h)
4	♗xd7+ (a)		d4	♕xd4
	♕xd7 (b)		♘f6	♘c6 (i)
5	c4	0-0	♘c3 (f)	♗b5
	♘c6	♘c6!? (c)	cxd4	♗d7
6	d4	c3	♕xd4	♗xc6
	cxd4	♘f6	e5	♗xc6
7	♘xd4	d4!?	♕d3	c4 (j)
	g6	♕xe4	h6	♘f6
8	♘c3	d5	♗e3	♘c3
	♗g7	♘e5	♗e7	g6
9	♗e3	♖e1	0-0	0-0
	♘f6	♘xf3+	0-0	♗g7
10	f3±	♕xf3 (d)	♗c4 (g)	♕d3±

(a) 4 a4!? ♘c6 5 0-0 ♘f6 6 ♖e1 e6 7 c3 (7 d3 △ ♘bd2-c4) 7 ... a6 8 ♗f1 ♗e7 9 d4 cxd4 10 cxd4 d5=.

(b) 4 ... ♘xd7 5 0-0 ♘gf6 6 ♖e1 e6 7 b3 ♗e7 8 ♗b2 0-0 9 c4 a6 10 d4±.

(c) 5 ... ♘f6 6 e5 dxe5 7 ♘xe5 ♕c7?! (7 ... ♕c8±) 8 d4 ♘c6 9 ♗f4!±; 5 ... e6 6 c4!♘c6 7 d4±; 6 c3 ♘f6 7 ♕e2=.

(d) 10 ... ♘f6 11 ♘a3∞/±.

(e) 3 ... ♘c6!? 4 0-0 ♗d7 (4 ... ♗g4±) 5 ♖e1 ♘f6 6 c3 a6 7 ♗xc6 ♗xc6 8 d4 ♗xe4 9 ♗g5∞.

(f) 5 e5?! ♕a5+ 6 ♘c3 ♘e4 7 ♗d2 ♘xc3 8 ♗xd7+ ♗xd7 9 ♗xc3 ♕a6 10 d5 ♘e5=.

(g) 10 ... ♘g4 11 ♖fd1 ♘b6 12 ♗b3 ♘xe3 13 ♖xe3=.

(h) 3 ... ♘f6:

(i) (1) 4 ♘c3 cxd4 5 ♘xd4.

(2) 4 ♗b5+ ♘d7!? col 43; 4 ... ♗d7!?

(3) 4 dxc5!? ♘xe4 5 cxd6 e6!=; 5 ... ♕b6!?; 5 ... ♘c6!?; 5 ... ♘xd6? 6 ♘c3 ♘c6 7 ♗f4 ♗g4 8 h3 ♗h5 9 ♕d5!±/±.

(i) (1) 4 ... a6 5 ♗g5 ♘c6 6 ♕d2±.

(2) 4 ... ♗d7 5 c4 ♘c6 6 ♕d2 g6 7 b3=/±.

(j) 7 ♘c3 ♘f6 8 ♗g5 e6 9 0-0-0 ♗e7 10 ♖he1 0-0=/±.

SICILIAN DEFENCE

1 e4 c5 2 ♘f3 d6 3 d4 cxd4 4 ♘xd4 ♘f6 5 ♘c3 (a) ♘c6

	Boleslavsky		Sozin	
	(45)	*(46)*	*(47)*	*(48)*
6	♗e2		♗e3	♗c4
	e5		e5! *(g)*	♕b6 *(i)*
7	♘b3 *(b)*		♘db5	♘b3 *(j)*
	♗e7		a6	e6!
8	0-0		♘a3	0-0
	0-0		b5	♗e7
9	♗e3		♘d5	♗e3
	a5	♗e6	♖b8!	♕c7
10	♘d2 *(c)*	f4	♘xf6+	♗d3
	d5!? *(d)*	d5	♕xf6	a6
11	♘xd5	f5	♘b1	f4
	♘xd5	d4	♗b7	b5
12	exd5	fxe6	♘c3	♕f3
	♕xd5	fxe6	♘d4!	♗b7
13	♘c4 *(e)*	♗c4 *(f)*	♗xd4 *(h)*	♖ae1± *(k)*

(a) 5 f3 e5 6 ♗b5+ ♘bd7 7 ♘f5 d5 8 exd5 a6 9 ♗xd7+ ♕xd7 10 ♘e3 b5=.

(b) 7 ♘f3 h6 (7 ... ♗e7 8 ♗g5=) 8 0-0 ♗e7 8 ♗e3 0-0=.

(c) 10 a4 ♘b4 △ ... d5=/∓; 10 a3 a4 11 ♘d2 ♘d4! 12 ♘c4 b5∓; 10 ♗f3 a4 11 ♘d2 ♗e6=/∓.

(d) 10 ... ♘d4(!) 11 ♘c4 b5=; 10 ... ♗e6!?

(e) 13 ... ♕xd1 14 ♖fxd1 ♗e6 15 c3 f5 16 ♘d6 ♘d4 17 ♗xd4 ♗xd6=.

(f) 13 ... dxc3 14 ♗xe6+ ♔h8 15 bxc3 ♕xd1 16 ♖axd1 ♘xe4=.

(g) 6 ... ♘g4!? 7 ♗b5 ♘xe3 8 fxe3 ♗d7 9 0-0 e6 10 ♗xc6 bxc6 11 e5 (11 ♕f3 ♕f6 12 ♕e2∞) 11 ... ♗e7!∞/=; 11 ... d5? 12 ♕f3 ♕e7 13 b4 g6 14 b5 c5 15 e4!±/±.

(h) 13 ... exd4 14 ♘d5 ♗xd5=.

(i) 6 ... ♗d7 7 0-0 g6 8 ♘xc6 ♗xc6 9 ♘d5 ♗g7 10 ♗g5 ♗xd5 11 exd5 0-0 12 ♖e1±.

(j) 7 ♘bd5!? a6 8 ♗e3 ♕a5 9 ♘d4 ♘e5!=; 7 ♘xc6 bxc6 8 0-0 g6!= (8 ... e6 9 ♗f4!±/±); 7 ♘de2 e6 8 0-0 ♗e7 9 ♗b3=.

(k) 12 ... ♖c8!? 13 ♕h3!? ♘b4 14 a3 ♘xd3 15 cxd3 0-0=.

SICILIAN DEFENCE
Sozin

**1 e4 c5 2 ♘f3 d6 3 d4 cxd4 4 ♘xd4 ♘f6 5 ♘c3 ♘c6
6 ♗c4 e6**

Velimirovic Attack

	(49)	(50)	(51)	(52)
7	♗b3	♗e3		
	a6 *(a)*	♗e7		
8	♗e3	♕e2		
	♗e7	a6 *(d)*		
9	0-0	0-0-0		
	0-0	♕c7		
10	f4	♗b3 [Dia]		
	♘xd4!	0-0 *(e)*		
11	♗xd4	♖hg1	g4 [Dia]	
	b5	♘a5 *(f)*	♘d7	♘xd4?!
12	a3 *(b)*	g4	♘f5!?	♖xd4
	♗b7	b5	exf5	b5 *(i)*
13	♕d3	g5	♘d5	g5
	a5! *(c)*	♘xb3+ *(g)*	♕d8 *(h)*	♘d7 *(j)*

(column 2)

(column 3)

(a) 7 ... ♗e7 8 ♗e3 0-0 9 0-0 a6! col 49; 9 ... ♘xd4 10 ♗xd4 b5 11 ♘xb5±; 9 ... ♗d7!?

(b) 12 e5 dxe5 13 fxe5 ♘d7 14 ♘e4 ♗b7 15 ♕g4 ♗xe4 16 ♕xe4 ♘c5=.

(c) 14 e5 dxe5 15 fxe5 ♘d7 16 ♘xb5 ♘c5 17 ♗xc5 ♗xc5+ 18 ♔h1 ♕g5∓ Fischer - Spassky, World Ch (4) 1972.

(d) 8 ... ♘xd4!? 9 ♗xd4 0-0 10 0-0-0 ♕a5 11 e5! (11 f4? e5 12 ♘d5 ♘xd5 13 exd5 exd4 14 ♕xe7 ♗f5!∓) 11 ... dxe5 12 ♗xe5 b6∞ (13 ♖d4 ♗b7 14 ♖hd1!± Velimirovic *ECO*).

(e) 10 ... ♘a5!? 11 g4 b5 12 g5 ♘xb3+ 13 axb3 ♘d7 14 h4 (14 ♘f5!?) 14 ... b4 15 ♘a4∞/±/±.

(f) 11 ... ♘d7 12 ♔b1 (12 g4 ♘c5 13 g5 b5 14 ♕h5 b4 15 ♘xc6 ♕xc6 16 ♗d5 ♕c7 17 ♗d4 bxc3 18 ♕h6 f6 19 gxf6 ♗xf6 20 ♗xf6 ♖xf6 21 ♕xf6 cxb2+ 22 ♕xb2 exd5 23 ♖xd5 ♗b7 24 ♖xd6 ♘xe4 25 ♖b6 ♘c3 26 ♖g3 ♘e2+ 27 ♔b1 ♗e4 28 ♖gb3 ♖c8 29 ♔a1 ♗xc2 30 ♖b7 h6 31 ♖xc7 ♖xc7 32 ♖b7 1-0 Hector - Plaskett, London (Watson, Farley & Williams) 1991) 12 ... ♘c5 13 ♕h5 (!Velimirovic) 13 ... ♗d7 (13 ... ♖e8) 14 g4 ♘xb3 15 axb3 ♘xd4 16 ♖xd4±.

(g) 14 axb3 ♘d7 15 f4 b4 16 ♘f5!? (16 ♘a4 Velimirovic - Ivanovic, Yugoslav Ch 1978) 16 ... exf5!? (16 ... ♖e8) 17 ♘d5 ♕d8 18 exf5 ♖e8∞ Velimirovic - Ivanovic, Niksic 1978.

(h) 14 gxf5 ♘f6 15 ♗b6 (15 ♖hg1 ♘xd5 16 ♗xd5 ♗f6 17 ♕h5 ♘e7 18 ♗b3 ♕a5 19 ♖xd6 ♕e5 20 ♕xf7+ Yakovich - Yudasin, Leipzig 1986) 15 ... ♕d7 16 ♖hg1 ♘xd5! 17 exd5 ♗f6!! 18 dxc6 ♕xc6 19 ♗d4 ♗xd4 20 ♖xd4 ♗xf5 21 ♕d2 ♖ae8!= Nunn - Liberzon, Hastings 1979/80.

(i) 12 ... e5?! 13 ♖c4 ♕d8 14 g5 ♘e8 15 ♖g1 ♗d7 16 ♘d5! ♗b5 17 ♗b6 ♕d7 18 ♕g4!±.

(j) (1) 14 e5?!∞;

(2) 14 ♕h5 ♖d8 15 ♖g1 g6! 16 ♕h4 ♘c5=/∓;

(3) 14 h4 ♘c5 15 f4 (15 h5 f5!=) 15 ... f5! 16 exf5 ♖xf5= (Byrne and Mednis).

1 e4 c5 2 ♘f3 d6 3 d4 cxd4 4 ♘xd4 ♘f6 5 ♘c3 ♘c6
6 ♗g5

	(53)	(54)	(55)	(56)
6	♗d7?! *(a)*	e6		
7	♕d2	♕d2		
	♖c8	♗e7	a6	
8	0-0-0	0-0-0	0-0-0	
	♘xd4	0-0	h6	♗d7
9	♕xd4	f4 *(d)*	♗f4	f4
	♕a5	♘xd4	♗d7	h6
10	f4!?	♕xd4	♘xc6	♗h4
	e6?! *(b)*	h6	♗xc6	♘xe4?!
11	e5	♗h4	f3	♕e1
	dxe5	♕a5	d5	♘f6
12	fxe5	♗c4 *(e)*	♕e1	♘f5
	♖xc3	e5	♗b4	♕a5 *(h)*
13	♗d2	fxe5	a3	♘xd6+
	♕xa2	dxe5	♗a5	♗xd6
14	♗xc3	♕d3	b4!?	♖xd6
	g6	♕c5	♗b6	0-0-0
15	b4!! *(c)*	♗xf6 *(f)*	exd5 *(g)*	♖d1!

(a) 6 ... ♕b6 7 ♘b3 e6 8 ♗f4 ♘e5 9 ♗e3 ♕c7 10 f4 ♘c6 11 g4 d5 12 e5 ♘d7 13 ♘b5 ♕d8 14 h4 f6 15 ♘d6+ ♗xd6 16 exd6± Speelman - Gulko, Hastings 1989/90.

(b) 10 ... ♖xc3! 11 bxc3 e5 12 ♕b4 ♕xb4 13 cxb4 ♘xe4 14 ♗h4 g5! 15 fxg5 ♗e7∓.

(c) 15 ... ♘d5 16 ♗c4 ♗h6+ 17 ♖d2! ♕a3+ 18 ♗b2 ♕xb4 19 ♗xd5 ♕xd2+ 20 ♕xd2 ♗xd2+ 21 ♔xd2 exd5 22 e6+-.

(d) 9 ♘b3!? e.g: 9 ... ♕b6 10 ♗e3 ♕c7 11 f3 a6 12 g4 b5 13 ♔b1 (13 g5) 13 .. ♘d7 14 f4 ♘b6 15 ♕f2 ♕a4 16 ♘e2∞/= Karpov - Sosonko, Waadinxveen 1979.

(e) 12 e5 dxe5 13 ♕xe5 ♕xe5 14 fxe5 ♘d5 15 ♗xe7 ♘xe7 16 ♗d3 b6 17 ♗e4 ♖b8=/±.

(f) 15 ... ♗xf6 16 ♕e2 a6 17 ♔b1 b5 18 ♗b3 ♗e6 19 ♘d5±.

(g) 15 ... ♘xd5 16 ♗c4 0-0 17 ♗e5 ♗c7 18 ♗xd5 exd5 19 ♗xc7 ♕xc7 20 ♘xd5± Byrne - Csom, Biel (izt) 1976.

(h) 12 ... ♕c7?! 13 ♗xf6 gxf6 14 ♘d5 ♕d8 15 ♕e3±.

SICILIAN DEFENCE
Richter - Rauzer

**1 e4 c5 2 ♘f3 d6 3 d4 cxd4 4 ♘xd4 ♘f6 5 ♘c3 ♘c6
6 ♗g5 e6 7 ♕d2 a6 8 0-0-0 ♗d7 9 f4**

	(57)	(58)	(59)	(60)
9	♗e7	b5		
10	♘f3	♗xf6(!)	♘xc6	
	b5	gxf6 (c)	♗xc6	
11	♗xf6 (a)	♔b1 (d)	♗d3	♕e3
	gxf6	♕b6	♗e7	♗e7
12	f5	♘ce2!	♖he1	♗xf6!?
	♕b6	0-0-0	0-0	♗xf6
13	♔b1	g3	e5	♘d5!? (h)
	0-0-0	♔b8	dxe5	♗xd5
14	g3	♗g2	♕f2!?	exd5
	♔b8	♗g7	h6	e5
15	fxe6 (b)	♖hf1	♗xb5(!) (f)	♗d3=/± (i)
	fxe6	♘e7 (e)	♕c7!	
16	♗h3±/=		♗xc6 (g)	

(a) 11 e5?! b4 12 exf6 bxc3 13 ♕xc3 gxf6 14 ♗h4 d5=.

(b) 15 ♗h3 b4 16 ♘e2 e5 17 c4= Boleslavsky - Taimanov, USSR 1970.

(c) 10 ... ♕xf6? 11 e5 dxe5 12 ♘dxb5±.

(d) 11 f5 ♘xd4 12 ♕xd4 ♗h6+ 13 ♔b1 ♗f4±/=; 11 ♘xc6 ♗xc6 12 ♕e3 ♕e7! 13 ♗d3 ♕a7=.

(e) △ ... ♗c8, ... ♗b7, ... d5±; 15 ... ♖he8? 16 ♕d3 ♔a7? 17 e5! dxe5 18 ♕xh7± Sax - Ribli, Warsaw (zt) 1979.

(f) (1) 15 ♗xf6?! ♗xf6 16 fxe5 ♗h4 17 g3 ♗g5+ 18 ♔b1 ♕c7∓ Karpov - Tal, USSR Ch 1976.

(2) 15 ♗h7+ ♔xh7 16 ♖xd8 ♖fxd8∓.

(g) 16 ... ♕xc6 17 ♗xf6 ♗xf6 17 fxe5±.

(h) 13 e5 ♗e7 14 exd6 ♗xd6 15 ♕d4=/∓.

(i) Radulov - Schneider, European Team Ch, Skara 1980.

1 e4 c5 2 ♘f3 d6 3 d4 cxd4 4 ♘xd4 ♘f6 5 ♘c3 g6
6 ♗e3 ♗g7 7 f3 0–0 8 ♕d2 ♘c6

	(61)	(62)	(63)	(64)
9	0–0–0	♗c4		
	d5 (a)	♗d7		
10	exd5	0–0–0 [Dia]		
	♘xd5	♕a5 (d)	♖c8	
11	♘xc6	♗b3	♗b3	
	bxc6	♖fc8	♘e5	
12	♗d4! (b)	h4	h4 [Dia]	
	e5	♘e5	♘c4	h5!?
13	♗c5	♔b1 (e)	♗xc4	♗g5 (i)
	♗e6!	♘c4	♖xc4	♖c5!
14	♘e4!	♗xc4	h5	♖he1!? (j)
	♖e8	♖xc4	♘xh5	b5
15	h4	♘b3!±(?)	g4	f4?!
	♖b8	♕c7!?	♘f6	♘c4
16	g4	♗d4	♘de2 (g)	♗xc4
	f5	♗e6	♖e8!?	♖xc4! (k)
17	gxf5	h5	e5	♗xf6
	gxf5 (c)	a5 (f)	♘xg4 (h)	♗xf6 (l)

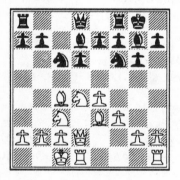

(column 2)

(column 3)

(a) 9 ... ♘xd4 10 ♗xd4 ♗e6 11 ♘d5! ♗xd5 12 exd5 ♖c8 13 g4 ♕c7 14 c3± Timman – Miles, England v. Holland 1977.

(b) 12 ♘xd5 cxd5 13 ♕xd5 ♕c7 14 ♕c5 ♕b7 15 ♕a3∞/=.

(c) 18 ♘d6 ♖f8 19 ♘c4 ♔h8 20 ♖g1 ♗f6 21 ♕h6 ♖f7 Timman – Miles, Bad Lauterberg 1977; 22 ♖g6!± Timman.

(d) (1) 10 ... ♕b8 11 h4! a5 12 ♗h6!± Spassky – Levy, Nice (ol) 1974.

(2) 10 ... ♕c7!? 11 ♗b3 ♘a5 12 ♔b1±/±.

(e) 13 h5 ♘xh5 14 ♗h6 ♗xh6 15 ♕xh6 ♖xc3 16 bxc3 ♖c8!∞.

(f) 18 hxg6 hxg6 19 a4 ♖b4 20 ♖h4! ♗xb3 21 cxb3 e5 22 ♗e3±.

(g) (1) 16 e5 ♘xg4 17 fxg4 ♗xg4 18 ♖dg1 (18 ♗h6? ♗xe5 19 ♗xf8 ♗xd1; 19 ... ♖xd4∓/∓) 18 ... dxe5 19 ♖xg4 h5 20 ♖xh5 ♖xd4 21 ♗xd4 exd4 22 ♘d5 gxh5 23 ♖xg7+ = (Nunn).

(2) 16 ♘b3 ♖e8 17 ♗h6 ♗h8 18 ♗g5 ♕c8 19 ♖h4 Short – Khalifman, Bundesliga 1991 19 ... ♘xg4!! 20 fxg4 ♗xg4 △ ... h5∞.

(3) 16 ♗h6 ♘xe4 17 ♕e3 ♖xc3 18 bxc3 ♘f6 19 ♗xg7 ♔xg7 20 ♖h2 ♖h8 21 ♘b3 ♗c6 22 g5 ♘h5 23 f4 ♖e8 24 f5± Kasparov – Piket, Tilburg 1989.

(h) 18 fxg4 ♗xg4 19 e6 ♗xe6 20 ♗d4 f6 21 ♘f4 ♗f7 22 ♕h2 h5!∞.

(i) 13 ♗h6?! ♗xh6 14 ♕xh6 ♖xc3; 13 ♔b1 ♘c4 14 ♗xc4 ♖xc4 15 ♘b3 ♕c7 16 ♗d4 ♗c6!= Tseshkovsky – Miles, Riga (izt) 1979.

(j) (1) 14 f4 (14 g4!? hxg4 15 f4) 14 ... ♘c4 15 ♕d3 b5 16 e5 ♘g4 17 ♘e4 Ljubojevic – Miles, Riga (izt) 1979; 17 ... ♖c8!∞.

(2) 14 ♔b1 b5 15 g4 a5 16 ♗xf6 ♗xf6 17 gxh5 a4 18 ♗d5 e6 19 hxg5 exd5 20 h5 ♗g5 21 f4 ♘c4 22 ♕g2∞.

(k) 16 ... bxc4? 17 ♗xf6 ♗xf6 18 e5±/± Karpov – Sosonko, Tilburg 1979.

(l) 18 e5 ♗g7 19 ♘cxb5 ♕b8!∓ Nunn – Miles, London 1980.

SICILIAN DEFENCE
Dragon

1 e4 c5 2 ♘f3 d6 3 d4 cxd4 4 ♘xd4 ♘f6 5 ♘c3 g6

Levenfish (65)	Classical (66)	(67)	Karpov (68)
6 f4	♗e2 (c)		
♘c6 (a)	♗g7		
7 ♘xc6	♗e3		0-0
bxc6	♘c6		0-0
8 e5	0-0	♘b3	♗g5
♘d7	0-0	0-0	♘c6
9 exd6	♘b3	f4	♘b3
exd6	♗e6	a5!? (f)	♗e6
10 ♗e3	f4	a4	♔h1
♗e7 (b)	♘a5 (d)	♗e6	a5
11 ♕f3	f5	0-0	a4
d5	♗c4	♕c8	♖c8
12 0-0-0	♗d3	♔h1	f4
♗f6=	♗xd3 (e)	♘b4±	♘b4=/± (g)

(a) (1) 6 ... ♘bd7 7 ♘f3 (7 ♗e2) 7 ... ♕c7 8 ♗d3 ♗g7∞.

(2) 6 ... ♗g7!? 7 e5 ♘h5! (7 ... dxe5? 8 fxe5 ♘h5 9 ♗b5+±) 8 ♗b5+ ♗d7 9 e6 fxe6 10 ♘xe6 ♗xc3+ 11 bxc3 ♕c8!∞.

(b) 10 ... ♕e7? 11 ♕d4 ♗g7 12 ♕xg7 ♕xe3+ 13 ♗e2 ♖f8 14 ♖f1 ♗a6 15 ♖f3 ♕g1+ 16 ♗f1±.

(c) 6 g3!? ♗g7 7 ♗g2 0-0 8 0-0 ♘c6 9 ♘de2 ♗d7 10 h3±.

(d) (1) 10 ... ♕c8 11 ♔h1 ♖d8 12 ♗f3 ♗c4 13 ♖e1 e5=.

(2) 10 ... b5?! 11 f5 b4?! 12 fxe6 bxc3 13 exf7+ ♔h8 14 bxc3 ♘e5 15 ♗d4± Spassky – Miles, Bugojno 1978.

(e) 13 cxd3 d5 14 ♘xa5 ♕xa5 15 e5 d4! 16 ♗xd4 ♘d7 17 f6 exf6 18 exf6 ♗xf6 (18 ... ♘xf6?? 19 ♗xf6 ♕b6+ 20 ♔h1 ♗xf6 21 ♘d5+-) 19 ♗xf6 ♕b6+ =; 19 ♖xf6!?

(f) 9 ... ♗e6!? 10 g4 ♘a5∞/=; 10 ... d5?! 11 f5 ♗c8 12 exd5 ♘b4 13 ♗f3! gxf5 14 a3! fxg4 15 ♗g2±; 10 ... ♖c8 11 g5!? ♘d7 12 ♕d2 ♘b6 13 0-0-0 ♘b4! 14 ♔b1 ♘c4 15 ♗xc4 ♖xc4=.

(g) 13 ♘d4 ♗c4 14 ♘db5:

(1) 14 ... d5!? 15 ♗xc4 ♖xc4 16 ♗xf6 ♗xf6 17 exd5 ♕b8 18 ♕e2! ♖xf4 19 d6 ♖xf1+ 20 ♖xf1±.

(2) 14 ... ♕b6 15 ♘h4 ♗xe2! 16 ♕xe2 ♕c5! 17 ♖ad1 ♕c4! 18 ♖fe1 ♖fe8 19 ♕xc4 ♖xc4 20 ♘a3=/±.

SICILIAN DEFENCE
Najdorf

1 e4 c5 2 Nf3 d6 3 d4 cxd4 4 Nxd4 Nf6 5 Nc3 a6

#	(69)	(70)	(71)	(72)
6	Be2		f4	Bc4 (i)
	e5 (a)		Qc7	e6
7	Nb3		Bd3	Bb3
	Be7 (b)		g6!? (e)	b5
8	0-0		0-0	0-0
	Be6		Bg7	Be7
9	f4		Nf3	f4
	Qc7		Nbd7	0-0
10	a4		Qe1	e5
	Nbd7		Nc5!? (f)	dxe5
11	Be3		e5!? (g)	fxe5
	0-0		dxe5	Nfd7
12	f5	Kh1	fxe5	Qh5
	Bc4	exf4	Nfd7	Nc6!
13	a5	Rxf4	Bf4	Nxc6
	Rfc8 (c)	Ne5 (d)	Ne6 (h)	Qb6+ (j)

(a) 6 ... Nbd7!? 7 Be3 Nc5?! 8 f3±.

(b) 7 ... Be6?! 8 f4 Qc7 9 g4!±/±.

(c) (1) 13 ... b5 14 axb6 Nxb6 15 Kh1 Rfc8 16 Bxb6 Qxb6 17 Bxc4 Rxc4 18 Qe2 Rac8 19 Ra2±.

(2) 13 ... Rfc8 14 Bxc4! (14 Kh1?! Bxe2 15 Qxe2 d5! 16 exd5 Bb4 17 Bd2 Bxc3 18 Bxc3 Nxd5∓ Sigurjonsson - Portisch, Buenos Aires (ol) 1978) 14 ... Qxc4 15 Ra4±.

(d) 14 a5! Rfe8 15 Bb6 Qd7 16 Ra4±.

(e) 7 ... e5 8 Nf3 Be7 9 0-0 0-0 10 Qe1 Nbd7 11 Kh1 b5=.

(f) 10 ... b5!?; 10 ... 0-0 11 Kh1 e6 12 Qh4 Nc5=.

(g) 11 Kh1.

(h) 14 Bg3 Qb6+ 15 Kh1 Qxb2∞.

(i) (1) 6 Be3 e5 7 Nb3 (7 Nf3 Qc7=) 7 ... Be6 8 Qd2 Nbd7 9 f3!? b5 10 g4 Nb6 11 g5 Nfd7∓(!).

(2) 6 a4!? Nc6=.

(3) 6 g3 e5 7 Nde2 Be7 8 Bg2 0-0 9 0-0 Nbd7!?=.

(4) 6 h3 e6 7 g4!? d5=.

(j) 14 Kh1 Qxc6 15 Rf3 Bb7 16 Bf4 Nc5∓ △ 17 Rg1 Ne4! 18 Nxe4 Qxe4; 17 Rg3 f5! 18 exf6 Rxf6∓/∓.

SICILIAN DEFENCE
Najdorf

1 e4 c5 2 ♘f3 d6 3 d4 cxd4 4 ♘xd4 ♘f6 5 ♘c3 a6
6 ♗g5

	(73)	(74)	(75)	(76)
6	♘bd7?!	e6		
7	♗c4	f4 (d)		
	♕a5	♗e7		♕c7!? (k)
8	♕d2	♕f3		♕f3 (l)
	e6	♕c7		b5
9	0-0-0	0-0-0		♗xf6!?
	b5	♘bd7 [Dia]		gxf6
10	♗b3! (a)	g4	♗d3	e5?! (m)
	♗b7	b5	h6 (h)	♗b7
11	♖he1	♗xf6	♗h4 (i)	♕h5
	♘c5 (b)	♘xf6 (e)	g5	dxe5!
12	♗xf6	g5	fxg5	♘xe6
	gxf6	♘d7	♘e5	♕b6
13	♕f4	f5 (f)	♕e2	♘xf8
	♗e7	♘c5	♘fg4 [Dia]	♕e3+!
14	♕g4 (c)	f6 (g)	♘f3 (j)	♕e2 (n)

(column 2)

(column 3)

(a) 10 Bd5?! b4! 11 Bxa8 bxc3 12 bxc3 (12 Qxc3?? Qxg5+) 12 ... Nb6 13 Nb3 Qb5 14 Nd4=; 10 Bxe6∞.

(b) 11 ... b4 12 Nd5! exd5 13 exd5+ Kd8 14 Nc6+ Bxc6 15 dxc6±.

(c) 14 ... 0-0-0 15 Bd5! b4 16 Bxb7+ Kxb7 17 Nd5!± Stein - Tal, USSR 1962.

(d) 7 Qf3 h6 8 Bxf6 Qxf6 9 Qxf6 gxf6=.

(e) 11 ... gxf6?! 12 f5! Nc5 13 fxe6 fxe6 14 b4! Na4 15 Nxa4 bxa4 16 Rd3!± Hübner - Hort, Wijk aan Zee 1979.

(f) 13 a3 Rb8 14 h4 b4 15 axb4 Rxb4 16 Bh3 Qc5! 17 Nb3 Qb6 18 h5 Nc5 19 Nxc5 dxc5! 20 g6 fxg6 21 hxg6 h6!∓ Bellin - Portisch, Teesside 1972.

(g) 14 ... gxf6 15 gxf6 Bf8 16 Qh5! Bd7! (16 ... b4 17 Nd5±; 16 ... Rg8!? 17 e5 Bd7 18 exd6 Bxd6 19 Qxh7 0-0-0 20 Qxf7 Rdf8 21 Qh5 b4 22 Nce2 Rxf6∞ Tsaturian - Makarov, Lvov 1984) 17 Bh3 b4 18 Nce2 0-0-0 19 Qxf7 Bh6+ 20 Kb1 Rdf8 21 Qh5 Rxf6=.

(h) 10 ... b5 11 Rhe1 Bb7 12 Qg3 (12 Nd5∞) 12 ... 0-0-0 13 Bxb5 axb5 14 Ndxb5 Qb6 15 e5 d5 16 f5!±.

(i) 11 Qh3 Nb6 12 f5 e5 13 Nb3 Bd7 14 Be3!?±/=.

(j) 14 ... hxg5! 15 Bg3 (15 Bxg5?! Bxg5+ 16 Nxg5 Qc5∓) 15 ... Bd7 16 h3 Nf6!= (16 ... Nxf3? 17 hxg4!±).

(k) 7 ... Nbd7 8 Qf3 Qc7 9 0-0-0 b5 10 e5!? Bb7 11 Qh3 dxe5 12 Nxe6∞/=.

(l) 8 Qe2 Nc6 9 0-0-0 Nxd4 10 Rxd4 Be7 11 e5 (11 g3 Bd7 12 Bg2 h6 13 Bh4 Bc6 14 f5 0-0= Ljubojevic - Kasparov, Belgrade 1989) 11 ... dxe5 12 fxe5 Nd5 13 Bxe7 Nxe7 14 Ne4 0-0 15 Qh5 Ng6 16 Ng5 h6 17 Nf3 b5 18 Bd3 Bb7 19 Bxg6 fxg6 20 Qxg6 Bd5∞ Ivanchuk - Kasparov, Tilburg 1989.

(m) 10 Qh5 Qc5!=; 10 Nd3=.

(n) 14 ... Qxf4 15 Qd3 Qh4+! 16 g3 Qd4∓.

SICILIAN DEFENCE
Najdorf

1 e4 c5 2 ♘f3 d6 3 d4 cxd4 4 ♘xd4 ♘f6 5 ♘c3 a6 6 ♗g5

	Poisoned Pawn			Polugaevsky
	(77)	(78)	(79)	(80)
6	e6			
7	f4			
	♕b6			b5!? [Dia]
8	♕d2			e5!? (g)
	♕xb2			dxe5
9	♘b3	♖b1		fxe5
	♘c6!? (a)	♕a3 [Dia]		♕c7
10	♗xf6	f5	e5?!	♕e2
	gxf6	♘c6	dxe5	♘fd7
11	♘a4	fxe6	fxe5	0-0-0
	♕a3	fxe6	♘fd7	♗b7
12	♘b6	♘xc6	♗c4	♘xe6!?
	♖b8	bxc6	♕a5!	fxe6
13	♘c4	e5 (b)	0-0	♕g4
	♕a4	dxe5!	♗c5!? (e)	♕xe5
14	♔f2!?	♗xf6	♘d5!	♗d3
	e5	gxf6	♗xd4+	♗e7
15	♗d3	♘e4!	♕xd4	♗xe7
	♗e6	♗e7 (c)	♘c6	♔xe7
16	♘b6∞	♗e2 (d)	♕f4∞/= (f)	♖he1 (h)

(column 2)

(column 4)

(a) 9 ... ♕a3!? 10 ♗xf6 gxf6 11 ♗e2 ♘c6 12 0-0 ♗d7 13 ♖f3 ♗e7 14 ♔h1 h5 15 ♘b1 ♕b4 16 ♕e3 ♗d8 17 c3 ♕b6∓ Kasparov - Magerramov, USSR 1982.

(b) 13 ♗e2 ♗e7 14 0-0 0-0 15 ♖b3 ♕c5+ 16 ♗e3 ♕e5 17 ♗f4 ♕c5+ 18 ♔h1 ♘g4 19 h3 e5 20 ♘a4 ♕a7 21 ♗c4+ ♔h8 22 hxg4 exf4 23 ♘b6 d5 24 exd5 cxd5 25 ♗xd5 ♖b8= Ivanchuk - Kasparov, Linares 1990.

(c) (1) 15 ... exf4!? 16 ♕xf4 ♘e5 17 ♘b6 ♕c6 18 ♘d5 ♘g4+ 19 ♔e2 ♗h6 20 ♕f1 ♗g7= Fernandez - Nunn, Budapest 1978.
(2) 15 ... ♗e6 16 ♘b6 ♕b4 17 ♕xb4 ♘xb4 18 f5 ♗d7 19 a3 ♘xd3+ 20 cxd3 ♗c6= Ligterink - Barczay, Wijk aan Zee 1977.

(d) 16 ... h5 17 ♖b3 ♕a4:
(1) 18 c4 f5 19 0-0 fxe4 20 ♔h1 (20 ♕c2) 20 ... c5 21 ♕c2 ♕c6 22 ♖fb1 ♗d8 23 ♗f3!=.
(2) 18 ♘xf6+!? ♗xf6 19 c4 ♖a7!? (19 ... ♗h4+ 20 g3 ♗e7 21 0-0 h4 22 ♕d3 ♕a5 23 ♗h5+ ♖xh5 24 ♕g6+ ♔d8 25 ♕xh5 ♕c5+ 26 ♔h1 e4∞ Martinez - Novikov, Mendoza 1985) 20 0-0 ♗e7 (20 ... ♖f7) 21 ♖b8 ♖c7 22 ♕d3 ♗c5+ 23 ♔h1 ♔e7 24 ♕g3 ♔d6! 25 ♖d1+ ♕xd1+ 26 ♗xd1 ♖f7∞/∓ Hübner - Portisch, Tilburg 1979.

(e) 13 ... ♘xe5!? 14 ♖be1 ♘bc6! 15 ♘xc6 ♘xc6∓ Boleslavsky.

(f) 16 ... ♘dxe5 17 ♖be1 ♕c5+ 18 ♔h1 ♕xc4 19 ♕xc4 ♘xc4 20 ♘c7+ ♔f8 21 ♘xa8 h6!∞/=.

(g) 8 ♗d3!?

(h) 16 ... h5 17 ♕b4+ ♕c5 18 ♕f4! g5 19 ♕g3 h4 20 ♕g4 ♔d8 21 ♖xe6 ♔c7 22 ♗e4± Umansky.

SICILIAN DEFENCE
Scheveningen

1 e4 c5 2 ♘f3 e6 3 d4 cxd4 4 ♘xd4 ♘f6 5 ♘c3 d6

	(81)	(82)	(83)	(84)
6	♗e2			f4 *(g)*
	a6 [Dia]		♗e7	♘c6
7	0-0	a4	0-0	♗e3
	♕c7	♘c6	♘c6	♗e7
8	f4	0-0	♗e3	♕f3
	♘c6	♗e7	0-0	e5
9	♗e3	♗e3	f4	♘xc6
	♗e7	0-0	♕c7 [Dia]	bxc6
10	♕e1	f4	♕e1 *(d)*	f5 *(h)*
	0-0	♕c7	♘xd4 *(e)*	♕a5
11	♕g3	♔h1	♗xd4	0-0-0
	♗d7	♖e8	e5	0-0
12	♔h1	♘b3 *(c)*	fxe5	♗c4
	b5	b6	dxe5	♗b7
13	a3 *(a)*	♗f3	♕g3	♗b3
	♘xd4	♗b7	♗c5	♖ad8! *(i)*
14	♗xd4	♕e2	♗xc5	g4
	♗c6 *(b)*	♘d7–	♕xc5+ *(f)*	d5 *(j)*

(column 1)

(column 3)

(a) 13 e5!?/! △ 13 ... dxe5 14 fxe5 ♘xe5 15 ♖xf6!! ♗xf6 16 ♗f4±; 14 ... ♘xd4 15 ♗xd4 ♘e8±/± Tal - Hartston, Hastings 1973/74; 13 ... ♘e8!?

(b) (1) 15 ♗d3 e5!? 16 fxe5 ♘h5! 17 ♕h3 dxe5 18 ♗xe5 ♕xe5 19 ♖f5 ♕d4 20 ♖xh5 g6!∞.

(2) 15 ♖ae1 ♕b7 16 ♗d3 g6!?=/±.

(c) (1) 12 ♕d2 ♗d7 13 ♘b3 b6 14 ♗f3 ♖ab8 15 g4 ♗c8 16 g5 ♘d7 17 ♕f2 ♗f8 18 h4 ♗b7 19 h5 ♘a5∞ Beliavsky - Kasparov, Barcelona 1989.

(2) 12 ♗f3 ♖b8 13 ♕d2 ♗d7 14 ♘b3 b6 15 g4!? ♗c8 16 g5∞ Karpov -Kasparov, World Ch (24) 1985.

(d) 10 ♔h1(!) ♗d7 11 ♕e1 ♘xd4 12 ♗xd4 ♗c6 13 ♕g3 ♖ad8 14 ♖ae1±.

(e) 10 ... a6 col 81.

(f) 15 ♔h1 ♔h8! 16 ♗d3!? (16 ♖xf6 gxf6 17 ♕h4 ♖g8 18 ♕xf6+ =) 16 ... ♗e6 17 ♕h4 ♘g8!= Unzicker - Andersson, Munich 1979; 17 ... ♖ae8? 18 ♖xf6 ♕e7 19 ♘d5± Unzicker - Penrose, Adelboden 1969.

(g) (1) 6 ♗e3 ♗e7 2 f4 ♘c6 - the column.

(2) 6 ♗c4?! a6 - Najdorf col 72; 6 ... ♘c6 - cols 49-52; 6 ... ♗e7! 7 ♗b3 ♘a6!

(h) 10 fxe5 dxe5 11 ♗c4 0-0=.

(i) 13 ... d5 14 ♗d2 ♕c7 15 exd5 cxd5 16 ♘xd5±/±.

(j) 15 exd5 (15 g5 d4!=) 15 ... ♘xd5 16 ♘xd5 cxd5 17 g5 ♗c5!=; 16 ♗d2?! ♘xc3 17 ♗xc3 ♗b4 18 g5 ♗xc3 19 bxc3 ♖d5!!∓(?) Sax - Schneider, European Team Ch, Skara 1980.

SICILIAN DEFENCE
Scheveningen

1 e4 c5 2 ♘f3 e6 3 d4 cxd4 4 ♘xd4 ♘f6 5 ♘c3 d6

Keres Attack

	(85)	(86)	(87)	(88)
6	g4 [Dia]			g3
	a6	♘c6	h6(!) (f)	♗e7 (j)
7	g5	g5	g5 (g)	♗g2
	♘fd7	♘d7	hxg5	0-0
8	♗e3	♗e3	♗xg5	0-0
	b5	♗e7	♘c6	♘c6
9	a3	h4	♕d2	b3 (k)
	♘b6 (a)	0-0!?	♕b6	♗d7
10	h4	♕d2 (e)	♘b3	♗b2
	d5	♘xd4	a6	♖c8
11	exd5	♗xd4	0-0-0	♘de2 (l)
	♗b7! (c)	a6	♕c7	♕a5
12	♗g2	0-0-0	f4 [Dia]	h3
	♘xd5	b5±	♗d7 (h)	♖fd8
13	♘xd5 (d)		♗e2 (i)	♔h1 (m)

(column 1)

(column 3)

- 68 -

SICILIAN DEFENCE
Scheveningen (continued)

(a) 9 ... ♗b7 10 ♕g4! ♘c6 11 0-0-0 ♘ce5?! 12 ♕h3 g6 13 f4 ♘c6 14 ♖g1 ♕c8 15 f5 ♘c5 16 fxe6 fxe6 17 ♗xb5!?∞/± Fedorowicz – Petrosian, Hastings 1977/78.

(b) 10 ... ♘8b7 11 h5 △ 12 ♖g1, 13 g6/12 ♖h3!?, 13 g6±/±.

(c) 11 ... exd5? 12 ♘de2! ♘c4 13 ♕xd5 ♘xe3 14 fxe3± Hort – Ree, Amsterdam 1978.

(d) 13 ... ♗xd5 14 ♕g4± (Hort).

(e) 10 ♕e2 ♘xd4 11 ♗xd4 b5!∞.

(f) 6 ... ♗e7 7 g5 ♘fd7 8 h4 ♘c6 9 ♗e3 col 86.

(g) 7 ♗g2 ♘c6 8 h3=; 7 h4 ♘c6 (7 ... ♗e7 8 ♖g1 d5 9 ♗f4 ♗b4 10 ♘db5 ♘c6 11 ♘c7+ ♔f8 12 ♘xa8 ♘xe4 13 a3 ♕h4⩲ Ivanchuk – Timman, Hilversum (6) 1991) 8 ♖g1 d5!= (8 ... h5 9 gxh5 ♘xh5 10 ♗g5 ♘f6 11 ♗e2 ♗d7 12 h5 a6 13 ♕d2 b5 14 a3 ♗e7 15 ♗e3 ♘xh5 16 0-0-0⩲ Kasparov – Sax, Tilburg 1989).

(h) 12 ... b5!? 13 ♗g2 b4! 14 ♘a4 e5 15 fxe5 dxe5 16 ♕f2=.

(i) 13 ... 0-0-0 14 h4 ♗e7 15 h5 ♔b8 16 ♔b1 ♗c8 17 ♗f3 ♘g8= Karpov – Andersson, European Team Ch, Skara 1980.

(j) 6 ... a6 7 ♗g2 ♕c7 8 0-0 ♘c6 9 ♖e1± Taimanov Variation – col 95.

(k) (1) 9 ♘xc6 bxc6 10 e5 dxe5 11 ♕xd8 ♖xd8 12 ♗xc6 ♖b8∓.

(2) 9 ♘ce2 ♗d7 10 c4 ♖c8 11 b3 a6 12 ♗b2 b5 13 cxb5 ♘xd4 14 ♘xd4 axb5=.

(l) 11 ♘ce2 ♘xd4 12 ♘xd4 b5!∓.

(m) 13 ... ♗e8 14 ♕e1 b5∓ Tarjan – Tal, Riga (izt) 1979.

SICILIAN DEFENCE
Taimanov

1 e4 c5 2 Nf3 e6 3 d4 cxd4 4 Nxd4 Nc6 5 Nc3 Qc7 (a)

	(89)	(90)	(91)	(92)
6	g3			Be2
	a6			a6
7	Bg2			f4
	Nf6		d6	Nxd4!
8	0-0		0-0	Qxd4
	Be7	Nxd4	Bd7	Nge7
9	Re1 (b)	Qxd4	Re1	Be3
	Nxd4	Bc5	Be7	b5!
10	Qxd4	Bf4!	Nxc6	0-0
	Bc5	d6 (e)	bxc6 (g)	Nc6
11	Qd1 (c)	Qd2	b3!	Qd2
	d6	h6	Rd8?!	Bb7
12	Be3	Rad1	Bb2	Rad1
	0-0	e5	Nf6	Be7
13	Qd2	Be3	Qe2	a4
	Rb8 (d)	Bg4 (f)	Qa5 (h)	b4 (i)

(a) 5 ... a6:

(1) 6 g3 Qc7 cols 89-91; 6 ... Nge7!? 7 Nb3! d6 (7 ... Na5 8 Qh5!±) 8 Bg2 Bd7 9 0-0 (9 Qxd6?? Nd5-+) 9 ... Nc8 10 a4±.

(2) 6 Be3 Qc7 cols 93-94; 6 ... Nge7?!/!?

(3) 6 Be2 Nge7 7 Bf4!? (7 Nb3±; 7 f4!? Nxd4 8 Qxd4 Ne7 9 Be3!? col. 92) 7 ... Ng6 8 Nxc6 bxc6 9 Bd6±.

(b) 9 Kh1 0-0 10 f4 d6=; 9 b3=.

(c) 9 Bf4?! d6 10 Qd2 Ng4!

(d) 14 Rad1 Ne8 15 Bxc5 Qxc5 16 Qd4±; 15 Bf4!? f6! (15 ... b5 16 e5) 16 Na4 Ba7! 17 Bxd6 Nxd6 18 Qxd6 Qxc2∞.

(e) 10 ... Bxd4 11 Bxc7 d5 12 exd5 Bxc3 13 bxc3 Nxd5 14 Be5 f6 15 c4!±/±.

(f) 13 ... Bxe3? 14 fxe3!±; 13 ... Bg4 14 Bxc5 dxc5 15 f3 Be6 16 f4! 0-0 17 Nd5 Bxd5 18 exd5 Qd6 19 fxe5±.

(g) 10 ... Bxc6 11 Qg4! h5 12 Qe2 (12 Qxg7?? Bf6) 12 ... h4 13 b3 hxg3 14 hxg3 Nf6 15 Bb2±.

(h) 14 Na4 c5 15 e5 dxe5 16 Bc3! Qc7 17 Qxa6±/+-.

(i) 14 Nd5 exd5 15 exd5 Qd6! 16 dxc6 Qxd2 17 Rxd2 Bxc6=

SICILIAN DEFENCE
Taimanov

1 e4 c5 2 Nf3 e6 3 d4 cxd4 4 Nxd4 Nc6

	(93)	(94)	(95)	(96)
5			Nb5	
			d6	
6	Be3		c4	Bf4
	a6		Nf6	e5
7	Bd3	Be2	N1c3	Be3
	Nf6	Nf6	a6	Nf6
8	0-0	0-0	Na3	Bg5
	Ne5!? (a)	Bb4	Be7	Be6
9	h3	Na4!	Be2	N1c3 (f)
	Bc5	0-0!	0-0	a6
10	Kh1! (b)	Nxc6	0-0	Bxf6
	d6	bxc6	b6	gxf6
11	f4	Nb6	Be3	Na3
	Nc6	Rb8	Bb7	d5!
12	e5!!	Nxc8	Rc1	Nxd5 (g)
	Nxe5	Rfxc8	Rc8	Bxa3
13	fxe5 (c)	Bxa6 (d)	Qd2 (e)	bxa3 (h)

(a) (1) 8 ... d6 9 Nb3 b5 10 f4 Bb7 11 Qf3/11 Qe2 col 52.

(2) 8 ... Bd6 9 Nxc6 bxc6 10 f4 e5 11 f5±.

(3) 8 ... b5 9 Nxc6 Qxc6 10 a3 Bb7 11 Qe2 Be7 12 f4 0-0 13 e5 Nd5 14 Nxd5 Qxd5 15 c4±.

(b) 10 f4? Nc6! 11 Nf5 (11 e5 Nxe5-+) 11 ... Ne7! 12 Nxg7+ Kf8 13 Bxc5 Qxc5+ 14 Kh1 Kxg7 15 e5 Ne8! 16 Ne4 Qc7∞/-+; 10 Qe2 d6 11 f4 Ng6 12 Nb3 Bxe3+ 13 Qxe3=.

(c) 13 ... dxe5 14 Bb5+ axb5 15 Ndxb5± Kasparov - Anand, Tilburg 1991.

(d) 13 ... Rd8 14 Bd3 Bd6 15 Kh1 Be5 16 c3 Rxb2 17 Qc1 Ng4! 18 f4 Nxe3 19 Qxb2 Bxf4 20 Qf2 Nxf1 21 Rxf1 g5 22 g3 Qd6 23 Be2 Be5=.

(e) 13 ... Ne5 14 Qd4 Ned7 15 Rfd1 Re8 16 Nc2 Qc7=.

(f) 9 Nd2 Be7 10 Bxf6 Bxf6 11 Nc4 0-0 12 Qxd6 Qc8∞/±.

(g) 12 exd5 Bxa3 13 bxa3 Qa5+ 14 Qd2 0-0-0 15 Bc4 Rhg8 16 Rd1 Bf5∓ Fischer - Petrosian (m) 1971.

(h) 13 ... Qa5+ 14 Qd2 Qxd2+ 15 Kxd2 0-0-0 16 c4 f5 ∞.

SICILIAN DEFENCE
Kan

1 e4 c5 2 Nf3 e6 3 d4 cxd4 4 Nxd4 a6

	(97)	(98)	(99)	(100)
5	Bd3		Nc3 (e)	c4!?
	Nf6	Bc5 (b)	Qc7	Nf6
6	0-0	Nb3	Be2 (f)	Nc3
	d6	Ba7	b5	Bb4
7	c4	Qe2	Nf3	Bd3
	Be7	Nc6	Bb7	Nc6
8	Nc3	Be3	0-0	Bc2
	0-0	Bxe3	Nc6	Qc7
9	Be3	Qxe3	Nxc6	0-0
	Nbd7	d6	dxc6	Nxd4 (j)
10	f3	Nc3 (c)	e5?! (g)	Qxd4
	Re8	Nf6 (d)	Qxe5	Ng4
11	Qd2	0-0-0	Re1	e5!
	Bf8	Qc7	Qd6!? (h)	Nxe5
12	Rfd1	f4±	Bg5	Bf4
	b6 (a)		Qxd1∞ (i)	f6!∞

(a) 13 Bf1 Bb7 14 Rac1 Rc8±.

(b) 5 ... Nc6!?/?! 6 Nxc6:

    (1) 6 ... dxc6 7 Nd2 e5 8 Nc4 Nf6 9 0-0 Bg4 10 Qe1! Nd7 11 f4±.

    (2) 6 ... bxc6 7 0-0 d5 8 c4! Nf6 9 Nc3 Be7 10 cxd5 cxd5 11 exd5 exd5 12 Qa4+! Qd7 13 Re1! Qxa4 14 Nxa4± Fischer - Petrosian (m) 1971.

    (3) 5 ... g6!? 6 0-0 Bg7 7 c3!?±.

(c) 10 c4!?±.

(d) 10 ... Nge7!?

(e) 5 Be2 Nf6 6 Nc3 Bb4=; 5 g3 d5=.

(f) 6 Bd3 b5!?; 6 ... Nc6 7 Nxc6 bxc6=.

(g) 10 a4 Bd6 11 axb5 (11 g3 Be5=) 11 ... cxb5 12 e5 Bxe5 13 Nxb5 axb5 14 Rxa8 Bxa8 15 Bxa8 Bxh2+ 16 Kh1 Bd6=.

(h) 11 ... Qc7 12 Bh5!∞ Kasparov - Polugaevsky, USSR Ch 1978.

(i) 13 Raxd1 Be7 14 Ne4?! Nf6! 15 Bxf6 gxf6 16 Bh5 Ra7∓.

(j) 9 ... Ne5 10 f4 Nxc4 11 e5 Bxc3 12 exf6 Nxb2 13 Bxb2 Bxb2 14 Rb1 Qc3 15 Rxb2∞/∓(?).

FRENCH DEFENCE
Tarrasch

1 e4 e6 2 d4 d5 3 Nd2

	(1)	(2)	(3)	(4)
3	a6 (a)	Nc6		c5
4	Ngf3	Ngf3 (b)		exd5 (h)
	c5	Nf6		Qxd5!?
5	dxc5	e5		Ngf3
	Bxc5	Nd7		cxd4
6	Bd3	Nb3	f6 (e)	Bc4
	Nc6	Be7		Qd6
7	0-0	Bb5	Bb5	0-0
	Nge7	a6?! (c)	fxe5 (f)	Nf6
8	Nb3	Bxc6	dxe5	Nb3
	Bd6	bxc6	Be7	Nc6
9	Qe2	0-0	Bf4	Nbxd4
	Qc7	c5	0-0	Nxd4
10	Bg5	Na5	Bg3	Nxd4
	dxe4	Nb8	Ncb8	a6
11	Bxe4±	c4! (d)	0-0 (g)	Re1 (i)

(a) 3 ... f5?! 4 exf5 exf5 5 Bd3 Bd6 6 Ndf3 Nf6 7 Ne2±; 3 ... b6!? 4 Ngf3 Bb7 5 Bd3 Nf6 6 Qe2±.

(b) 4 c3 e5 5 exd5 Qxd5 6 Ngf3 exd4 7 Bc4 Qh5 8 cxd4 (8 0-0 Nf6 9 Re1+ Be7=) 8 ... Nf6 9 0-0 Be7 10 Ne5 Qxd1 11 Rxd1 Nxd4 12 Bxf7+ Kf8 13 Bc4 b5 14 Bd3 Bb7=.

(c) 7 ... Ncb8 8 c3 b6 9 h4 c5 10 Rh3 Ba6 11 Bxa6 Nxa6 12 h5 h6 13 Rg3±/± Andersson – Hug, Skopje (ol) 1972.

(d) 11 ... 0-0 12 Be3 cxd4 13 Nxd4 Bd7 14 c5!±.

(e) 6 ... a5!? 7 a4 Be7 8 h4! b6 9 Bg5 h6 10 Bxe7 Nxe7 11 h5±; 11 Nc1 Ba6 12 Nd3±.

(f) 7 ... a6!? 8 Bxc6 bxc6 9 0-0 c5 10 exf6 Qxf6±; 7 ... Be7 (=6 ...Be7 7 Bb5 f6) 8 Bf4 0-0 9 exf6 gxf6 10 0-0 Nb6±.

(g) 11 ... a6 12 Bd3 c5 13 c4±.

(h) 4 Ngf3 Nc6 5 exd5 – cols 5-6; 5 Bb5 dxe4 (5 ... cxd4) 6 Nxe4 Bd7 7 Bg5 Qa5+ 8 Nc3 cxd4 9 Nxd4 Be7!∞/=.

(i) 11 ... Bd7 12 c3 Qc7 13 Bb3 0-0-0 14 Qe2 Bd6 15 h3 Kb8 16 a4 h6 17 Be3 Rhe8 18 Nf3 Bc6 19 a5 Nd7 20 Nd4 Be4 21 Ba4±/± Adams – Speelman, English Ch 1991.

FRENCH DEFENCE
Tarrasch

1 e4 e6 2 d4 d5 3 Nd2 c5 4 exd5 exd5

	(5)	(6)	(7)	(8)
5	Ngf3 (a)		Bb5+ [Dia]	
	Nc6		Bd7	Nc6
6	Bb5		Qe2+ (f)	Qe2+!? (j)
	Bd6		Be7!? (g)	Be7
7	0-0		dxc5	dxc5
	Ne7		Nf6	Nf6
8	dxc5		Nb3	Nb3
	Bxc5		0-0	0-0
9	Nb3 [Dia]		Nf3	Nf3
	Bd6 (b)		Re8	Re8
10	Nbd4	Bg5 (d)	Be3	Be3?! (k)
	0-0	0-0	a6 (h)	a6!
11	c3	Bh4	Bd3!	Ba4
	Bg4	Bg4	Ba4	Ne4
12	Qa4	Be2	Nfd4	0-0-0
	Bh5	Re8!	Nbd7	Bxc5∓ (l)
13	Be3 (c)	Re1 (e)	0-0-0! (i)	

(column 1)

(column 3)

FRENCH DEFENCE
Tarrasch (continued)

(a) 5 ... ♘f6 6 ♗b5+ ♗d7 7 ♗xd7+ ♘bxd7 8 0-0 ♗e7 9 dxc5
♘xc5 10 ♘d4 ♕d7 11 ♘2f3 0-0 12 ♗f4 ♖fe8 13 ♖e1 ♘ce4 14
♘e5 ♕d8 15 ♘d3 ♖c8 16 c3 ♗f8 17 ♕b3 ♘h5 18 ♗g3 ♘hxg3
19 hxg3 ♕d7 20 ♖ad1 ♖cd8 21 ♘f3 ♕c8 22 ♖e2± Adams –
Short, English Ch 1991.

(b) 9 ... ♗b6!? 10 ♖e1 0-0 11 ♗e3 ♗f5 12 c3 ♗e4 13 ♘bd4
♕d6 14 ♗f1±.

(c) 13 ... ♕c7 14 h3 ♘a5! 15 ♗d3 ♘c4! 16 ♘b5 ♕d7 17 ♗xc4
dxc4 18 ♖fd1 ♘f5! 19 ♕xc4 ♗xf3 20 gxf3 ♘xe3 21 fxe3
♕xh3 22 ♘xd6 ♕g3+= Karpov – Korchnoi, World Ch (12)
1974; 13 ♖e1 ♕c7 14 h3 ♗g6 15 ♗g5 a6 16 ♗f1 h6 17 ♗xe7
♘xe7= Karpov – Korchnoi, World Ch (8) 1974.

(d) 10 ♖e1 0-0 11 ♗g5 ♗g4 12 ♗h4 ♖e8 13 ♗g3 ♗xg3 14
hxg3 ♕b6 15 a4!± Ivanchuk – Yusupov, Brussels (m) 1991.

(e) 13 ... ♕b6 14 ♘fd4 (14 ♗xe7 ♖xe7!) 14 ... ♗xe2 15 ♖xe2
♗e5!= Schmid – Portisch, Nice (ol) 1974.

(f) 6 ♗xd7+ ♘xd7 7 ♘e2 ♗d6 8 0-0 ♘gf6! 9 ♘f3 0-0 10
dxc5 ♘xc5 11 ♗e3 ♖e8= Larsen – Uhlmann (m) Las Palmas
1971.

(g) 6 ... ♕e7 7 ♗xd7+ ♘xd7 8 dxc5 ♘xc5 9 ♘b3 ♕xe2+ 10
♘xe2 ♘xb3 11 axb3± Karpov – Korchnoi, World Ch (16)
1978.

(h) 10 ... ♗xc5 11 ♘xc5 ♕a5+ 12 ♕d2 ♕xb5 13 0-0-0± Karpov – Korchnoi, World Ch (22) 1978.

(i) 13 ... ♘xc5 14 ♘f5 ♗f8 15 ♘xc5 ♗xc5 16 ♕f3 ♗xe3+ 17
♘xe3± Tal – Portisch, Montreal 1979.

(j) 6 ♘e2 ♗d6 7 dxc5 ♗xc5 8 0-0± Karpov – Unzicker,
Munich 1979.

(k) 10 0-0 ♗xc5 11 ♕d3 ♗b6 12 ♗g5± Keres.

(l) Sax – Petrosian, Rio (izt) 1979.

FRENCH DEFENCE
Tarrasch

1 e4 e6 2 d4 d5 3 ♘d2 ♘f6 4 e5 ♘fd7 *(a)*

	(9)	*(10)*	*(11)*	*(12)*
5	f4		♗d3	
	c5		c5	
6	c3		c3 [Dia]	
	♘c6		♘c6 *(h)*	
7	♘df3		♘e2	♘gf3
	cxd4 *(b)*		cxd4	♕b6!? *(k)*
8	cxd4 [Dia]		cxd4	0-0
	♕b6	h5 *(f)*	♕b6 *(i)*	cxd4
9	g3! *(c)*	♗d3	♘f3	cxd4
	♗b4+	♘b6	f6	♘xd4
10	♔f2	♘h3	exf6	♘xd4
	f6 *(d)*	♗d7	♘xf6	♕xd4
11	♔g2	0-0	0-0	♘f3
	♕d8	g6	♗d6	♕b6
12	♗d3	a3	♘c3!	♕c2
	♘b6 *(e)*	a5 *(g)*	0-0 *(j)*	♕c5 *(l)*

(column 1)

(column 3)

(a) 4 ... ♘g8!? △ ... b6, ... ♗a6; 4 ... ♘e4!? 5 ♘xe4 - col 17 note (a); 5 ♗d3 ♘xd2 6 ♕xd2 c5 7 c3 ♕b6 8 ♘f3 (8 ♘e2!?)±/±.

(b) 7 ... ♕a5 8 ♔f2 (8 dxc5!±) 8 ... b5 9 ♗d3 b4 10 ♘e2 ♘b6 11 g4 bxc3 12 bxc3= Portisch.

(c) 9 h4 ♗b4+ 10 ♔f2 f6 11 ♕e3 ♗e7 12 ♕d2 0-0 13 ♖d1∞ Beliavsky - Kindermann, Munich 1991.

(d) 10 ... f5!? 11 ♔g2 ♕d8 12 ♗d3 ♘b6±; 10 ... g5!? 11 fxg5 ♘dxe5 12 ♘xe5 ♘xe5 13 ♔g2 ♘c4 14 ♘f3 ♗d7 15 b3 ♘d6 16 ♗f4 ♘e4 17 ♖c1 ♗d6 18 ♗d3± Glek - Vaiser, Tallinn 1986.

(e) 13 ♘e2± Uhlmann; 13 ♕c2?! f5 14 ♘e2 ♗e7 15 a3 ♗d7 16 b3 ♖c8= Bronstein - Uhlmann, Budapest 1961.

(f) 8 ... ♘b6 9 g4!?/! h5 10 gxh5 ♖xh5 11 ♘e2 g6 12 ♘g3 ♖h8 13 h4! ♗e7 14 h5 gxh5 15 ♘xh5±.

(g) 13 ♕e2 ♗e7 14 ♘hg5 a4 15 ♕f2± Maric - Uhlmann. Skopje 1968.

(h) 6 ... b6 7 ♘e2 ♗a6 8 ♗xa6 ♘xa6 9 0-0 ♗e7 10 ♘g3!? 0-0 11 ♕g4± Kotov - Keres, Moscow 1948.

(i) 8 ... f6!? 9 exf6 ♘xf6 10 ♘f3 ♗d6 11 0-0 ♕c7 12 ♗g5 0-0 13 ♖c1 ♘g4 14 ♘g3∞ A Sokolov - Yusupov, Riga (m) 1986.

(j) 13 ♗e3 ♗d7 14 a3 ♕d8 15 h3 ♖c8 16 ♖e1 ♔h8 17 ♖c1 ♕e8±.

(k) (1) 7 ... cxd4 8 cxd4 f6 9 exf6 (9 ♘g5!?) 9 ... ♕xf6 10 0-0±.

(2) 7 ... f6 8 exf6 ♕xf6 9 0-0 ♗d6 10 c4 0-0 11 ♘b3 ♘xd4 12 ♘bxd4 cxd4 13 cxd5 exd5 14 ♗g5 ♕f7 15 ♗h4 h6 16 ♗g3±.

(l) 13 ♕e2 ♗e7 14 ♗d2! 0-0 15 ♖ac1 ♕b6 16 ♗b1 f5 17 exf6 ♘xf6 18 ♗c3 ♗d7 19 ♖fe1 ♗b4 20 ♗d4 ♕a5?! (20 ... ♕d8) 21 ♖ed1± Nunn - Mednis, Budapest 1978; 12 ... h6 13 ♗f4 ♗e7 14 ♖ac1 0-0 15 ♗e3 ♕d8 16 ♕d2?! Nunn - Sisniega, Mexico 1977 - 16 ♕e2! f5 17 exf6 ♘xf6 18 ♗d4±.

FRENCH DEFENCE

1 e4 e6 2 d4 d5 3 ♘c3

	Rubinstein		Burn	
	(13)	*(14)*	*(15)*	*(16)*
3	dxe4		♘f6	
4	♘xe4		♗g5	
	♘d7		dxe4	
5	♘f3		♘xe4	
	♘gf6		♗e7	
6	♘xf6+		♗xf6	
	♘xf6		♗xf6	gxf6
7	♗d3		♘f3	♕d2 *(i)*
	♗e7	b6?! *(d)*	♘d7 *(g)*	f5
8	♕e2	♕e2 *(e)*	♕d2	♘c3
	0-0	♗b7	b6	c6
9	♗g5	♗g5	♗b5	g3
	c5 *(a)*	♗e7	♗b7	b6
10	0-0-0!? *(b)*	0-0	♘xf6+	♗g2
	cxd4	0-0	gxf6	♗b7
11	h4 *(c)*	♖ad1 *(f)*	♕c3 *(h)*	0-0-0 *(j)*

(a) 9 ... b6?? 10 ♗xf6 ♗xf6 11 ♕e4+-.

(b) 10 dxc5 ♕a5+ 11 c3 ♕xc5 12 0-0-0 ♖d8 13 ♘e5±.

(c) 11 ... ♕a5 12 ♔b1 ♗d7 13 ♘xd4 ♗c6±.

(d) 7 ... c5 8 dxc5 ♗xc5 9 ♕e2 0-0 10 ♗g5 ♕a5+ 11 c3±/∞ Karpov – Speelman, Reykjavik 1991.

(e) 8 ♘e5 ♗b7 9 ♗b5+!? c6 10 ♕f3 (10 ♘xc6!? ♕d5 11 c4) 10 ... ♕d5 11 ♕xd5 ♘xd5 12 ♗xc6+ ♗xc6 13 ♘xc6 ♖c8 14 ♘xa7 ♖xc2∞.

(f) 11 ... h6 12 ♗f4 ♕d5?! 13 c4±.

(g) 7 ... 0-0 8 ♕d2 ♗e7 9 0-0-0 ♗b7 10 ♗d3 ♘d7 11 h4=/∞ Kosten – Bareev, Hastings 1990/91.

(h) 11 ... a6 12 ♗c6 ♗xc6 13 ♕xc6 ♖a7 14 0-0-0 ♕a8 15 ♕c3 ♕d5± Persitz – Czerniak, Israel 1961.

(i) 7 g3!? f5!? (7 ... ♗d7 d5!? exd5 9 ♕xd5 ♗c6 10 ♕xd8+ ♗xd8 11 f3 ♘d7 12 ♗h3 Kuzmin – Hort, Reykjavik 1978/79, 12 ... ♘e5!=) 8 ♘c3 ♗f6 9 ♘ge2 ♘c6! 10 d5 exd5 11 ♘xd5 ♗xb2 12 ♗g2 0-0 13 0-0 ♗h8?! Fischer – Petrosian, Buenos Aires (3) 1971; 13 ... ♗e5(!)∞/∓.

(j) 11 ... ♘d7 12 ♘h3 ♘f6 13 ♖he1±.

FRENCH DEFENCE

1 e4 e6 2 d4 d5 3 Nc3 Nf6

	(17)	(18)	(19)	(20)
4	e5		Bg5	
	Nfd7 (a)		Bb4	
5	f4	Nf3!? (d)	e5 (f)	
	c5	c5	h6	
6	Nf3	dxc5	Bb2	
	Nc6	Nc6	Bxc3	
7	Be3	Bf4	bxc3	
	cxd4 (b)	Bxc5	Ne4	
8	Nxd4	Bd3	Qg4	
	Nxd4	f6	g6	Kf8
9	Bxd4	exf6	Bd3 (g)	h4
	Nb8	Nxf6	Nxd2	c5?!
10	Bd3	0-0	Kxd2	Rh3
	Nc6	0-0	c5	Qa5
11	Bf2	Ne5	Qf4	Bd3
	Qa5 (c)	Bd7 (e)	Nc6±	Nxd2±

(a) 4 ... Ng8!?; 4 ... Ne4!? 5 Nxe4 dxe4 6 Bc4 (6 Be3) 6 ... c5 7 d5 Nd7 8 dxe6 fxe6 9 Qxe6 Qe7 10 Qxd7+ Bxd7 11 f4!±.

(b) (1) 7 ... a6 8 Qd2 b5 9 dxc5 Nxc5 10 a3 Bb7 11 Rd1 Ne4!? 12 Nxe4 dxe4 13 Qf2 Rc8! 16 Nd2 Nd7∞/=.

(2) 7 ... Qb6!? 8 Na4 Qa5+ 9 c3 cxd4 10 b4! Nxb4 11 cxb4 Bxb4+ 12 Bd2 Bxd2+ 13 Nxd2∞.

(b) 7 ... Qb6 8 Na4 Qa5+ 9 c3 cxd4 10 b4 Nxb4 11 cxb4 Bxb4+ 12 Bd2 Bxd2+ 13 Nxd2 g5 14 Nb2 gxf4 15 Nd3 b6 16 Kf2 Ba6 17 Nf3 Rc8∞ Anand - Dreev, Madras (m) 1991.

(c) 12 0-0 Bc5!= Boleslavsky-Tröger, Hamburg 1960.

(d) (1) 5 Qg4?! c5 6 Be3 cxd4 7 Bxd4 Nc6 8 0-0-0 Nxd4 9 Rxd4 f5 10 exf6 Qxf6∓;

(2) 5 Nce2 c5 6 c3 Nc6 7 f4 f5 (7 ... f6) 8 Nf3 Be7 9 Ng3 cxd4 10 cxd4 0-0 11 Be2 Qb6 12 a3=.

(e) 12 Nxc6 Bxc6 13 Qe2 Qe7=; 13 ... Ne4!?∞/=.

(f) (1) 5 Ne2 dxe4 6 a3 Be7 7 Bxf6 gxf6 8 Nxe4 b6=.

(2) 5 Bd3 dxe4 6 Bxe4 c5 7 dxc5 Qxd1+ 8 Rxd1 Nbd7 9 Bxf6 Nxf6 10 Bf3 Bxc5=.

(g) 9 Bc1!? c5 10 Bd3 Nxc3 11 dxc5 Qa5 12 Bd2 Qa4 13 h3 h5! 14 Qxa4 Nxa4= Keres.

FRENCH DEFENCE

1 e4 e6 2 d4 d5 3 ♘c3 ♘f6 4 ♗g5 ♗e7 5 e5 *(a)* **♘fd7** *(b)*

	Classical		Alekhine Attack	
	(21)	*(22)*	*(23)*	*(24)*
6	♗xe7		h4 [Dia]	
	♕xe7 [Dia]		a6	♗xg5!? *(j)*
7	f4	♕d2 *(e)*	♕g4	hxg5
	0-0	0-0	f5 *(h)*	♕xg5
8	♘f3	♘ce2 *(f)*	♕h5+ *(i)*	♘h3
	c5	c5	g6	♕e7
9	♕d2 *(c)*	c3	♕h6	♘f4
	♘c6	f6	♗xg5!	a6
10	dxc5	f4	hxg5	♕g4
	♘xc5 *(d)*	cxd4	♔f7	g6!
11	0-0-0	cxd4	♘ge2	0-0-0 *(k)*
	f6	fxe5	♘f8	♘b6
12	exf6	fxe5	0-0-0	♗d3
	♕xf6	♘c6 *(g)*	♖g8	♘8d7
13	g3	♘f3	g4±	♖h6
	♖d8±	♘b6=		♘f8∞

(column 1)

(column 3)

(a) 5 ♗xf6?! ♗xf6 6 ♘f3 c5 (6 ... 0–0!? 7 ♗d3 △ e5, ♗xh7+ 7 ... c5 8 e5 ♗e7 9 h4 f5! 10 exf6 gxf6=) 7 exd5 exd5 8 ♗b5+ ♘c6 9 0–0 0–0 10 dxc5=.

(b) 5 ... ♘g8!? 6 ♗e3!±; 5 ... ♘e4 6 ♗xe7 ♘xc3 7 ♕g4 ♕xe7 8 ♕xg7 ♕b4 9 ♕xh8+ ♔d7 10 ♗d3! ♕xb2 11 ♖d1 ♘xd1 12 ♔xd1 ♕xd4 13 ♕xh7±.

(c) (1) 9 ♗d3 cxd4!? 10 ♗xh7+ ♔xh7 11 ♘g5+ ♕xg5! 12 fxg5 dxc3∞.

(2) 9 dxc5 ♕xc5 10 ♕d2 ♘b6 11 ♘b5 ♘c6 12 c3 f6 13 exf6 ♖xf6= van der Sterren – Korchnoi, Wijk aan Zee 1984.

(d) 10 ... ♕xc5 11 ♗d3 f6 12 exf6 ♘xf6 13 0–0–0 ♖b8 14 ♖he1 b5∞ Kupreichik – Bareev, USSR Ch 1987.

(e) (1) 7 ♕g4?! 0–0 8 ♘f3 c5 9 ♗d3 f5 10 exf6 ♖xf6 11 ♕h4 ♘f8∓ Bernstein – Lasker, Zurich 1934.

(2) 7 ♘b5 ♘b6 8 c3 a6 9 ♘a3 c5 10 f4 ♘c6 11 ♘c2 ♘c4 12 ♖b1 b5=.

(f) 8 f4 c5 9 ♘f3 – col 21; 8 ♘d1!?.

(g) 12 ... ♕h4+!? 13 ♘g3 ♘c6 14 ♖d1! △ 15 ♘f3 – 14 ♘f3? ♖xf3!∓.

(h) 7 ... ♗xg5!? 8 hxg5 c5 9 g6 f5 10 ♕g3 h6 11 0–0–0 cxd4 12 ♘ce2∞.

(i) 8 ♕g3!? c5 9 ♗e3 0–0 10 ♘ge2 ♘c6 11 ♘f4 ♘db8∞/±.

(j) (1) 6 ... h6?! 7 ♗xe7 (7 ♗e3) 7 ... ♕xe7 8 f4 a6 9 ♕g4 ♔f8 10 0–0–0±.

(2) 6 ... f6?! 7 ♕h5+ ♔f8 (7 ... g6 8 exf6! ♘xf6 9 ♕e2±) 8 exf6 ♘xf6 9 ♕e2 (9 ♕f3) 9 ... c5 10 dxc5 ♘c6 11 ♘f3 ♘xc5 12 0–0–0 b5 13 ♕e3±/±.

(3) 6 ... c5 7 ♗xe7 ♕xe7?! 8 ♘b5 0–0 9 ♘c7 cxd4 10 ♘xa8 f6∞/±; 7 ... ♔xe7 8 f4! ♕b6 9 ♘f3 ♘c6 (9 ... ♕xb2 10 ♘b5 ♕b4+ 11 ♔f2! ♘c6 12 c4!±) 10 ♘a4! ♕a5+ 11 c3 cxd4 12 b4 ♕c7 13 ♘xd4 a6 14 ♖h3±.

(k) 11 ♕g3!? △ 11 ... c5 12 ♘cxd5!

FRENCH DEFENCE
Winawer

1 e4 e6 2 d4 d5 3 Nc3 Bb4 4 e5 c5 5 a3 Bxc3+ 6 bxc3

	(25)	(26)	(27)	(28)
6	Ne7			Qc7
7	Nf3 (a)		Qg4	Qg4
	Qc7	Bd7	Nf5 (h)	Ne7 (i)
8	a4	a4 (d)	Bd3	Qxg7
	b6	Qa5	h5	Rg8
9	Bb5+	Bd2 (e)	Qf4	Qxh7
	Bd7	Nbc6	cxd4	cxd4
10	0-0 (b)	Be2	cxd4	Ne2
	Bxb5	f6!	cxd4	Nbc6
11	axb5	c4 (f)	Qxh4	f4
	Nd7	Qc7	Nxh4	Bd7
12	Qd3	exf6	Bg5!	Qd3
	h6	gxf6	Nf5	dxc3
13	Ba3	cxd5	Ne2	Ng3 (j)
	0-0	Nxd5 (g)	Nc6	0-0-0
14	c4 (c)		c3±	Be2 (k)

(a) 7 h4! Nbc6 8 h5 Qa5 9 Bd2 cxd4 10 cxd4 Qa4 11 Nf3!! (11 Bc3=) 11 ... Nxd4 12 Bd3 Nec6 13 Kf1! Nxf3 14 Qxf3 b6 15 h6!± Kasparov - Anand, Linares 1992.

(b) 10 Bd3 Nbc6 11 0-0 h6 12 Qd2 c4 13 Be2 0-0-0 14 Ba3 Be8 15 Bd6 Rxd6 16 exd6 Qxd6∞.

(c) 14 ... dxc4 15 Qxc4 Rfc8 16 Qe2 Qb7=.

(d) 8 dxc5!? Qc7 9 Bd3 Ba4 10 Rb1! Nd7 11 Rb4 Bc6 12 0-0 Nxc5 13 Rg4 Ng6 14 Nd4!± Spassky - Korchnoi (m) 1977.

(e) 9 Qd2!?

(f) 11 Rb1!? Qc7 12 Bf4 Ng6 13 Bg3 fxe5 14 0-0∞.

(g) (1) 14 c4 Nde7 15 dxc5 0-0-0 16 Bc3 e5 17 Qd6 Nf5 18 Qxc7+ Kxc7= Timman - Korchnoi, Leeuwarden (3) 1976.

(2) 14 c3 0-0-0 15 0-0 Rhg8 16 Re1 e5 17 c4 Bh3 18 Bf1 Nb6 19 d5 Nxc4!= Spassky - Korchnoi (m) 1977.

(h) 7 ... Qc7 col 28; 7 ... 0-0!? 8 Nf3 Nbc6 9 Bd3 f5 10 exf6 Rxf6 11 Bg5∞/±/±?

(i) 7 ... f5!? 8 Qg3 cxd4 9 cxd4 Ne7 10 Bd2 0-0 11 Bd3±.

(j) 13 Rb1 0-0-0 14 Nxc3 Na5 15 Nb5 Bxb5∞.

(k) 14 ... Nf5 15 Nxf5 exf5 16 0-0 d4=.

FRENCH DEFENCE
Winawer

1 e4 e6 2 d4 d5 3 ♘c3 ♗b4

	(29)	(30)	(31)	(32)
4	e5		a3!?	♘ge2 (j)
	c5	b6 (e)	♗xc3+	dxe4
5	a3 (a)	♕g4!? (f)	bxc3	a3
	♗a5!? (b)	♗f8	dxe4	♗e7
6	b4	♗g5	♕g4	♘xe4
	cxd4 (c)	♕d7	♘f6	♘c6
7	♘b5 (d)	♘f3	♕xg7	♗e3
	♗c7	♘c6?! (g)	♖g8	♘f6
8	f4	a3	♕h6	♘2c3
	♘e7	♗b7	♘bd7	♘xe4
9	♘f3	♗d3	♘e2 (h)	♘xe4
	♘bc6	h6	b6	e5!?
10	♗d3	♗d2	♗g5	dxe5±
	a6	0-0-0	♕e7!	
11	♘xc7+	h4	♕h4	
	♕xc7±	♘ge7±/±	♗b7 (i)	

(a) (1) 5 ♗d2 ♘c6 6 ♘b5 ♗xd2+ 7 ♕xd2 ♘xd4 8 ♘xd4 cxd4 9 ♘f3 ♘e7=.

(2) 5 ♕g4!? ♘e7 6 ♕xg7 ♖g8 7 ♕h6 cxd4 8 a3 ♗a5 9 b4 ♕c7 10 ♘b5 ♕xe5+ 11 ♘e2 ♗b6 12 ♗f4 ♕g7∞/=.

(b) 5 ... cxd4? 6 axb4 dxc3 7 ♘f3! ♕c7 8 ♕d4±.

(c) 6 ... cxb4? 7 ♘b5 ♘c6 8 axb4 ♗xb4+ 9 c3 ♗e7 10 ♗d3 a6 11 ♕g4 ♔f8 12 ♗a3±.

(d) 7 ♕g4 ♘e7 8 bxa5 dxc3 9 ♕xg7 ♖g8 10 ♕xh7 ♘bc6∞.

(e) 4 ... ♕d7 △ 5 ♕g4 f5!?; 5 ♘f3 b6 6 ♗d2 ♗a6 7 ♗xa6 ♘xa6 8 0-0 ♘b8 9 ♘e2!± ♗e7? 10 ♖c1!± △ c4 Geller - Karpov, USSR Ch 1976; 9 ... ♗xd2 10 ♕xd2±.

(f) 5 a3 ♗xc3+ (5 ... ♗f8!?) 6 bxc3 ♘e7±; 5 ♘f3.

(g) 7 ... ♗a6!?; 7 ... c5?!

(h) 9 ♗b2 ♘b6 △ ... ♘a4; 9 ♗g5!?

(i) 12 ♘g3 h6!∓ Fischer - Kovacevic, Zagreb 1970.

(j) 4 ♗d2!? dxe4 5 ♕g4 ♕xd4 6 0-0-0?! (6 ♘f3 ♘h6 7 ♕f4 e5 8 ♕xe5+ ♕xe5 9 ♘xe5 ♘g4 10 ♘xg4 ♗xg4 11 ♘xe4=) 6 ... h5! 7 ♕g3 ♗d6 8 ♗f4 h4 9 ♕g5 ♕f6 10 ♕xf6 ♘xf6 11 ♗xd6 cxd6 12 ♘b5 ♘a6∓.

FRENCH DEFENCE

1 e4 e6

	(33)	(34)	(35)	(36)
2	d4			d3 *(i)*
	d5			d5
3	e5		exd5	♘d2
	c5		exd5	♘f6
4	c3 *(a)*		♗d3 *(g)*	g3
	♕b6 *(b)*		♗d6	c5!?
5	♘f3		♘f3 *(h)*	♗g2
	♘c6 *(c)*		♘f6	♘c6
6	♗d3!?	a3 *(e)*	0-0	♘gf3
	cxd4	c4! *(f)*	0-0	♗e7
7	cxd4	g3	♗g5	0-0
	♗d7	♘a5	♗g4	0-0
8	♘c3	♘bd2	♘bd2	♖e1
	♘xd4	♗d7	♘bd7	b5
9	♘xd4	♗h3	c3	e5
	♕xd4	0-0-0	c6	♘d7
10	0-0 *(d)*	0-0=	♕c2=	♘f1=

(a) 4 ♘f3 ♘c6 5 ♗d3 cxd4 6 0-0 f6 (6 ... ♘ge7) 7 ♗b5 ♗d7 8 ♗xc6 bxc6 9 ♕xd4 ♕b6 10 ♕f4 f5∞/=.

(b) 4 ... ♘c6 5 ♘f3 ♕b6 – column; 4 ... ♘c6 5 ♘f3 ♗d7!?: 5 ... ♘ge7!? 6 ♘a3 ♘f5 7 ♘c2 ♗d7 8 ♗d3±.

(c) 5 ... ♗d7!? (Wade △ ... ♗b5) 6 ♗e2 ♗b5 7 c4 ♗xc4 8 ♗xc4 ♕b4+!? 9 ♘bd2 dxc4 10 0-0 cxd4 11 ♘xd4∓.

(d) (1) 10 ... a6 11 ♕e2 ♘e7 12 ♖d1 (12 ♔h1!? △ 13 f4) 12 ... ♘c6 (12 ... ♕b6!?) 13 ♗xa6 ♕xe5 14 ♕xe5 ♘xe5 15 ♗xb7=/∓:

(2) 10 ... ♕xe5!? 11 ♖e1 ♕b8! 12 ♘xd5 ♗d6 13 ♕g4 ♔f8!?∞/∓?

(e) 6 ♗e2 cxd4 7 cxd4 ♘h6 8 b3 (8 ♗xh6? ♕xb2; 8 ♘c3!? ♘f5 9 ♘a4=) 8 ... ♘f5 9 ♗b2 ♗b4+ 10 ♔f1 h5 11 ♘c3 ♗xc3∓.

(f) 6 ... a5?! 7 ♗e2 (7 ♗d3!?) 7 ... cxd4 8 cxd4 ♘ge7 9 ♘c3 ♘f5 10 ♘b5±; 6 ... ♗d7?! 7 b4 cxd4 8 cxd4 ♘ge7 9 ♘c3±.

(g) 4 ♘f3 ♘c6 5 ♗b5± Kasparov – Bareev, Paris 1991.

(h) 5 ♘e2 ♕h4!?; 5 c3 △ 5 ... ♘e7 6 ♕h5; 5 ... ♘f6 6 ♘e2.

(i) (1) 2 ♕e2 c5 3 f4 ♘c6 4 ♘f3 ♘ge7 5 g3 g6 6 d3 ♗g7=.

(2) 2 b3 d5 3 ♗b2?! dxe4 4 ♘c3 ♘f6 5 ♕e2 ♗e7=.

(3) 2 ♘f3 d5 3 ♘c3 d4!? 4 ♘e2 c5 5 c3=/±.

CARO-KANN DEFENCE

1 e4 c6

	(1)	(2)	(3)	(4)
2	d3 (a)	Nc3		d4
	d5	d5		d5
3	Nd2	Nf3		e5!?
	g6	Bg4		Bf5
4	Ngf3	h3	Bh5!?	Bd3 (h)
	Bg7	Bxf3		Bxd3
5	g3	Qxf3	exd5	Qxd3
	dxe4 (b)	Nf6 (d)	cxd5	e6
6	dxe4	d3	Bb5+	Nc3
	b6	e6	Nc6	Qb6
7	Bc4	Bd2!? (e)	g4	Nge2
	Nf6	Nbd7	Bg6	Qa6
8	0-0	g4!?	Ne5	Qh3
	0-0	g6	Rc8	Ne7!= (i)
9	Re1= (c)	Bg2=/± (f)	d4 (g)	

(a) 2 Ne2 d5 3 e5 c5 4 d4 Nc6 5 c3 Bf5!? 6 dxc5=/±.

(b) 5 ... e5 6 Bg2 Ne7 7 0-0 0-0 8 b4 a5 9 bxa5=/±.

(c) 9 ... Qc7 10 c3 e5 11 a4 a5=.

(d) 5 ... e6 6 d3 Nd7 7 Be2 g6 8 0-0 Bg7 9 Qg3 Qb6!?∞ Anand - Karpov, Brussels (3) 1991.

(e) 7 g3? Bb4 8 Bd2 d4 9 Nb1 Qb6 10 b3 Nbd7∓ Fischer - Keres, Bled - Belgrade Candidates 1959; 7 a3!?=/±.

(f) 9 ... Bd6 10 exd5 cxd5 11 Qe2 Qb6 12 g5 d4! 13 gxf6 bxc3 14 Bxc3 Bb4 15 Bxb4 Qxb4+ 16 c3±.

(g) 9 ... e6 10 Qe2! (10 h4?! f6 11 Nxg6 hxg6±) 10 ... Bb4 11 h4 Ne7 12 h5 Be4 13 f3 0-0! 14 Bxc6 (14 fxe4 Nxd4 15 Qd3 dxe4∓; 14 Nxc6 Nxc6 15 Be3 Qf6 16 fxe4 Nxd4 17 Bxd4 Qxd4 18 Rd1∞ van der Wiel - van der Sterren, Dutch Ch 1991) 14 ... Nxc6 15 Nxc6 Rxc6 16 0-0! Bxc3 17 bxc3 Rxc3 18 Bd2! Rxc2 19 fxe4 dxe4∞/=.

(h) 4 g4 Be4 5 f3 Bg6 6 h4 h5∓; 4 h4!? h5=; 4 Ne2?! e6 5 Ng3 Bg6 6 h4 h5 7 Be2 c5 8 dxc5 Nc6∓/∓(?); 4 Nf3 e6 5 Be2 c5 6 0-0 Nc6 7 c3 Bg4 8 Nbd2 cxd4 9 cxd4 Nge7= Anand - Karpov, Reggio Emilia 1991/92; 4 Nc3 e6 5 g4 Bg6 6 Nge2∞.

(i) 8 ... c5? 9 Nxd5!±.

CARO-KANN DEFENCE
Panov Attack and 2 c4

1 e4 c6

	(5)	(6)	(7)	(8)
2	d4		c4	
	d5		d5 *(g)*	
3	exd5		cxd5	
	cxd5		cxd5	
4	c4		exd5	
	♘f6		♘f6	
5	♘c3		♘c3 *(h)*	
	e6	g6 *(d)*	♘xd5!	g6?
6	♘f3	♕b3	♘f3	♗c4
	♗e7 *(a)*	♗g7	♘c6	♗g7
7	c5!? *(b)*	cxd5	d4	♘f3
	0–0	0–0	♗g4	0–0
8	♗d3	♗e2 *(e)*	♕b3	0–0
	b6	♘bd7	♗xf3	♘bd7
9	b4	♗f3	gxf3	d3!±/±
	a5 *(c)*	♘b6± *(f)*	e6 *(i)*	

(a) (1) 6 ... ♘c6 7 c5 ♗e7 8 ♗b5 0–0 9 0–0 ♗d7 10 a3±;
(2) 6... ♗b4!? 7 ♗d3 0–0 8 0–0 dxc4 9 ♗xc4 b6±.

(b) 7 cxd5(!) exd5 8 ♗b5+ ♗d7 9 ♗xd7+ ♘bxd7 10 0–0 0–0 11 ♕b3±; 7 ... ♘xd5 – Queen's Gambit Declined, col 2.

(c) 10 ♘a4 ♘fd7 11 h4 (△ ♘g5, ♗g5) 11 ... f5 12 ♘g5 ♕e8 13 ♔f1 axb4 14 ♘xe6∞ Karlsson – Mahlin, corr 1970.

(d) 5 ... ♘c6 6 ♗g5! ♕a5 7 ♗xf6 exf6 8 cxd5 ♗b4 9 ♕d2 ♗xc3 10 bxc3 ♕xd5 11 ♘f3 ♗g4 12 ♗e2 0–0 13 0–0±; 6 ♘f3 ♗g4 7 cxd5 ♘xd5 8 ♕b3 – col 7.

(e) 8 ♘ge2 ♖e8 9 ♘f4!? ♘g4 10 ♗b5 e5 11 dxe5 ♖xe5+ 12 ♗e2 ♘a6 13 0–0 b6∞.

(f) 10 ♗g5 ♗g4 (10 ... a5!?) 11 ♗xf6 ♗xf3 12 ♘xf3 △ a4±.

(g) (1) 2 ... e6 3 ♘c3 d5 4 cxd5 exd5 5 exd5 cxd5 6 ♘f3 ♘f6 7 ♗b5+ ♘c6 8 0–0 ♗e7 9 ♘e5 ♗d7 10 d4±.
(2) 2 ... e5 3 ♘f3 d6 4 d4 ♗g4 5 ♗e2 ♘d7 6 ♘c3±.

(h) 5 ♗b5+!? ♘bd7 6 ♘c3 g6 7 d4 ♗g7 8 d6 exd6 9 ♕e2+ ♕e7 10 ♗f4 ♕xe2+ 11 ♘gxe2 ♔e7=/±.

(i) 9 ... ♘b6!? 10 ♗e3 e6 11 0–0–0∞/=; 9 ... e6 10 ♕xb7 ♘xd4 11 ♗b5+ ♘xb5 12 ♕c6+! ♔e7 13 ♕xb5 ♕d7 14 ♘xd5+=/±.

CARO-KANN DEFENCE

1 e4 c6 2 d4 d5

	(9)	(10)	(11)	(12)
3	exd5	♘c3 (b)	dxe4	
	cxd5	g6!?		
4	♗d3	♘f3	♘xe4	
	♘c6	♗g7	♘d7	
5	c3	h3!	♘f3	♗c4
	♘f6	♘f6!? (c)	♘gf6	♘gf6
6	♗f4	e5	♘xf6+	♘g5
	♗g4 (a)	♘e4	♘xf6	e6
7	♕b3	♘xe4	♘e5!	♕e2
	♕c8	dxe4	♗e6! (f)	♘b6
8	♘d2	♘g5	♗e2	♗d3
	e6	c5	g6	h6! (h)
9	♘gf3	dxc5!? (d)	0-0	♘5f3
	♗e7±	♕xd1+ (e)	♗g7 (g)	c5 (i)

(a) 6 ... e6±; 6 ... g6 7 ♘f3 ♗g7 8 ♘bd2 ♘h5 9 ♗e3±.

(b) 3 ♘d2 dxe4 4 ♘xe4 - cols 11-16; 3 ♘d2 g6!? 4 ♘gf3 ♗g7±.

(c) 5 ... dxe4 6 ♘xe4±; 5 ... ♘h6!?.

(d) 9 ♗c4 0-0∞.

(e) 10 ♔xd1 ♗xe5 11 ♗c4 0-0 12 c3±; 9 ... ♕a5+!? 10 ♗d2 ♕xc5 11 ♗c3±.

(f) 7 ... ♗f5? 8 c3! (± △ 9 ♕b3) 8 ... e6? (8 ... ♗e6!±) 9 g4 ♗g6 10 h4 h5 11 g5 ♘d5 12 ♘xg6 fxg6 13 ♕c2! ♔f7 14 ♖h3 ♘e7 15 ♗c4 ♘f5 16 ♖f3 ♕d7 17 ♖xf5+!+- Karpov - Hort, Bugojno 1978.

(g) 10 c4 0-0 11 ♗e3 ♘d7 12 ♘f3! ♗g4 13 h3 ♗xf3 14 ♗xf3±.

(h) 8 ... ♕xd4? 9 ♘1f3 △ 10 ♘e5±.

(i) 10 dxc5 (10 ♗f4 ♘bd5 {10 ... ♗d6 11 ♗g3 ♕e7 12 dxc5 ♗xc5 13 ♘e5 ♗d7 14 ♘gf3±} 11 ♗e5 ♕a5+ 12 ♘d2 b5∞) 10 ... ♗xc5 (10 ... ♘bd7!? 11 b4!?∞/=) 11 ♘e5 ♘bd7 12 ♘gf3 ♘xe5 13 ♘xe5 0-0 14 0-0 (14 ♗d2!? ♕d5 15 0-0-0 ♕xa2 16 c3=) 14 ... b6=/±.

CARO-KANN DEFENCE

1 e4 c6 2 d4 d5 3 ♘c3 dxe4 4 ♘xe4

	(13)	(14)	(15)	(16)
4	♗f5		♘f6	
5	♘g3		♘xf6+ (d)	
	♗g6		exf6	gxf6
6	h4	♘f3	c3 (e)	♘f3 (g)
	h6	♘d7	♗d6	♗f5! (h)
7	♘f3	♗c4 (b)	♗d3	♗e2
	♘d7	e6	0-0	♕c7
8	h5	0-0	♕c2	0-0
	♗h7	♘gf6	♖e8+	e6
9	♗d3	♕e2	♘e2	c4
	♗xd3	♗e7	h6!? (f)	♘d7
10	♕xd3	♖e1	♗e3!?±/=	d5!?
	♕c7	0-0		0-0-0
11	♗d2 (a)	c3 (c)		♗e3 (i)

(a) 11 ... e6 12 0-0-0 ♘gf6 13 ♘e4 (13 ♘e5!? ♘xe5 14 dxe5 ♕xe5 15 ♖he1∞ Shamkovich) 13 ... 0-0-0 14 g3 ♘xe4 15 ♕xe4±.

(b) (1) 7 h4 h5!? (7 ... h6 - col 13) 8 ♗d3 ♗xd3 9 ♕xd3 e6 10 ♘e4 ♕a5+ 11 ♗d2 ♕f5 12 0-0-0 0-0-0= Karpov - Larsen, Bugojno 1978.

(2) 7 ♗d3 ♘fg6 8 ♗xg6 hxg6 9 0-0 e6 10 c4 ♗e7=.

(c) 11 ... ♕c7 12 ♗g5 h6 13 ♗h4 ♖ad8= Hübner - Portisch, Montreal 1979.

(d) 5 ♘g3 g6 6 ♘f3 ♗g7 7 ♗e2 0-0 8 0-0 ♗g4=.

(e) (1) 6 ♗c4 ♕e7+ 7 ♕e2 ♗e6 8 ♗b3=/±.

(2) 6 ♗c4 ♘d7!? 7 ♘e2 ♗d6 8 0-0 0-0 9 ♗f4 ♘b6 10 ♗d3± Karpov - Korchnoi, World Ch (20) 1978.

(3) 6 ♘f3 ♗d6 7 ♗e2 ♘a6!? 8 0-0 ♘c7 9 c4 0-0= Torre - Korchnoi, Buenos Aires (ol) 1978.

(f) 9 ... g6 10 h4 ♘d7 11 h5 ♘f8 12 ♗h6± e.g. 12 ... ♕e7 13 0-0-0 ♗f5 or 12 ... ♗e6 13 0-0-0 b5.

(g) (1) 6 ♘e2 h5!? 7 h4?! (7 ♕d3) 7 ... ♗g4 8 ♕d3 e5!? 9 ♗e3 ♘a6 10 a3?! ♕a5+ 11 ♗d2 ♕b6∓/∓ Mihalcisin - Speelman, Frunze 1979.

(2) 6 ♗c4 ♗f5 7 ♗f4 ♘d7 8 ♘e2 ♘b6 9 ♗b3 a5=.

(h) 6 ... ♗g4?! 7 ♗e2 ♘d7 8 0-0 ♕c7 9 ♘h4±.

(i) 11 ... c5= Spassky - Larsen, Buenos Aires (Clarin) 1979.

PIRC DEFENCE

1 e4 d6 2 d4 ♘f6 3 ♘c3 g6

Byrne

	(1)	(2)	(3)	(4)
4	♗g5	f3	g3	♗c4!? (g)
	c6	c6	♗g7	♗g7
5	♕d2	♗e3	♗g2	♕e2
	b5	♘bd7	0-0	♘c6
6	♗d3	♕d2	♘ge2	e5
	♗g7	b5	e5	♘d7!?/! (h)
7	f4!? (a)	♘ge2 (c)	0-0	♘f3
	0-0	♘b6	♘c6 (e)	0-0!? (i)
8	♘f3	b3	dxe5	e6
	♘bd7	♕c7	dxe5	♘b6
9	0-0	g4!?	♗g5	exf7+
	b4	e5	♘d4	♔h8∞/∓/∓
10	♘d1	♗g2	♘d4	
	♕b6 (b)	b4 (d)	exd4 (f)	

(a) (1) 7 ♗h6 ♗xh6! 8 ♕xh6 ♕b6=.

(2) 7 ♘ge2!? 0-0 8 ♗h6 e5 9 ♗xg7 ♔xg7 10 0-0 ♖e8 11 dxe5 dxe5 12 ♘g3 ♘bd7∓ Aaron – Torre, Penang 1978.

(b) 11 ♘f2 e5!? 12 c3 bxc3 13 bxc3 ♕a5=.

(c) (1) 7 ♘h3 ♗b7 8 ♗e2 e5 9 0-0 a6=.

(2) 7 g4 ♗b7 8 ♘ge2 e5?! (8 ... ♘b6) 9 g5 ♘h5 10 ♘g3 ♘g7 11 d5± Ehlvest – Ftacnik, Philadelphia 1991.

(d) 11 ♘d1 a5 12 0-0 c5= Hennings – Smyslov, Havana 1967.

(e) 7 ... ♘bd7 8 h3 c6 9 a4±.

(f) 11 ♘d5 ♗e6 (11 ... c6?? 12 e5! cxd5 13 ♕xd4+−) 12 ♕f3 ♗xd5 13 exd5±; 12 e5 ♗xd5 13 exf6 ♖e8!! 14 ♕xd4 ♗xg2 15 ♕xd8 ♖axd8 16 ♔xg2 h6! 17 ♗e3 ♗xf6= ½–½ Speelman – Nunn, Hastings 1979/80.

(g) 4 ♗e2 ♗g7 5 h4!? (5 ♘f3 – cols 5-8) 5 ... h5 6 ♘h3 ♘c6! 7 ♘g5 0-0 8 ♗e3 e5 9 d5 ♘d4! 10 ♗xd4 exd4 11 ♕xd4 c6 12 dxc6 bxc6 Wade – Smylsov, Havana 1962 13 ♕d2!∓/∓.

(h) 6 ... ♘xd4 7 exf6 ♘xe2 8 fxg7 ♖g8 9 ♘gxe2∞/±.

(i) 7 ... dxe5 8 ♗xf7+ ♔xf7 9 ♘g5+ ♔e8 10 ♕c4! e6∞/±.

PIRC DEFENCE
Classical

1 e4 d6 2 d4 Nf6 3 Nc3 g6 4 Nf3 Bg7 5 Be2 O-O 6 O-O *(a)*

	(5)	*(6)*	*(7)*	*(8)*
6	Bg4		c6	Nc6 *(g)*
7	Be3		a4	d5!
	Nc6		Qc7 *(f)*	Nb8 *(h)*
8	Qd2 *(b)*		h3	h3
	e5		Nbd7	c6!? *(i)*
9	d5	dxe5	a5	Bg5
	Ne7	dxe5	e5	Nbd7
10	Rad1	Rad1	dxe5	Re1
	Nd7!? *(c)*	Qc8	dxe5	Re8
11	Ng5!?	Qc1	Be3±	Qd2
	Bxe2	Rd8		a6
12	Qxe2	Rxd8		a4
	h6	Qxd8 *(d)*		Qc7±
13	Nh3±	Rd1 *(e)*		

(a) (1) 6 h3 Na6!? (6 ... c6 7 O-O - col 7, 6 ... c5 7 dxc5
Qa5 8 O-O Qxc5=/±) 7 Be3 c5 8 d5 Nc7 9 a4 a6 10 Nd2
Rb8 11 a5 Bd7 12 Na4 e6∞/= Hübner - Keene, Southport
1969.

(2) 6 Bg5 c5 7 dxc5 Qa5=.

(b) (1) 8 Nd2 Bxe2 9 Qxe2 e5 10 d5 Ne7 11 Rfd1 Qc8 12
Nc4!? (12 f3=) 12 ... Ng4=.

(2) 8 Qd3!? Nd7 (8 ... e5 9 d5 Nb4!? 10 Qd2 a5± Karpov - Korchnoi, World Ch (20) 1978) 9 Nd2 Nb4! 10 Qc4
Bxe2 11 Nxe2 c5!=.

(c) 10 ... Bd7 11 Ne1 Ng4 12 Bxg4 Bxg4 12 f3 Bd7 13
f4=/±; 10 ... Kh8; 10 ... Nc8!?

(d) 12 ... Nxd8∞ Pritchett - Keene, China 1981.

(e) 13 ... Qf8 14 h3 Bxf3 15 Bxf3 h5! △ ... Kh7, Bh6±; 15
... Rd8 16 Nb5!±; 15 .... a6 16 Nb1! Rd8 17 Rxd8 Qxd8 18 c3±.

(f) 7 ... Nbd7 8 e5 Ne8 9 Bf4±; 7 ... a5 8 Bf4 Na6 9 h3±.

(g) (1) 6 ... Na6?! 7 Re1 c5 8 e5! Ne8 9 Bg5 f6 10 exf6±/±.

(2) 6 ... Nbd7 7 e5! Ne8 8 Bf4 c6±.

(h) 7 ... Nb4!? 8 Re1± △ 8 ... e6?! 9 a3 Na6 10 dxe6 Bxe6
11 Nd4 Bd7 12 Bg5±.

(i) 8 ... e5!? 9 dxe6 Bxe6±.

PIRC DEFENCE
Austrian Attack

1 e4 d6 2 d4 ♘f6 3 ♘c3 g6 4 f4 ♗g7 5 ♘f3 *(a)*

	(9)	*(10)*	*(11)*	*(12)*
5	0-0			c5
6	♗d3	♗e3	e5!?	dxc5 *(i)*
	♘c6 *(b)*	c5 *(e)*	♘fd7!	♕a5
7	0-0 *(c)*	dxc5	h4!? *(f)*	♗d3
	♗g4 *(d)*	♕a5	c5	♕xc5
8	e5	♗d3	h5	♕e2
	dxe5	♘g4!?	cxd4	♘c6
9	dxe5	♗d2	hxg6 *(g)*	♗e3
	♘d5	♕xc5	dxc3	♕a5
10	h3!	♕e2	exf7+	0-0
	♘xc3	♘f6	♖xf7∓ *(h)*	♗g4
11	bxc3	0-0-0!?		h3!?
	♗f5			♗xf3
12	♗e3±			♕xf3=

(a) 5 e5 dxe5 6 dxe5 ♕xd1+ 7 ♔xd1 ♘g4 8 ♔e1 f6 9 h3 ♘h6 10 exf6 exf6 11 g4=/±.

(b) 6 ... ♘a6!? 7 0-0 (7 e5!?) 7 ... c5 8 d5=/±.

(c) 7 e5 dxe5 8 fxe5 ♘h5! 9 ♗e2 ♗g4 10 ♗e3 f6 11 exf6=; 11 e6!?∞; 8 dxe5 ♘d5 9 ♗d2 ♘cb4 10 ♗e4 ♘b6=/±.

(d) 7 ... e5!? 8 fxe5 dxe5 9 d5 ♘e7±; 9 ... ♘d4!?; 8 dxe5 dxe5 9 f5 gxf5 10 exf5 ♘b4 11 ♔h1 ♘xd3 12 cxd3 ♗xf5 13 ♘xe5 ♘d7 14 ♖xf5 ♘xe5 15 d4±.

(e) (1) 6 ... b6 7 e5! ♘g4 8 ♗g1 c5 9 h3 ♘h6 10 d5 ♗b7 11 ♕d2 ♘f5 12 ♗h2 dxe5 13 fxe5 e6 14 0-0-0 exd5 15 ♘xd5 ♘c6∞ Beliavsky - Anand, Munich 1991.

(2) 6 ... ♘c6 7 ♗e2 a6! 8 e5 ♘g4 △ ... b5∞.

(f) 7 e6!? fxe6 8 h4 ♘f6 9 ♗d3 ♘c6 10 h5 gxh5! 11 a3 ♗d7!∓; 7 ♗g5 ♘b6 8 ♗d3 ♘c6∓; 7 ♗c4!? ♘b6 8 ♗e2 dxe5 9 fxe5 ♘c6 10 0-0 ♗g4=/∓.

(g) 9 ♕xd4 dxe5 10 ♕f2 e4!; 10 ♕g1 e4!

(h) (1) 11 ♘g5? cxb2 12 ♗c4 ♘xe5 13 ♕h5 ♕a5+ 14 ♔f1 d5!-+.

(2) 11 ♗c4 e6! 12 ♘g5 ♘xe5 13 ♕h5 h6-+/∓.

(i) 6 ♗b5+!? ♗d7 7 e5 ♘g4 8 h3 (8 ♗xd7+!? ♕xd7 9 d5±) 8 ... cxd4 9 ♕xd4 ♗xb5 10 ♘xb5 ♘c6 11 ♕e4 ♕a5+ 12 ♘c3±.

MODERN DEFENCE

1 e4 g6 2 d4 d6

	(1)	(2)	(3)	(4)
3	♘c3		♘f3	c3 *(j)*
	♗g7		♗g7	♗g7
4	♗e3	f4	♗c4!? *(f)*	f4!? *(k)*
	a6!? *(a)*	c6 *(c)*	♘f6	♘f6
5	♕d2	♘f3 *(d)*	♕e2!	e5 *(l)*
	b5	♗g4	c6	dxe5
6	f3	♗e3	♗b3	fxe5
	♘d7	♕b6	0-0 *(g)*	♘d5
7	♘h3!? *(b)*	♕d2!? *(e)*	0-0	♘f3
	♗b7	♗xf3	a5	0-0
8	♘f2	gxf3	a4?! *(h)*	♗c4
	c5	♘d7∞/=	♗g4	c5!
9	♗e2=/±		♘bd2 *(i)*	0-0 *(m)*

(a) 4 ... c6 5 ♕d2 b5 6 h4 h5 7 ♘h3 a6 8 ♗d3 ♘d7 9 ♘e2=/±.

(b) 7 h4!? h5 8 ♘h3=/±.

(c) 4 ... ♘f6 – Pirc Defence cols 9–12; 4 ... a6!?; 4 ... ♘c6!? 5 ♗e3!±.

(d) 5 ♗e3!? ♕b6 6 ♖b1 f5 (Botvinnik) 7 e5! dxe5 8 fxe5 ♗xe5 9 ♘f3! ♗g7 10 ♗c4!⩱ (Keene).

(e) 7 ♕d3 ♘f6 8 0-0-0 d5! 9 e5 ♘e4 10 ♘e2 ♘a6=; 7 ♖b1!?

(f) 4 ♗e2 ♘f6 5 ♘c3 / 4 ♘c3 ♘f6 5 ♗e2 – Pirc Defence cols 5–8; 4 ♘c3 a6!? 5 ♗c4!?±.

(g) 6 ... e5 7 dxe5 dxe5 8 ♗d2!? ♕e7 9 ♘a3!? b5! 10 c4!= Speelman – Zilberman, Frunze 1979.

(h) 8 c3!± Keene.

(i) 9 ... d5 10 e5 ♘fd7 11 h3 ♗xf3 12 ♘xf3 e6=.

(j) (1) 3 c4
(2) 3 ♗c4!? ♗g7 4 ♕f3!? e6 5 ♘ge2±.
(3) 3 h4!? ♘f6 4 ♘c3 ♗g7 5 ♗e2 h5! Pirc Defence col 4 note *(g)*.

(k) 4 ♘f3 ♘f6 5 ♘bd2 0-0 6 ♗e2 ♘c6 7 0-0 ♖e8! 8 ♖e1 e5 9 dxe5 ♘xe5 10 ♘xe5 ♖xe5=.

(l) 5 ♗d3 e5!? 6 ♘f3 exf4 7 ♗xf4 0-0 8 0-0 c5=.

(m) 9 ... cxd4 10 cxd4 ♘c6 11 ♘c3 ♘b6!?=/∓.

ALEKHINE'S DEFENCE

1 e4 ♘f6 2 e5 *(a)* ♘d5

	(1)	*(2)*	*(3)*	*(4)*
3	♘c3	c4	d4	
	e6 *(b)*	♘b6	d6	
4	d4	c5!?	♗c4!?	c4
	d6	♘d5	♘b6 *(f)*	♘b6
5	♘f3 *(c)*	♗c4	♗b3	exd6
	♘xc3	e6 *(d)*	dxe5 *(g)*	cxd6!? *(i)*
6	bxc3	♘c3	♕h5	♘c3
	dxe5	♘xc3	e6	g6
7	♘xe5	dxc3	dxe5	h3 *(j)*
	♘d7	♘c6	a5	♗g7
8	♗f4	♗f4	a4	♘f3
	c5=	♕h4!? *(e)*	♘c6!? *(h)*	0-0=/±

(a) 2 ♘c3 d5 (2 ... e5 – Vienna Game) 3 exd5 ♘xd5 4 ♗c4
e6 5 ♘f3 ♗e7 6 0-0 0-0 7 d4 b6=.

(b) 3 ... ♘xc3 4 dxc3 d6 5 ♘f3 dxe5 6 ♕xd8+ ♔xd8 7
♘xe5 ♔e8±; 4 bxc3 d6 5 f4 g6 6 ♘f3 ♗g7 7 d4 0-0 8 ♗d3 c5
9 0-0 dxe5 10 dxe5 ♗f5±/=.

(c) 5 ♘e4!? ♘c6 6 ♘f3±/=:

(d) 5 ... c6 6 ♕e2!? (6 ♘c3 d6 7 cxd6 exd6 8 ♕b3 dxe5=) 6
... ♕a5!? 7 ♘f3 ♕xc5 8 d4 ♕b4+ 9 ♘bd2 b6 10 0-0∞ Maka-
richev – Alburt, USSR Ch, 1st League 1978.

(e) (1) 8 ... b6 9 cxb6 axb6 10 ♘f3 ♗e7±.

(2) 8 ... ♗xc5 9 ♕g4 g5 10 ♗xg5 ♖g8 11 ♗xd8 (11
♘h3!?) 11 .. ♖xg4 12 ♗e2 ♖xg2 13 ♗xc7 ♗xf2+ 14 ♔f1 ♖xg1+
15 ♔xf2±.

(3) 8 ... ♕h4!? 9 g3 ♕e7 10 ♘f3 ♕xc5 11 ♕e2∞.

(f) 4 ... c6 5 ♕e2 g6 6 h3 ♗g7 7 ♘f3±; 4 ... e6 5 ♘f3 ♗e7 6
0-0 0-0±.

(g) 5 ... ♘c6 6 e6!? fxe6 7 ♘f3 g6 8 ♘g5∞/±; 5 ... ♗f5!? 6
♕f3 ♕c8 7 ♘h3 e6=/± △ 8 ♘g5 ♗e7 9 ♘xf7 ♖f8!=.

(h) 8 ... ♘c6!? 9 ♘f3 ♘d7! 10 ♗xe6!? ♘xde5 11 ♘xe5 (11
♗xc8 g6!±) 11 ... ♗xe6 12 ♘xc6 bxc6=; 8 ... ♘a6!? 9 ♘f3
♘c5 10 ♗a2 ♗d7 11 ♘c3 ♘bxa4 12 ♗g5∞.

(i) 5 ... exd6 6 ♘c3 ♗e7 7 h3 0-0 8 ♘f3 ♗f6 9 ♗e2
♖e8=/±.

(j) 7 ♗e3 ♗g7 8 ♗d3 0-0 9 ♘ge2 ♘c6 10 0-0 ♗g4 11 f3 ♗f5=.

ALEKHINE'S DEFENCE

1 e4 ♘f6 2 e5 ♘d5 3 d4 d6

	Modern		Four Pawns Attack	
	(5)	*(6)*	*(7)*	*(8)*
4	♘f3 [Dia]		c4	
	♗g4	g6 *(d)*	♘b6	
5	♗e2	♗c4! *(e)*	f4	
	e6	♘b6	dxe5	
6	0-0	♗b3	fxe5	
	♗e7 *(a)*	♗g7	♗f5 *(h)*	
7	h3	♘g5! *(f)*	♘c3	
	♗h5	d5	e6	
8	c4	0-0	♘f3	
	♘b6	♘c6	♘c6	
9	♘c3	c3	♗e3 [Dia]	
	0-0 *(b)*	0-0 *(g)*	♗e7 *(i)*	
10	♗e3	f4	♗e2	d5!?
	d5	f6	0-0	exd5!
11	c5	♘f3	0-0	cxd5
	♗xf3	♗f5±	f6	♘b4
12	gxf3!?± *(c)*	♘h4±	exf6±	♘d4∞ *(j)*

(column 1)

(column 3)

(a) 6 ... ♘c6?! 7 c4 ♘b6 8 exd6 cxd6 9 d5 exd5 10 cxd5 ♗xf3 11 gxf3! ♘e5 12 ♗b5+ ♘ed7 13 ♕d4 ♕f6 14 ♖e1+ ♔d8 15 ♕d1± Boleslavsky.

(b) 9 ... ♘c6? 10 exd6 cxd6 11 d5 exd5 12 ♘xd5±.

(c) (1) 12 ♗xf3 ♘c4 13 ♗f4 ♘c6 14 b3 ♘4a5 15 ♖c1 ♕d7 16 ♗e3 f6= Geller – Bagirov, USSR Ch 1978.

(2) 12 gxf3!? ♘c8 13 f4 ♘c6 14 f5 exf5 15 ♗f3∞/± Sax – Ivanchuk, Tilburg 1989.

(d) (1) 4 ... ♘c6 5 c4 ♘b6 6 e6!? fxe6 7 h4!? e5 8 d5 ♘d4 9 ♘xd4 exd4 10 ♕xd4±;

(2) 4 ... ♘b6!? 5 a4 a5 6 ♗e2±;

(3) 4 ... dxe5 5 ♘xe5 ♘d7!? 6 ♘xf7!? ♔xf7 7 ♕h5+ ♔e6 8 c4 (8 ♕g4+ ♔f7! 9 ♕h5+=; 8 g3!?) 8 ... ♘5f6 9 d5+ ♔d6 10 ♕f7 ♘b6∞/±.

(e) 5 c4 ♘b6 6 exd6 cxd6!? 7 ♗e2 ♗g7 8 0-0 0-0 9 ♗e3 ♘c6 10 ♘c3 ♗g4±.

(f) 7 a4 dxe5!? (7 ... a5±) 8 a5 ♘6d7 9 ♗xf7+ ♔xf7 10 ♘g5+ ♔g8 11 ♘e6 ♕e8 12 ♘xc7 ♕d8!⩲ Christiansen – Alburt, USA Ch 1990.

(g) 9 ... ♗f5?! 10 g4 ♗xb1 11 ♕f3!± Olafsson – Larsen, Reykjavik 1978.

(h) 6 ... c5!? 7 d5 e6 8 ♘c3 exd5 9 cxd5 c4 10 ♘f3 ♗b4! 11 ♗xc4 ♗xc3+ 12 bxc3 ♘xc4 13 ♕a4 ♘d7 14 ♕xc4∞ Minasian – Shabalov, Minsk 1990.

(i) (1) 9 ... ♕d7 10 ♗e2 0-0-0 11 0-0 ♗g4 12 c5 ♘d5 13 ♘xd5 ♕xd5 14 ♘g5!±;

(2) 9 ... ♘b4 10 ♖c1 c5 11 ♗g5! f6 12 exf6 gxf6 13 ♗e3 ♗g4 14 ♗e2±/±.

(3) 9 ... ♗g4 10 ♕d2 ♗b4 11 a3 ♗e7 12 ♘e4 ♕d7∞ Hübner – Hort, Biel 1987.

(j) 12 ... ♗d7 13 e6 fxe6 14 dxe6 ♗c6 15 ♕g4 ♗h4+ 16 g3 ♗xh1 17 0-0-0 ♕f6 18 gxh4 0-0∞.

1 e4 VARIOUS

1 e4

	Centre-Counter (1)	(2)	Nimzowitsch (3)	1 ... b6 (4)
1	d5		♘c6	b6 *(i)*
2	exd5		d4	d4
	♘f6	♛xd5	d5 *(g)*	♗b7
3	d4 *(a)*	♘c3	♘c3!	♘c3 *(j)*
	♘xd5	♛a5	dxe4	e6
4	♘f3	d4	d5	♘f3
	♗g4?! *(b)*	♘f6	♘e5 *(h)*	♗b4
5	c4	♘f3	♗f4	♗d3
	♘b6	♗f5 *(e)*	♘g6	♘f6
6	c5!	♗d2	♗g3	♛e2
	♘6d7 *(c)*	♘bd7	f5	d5
7	♗c4	♗c4	♘h3!	e5
	e6	c6	e5	♘e4
8	♗e3 *(d)*	♛e2! *(f)*	dxe6±	0-0!?∞/± *(k)*

(a) (1) 3 c4 c6 (3 ... e6!? 4 dxe6 ♗xe6 5 d4 ♗b4+ △ ... ♛e7⩲ A Sokolov - Speelman, Madrid 1988) 4 d4! cxd5 5 ♘c3 - Caro-Kann cols 5-6.

(2) 3 ♘c3 ♘xd5 Alekhine - cols 1-4 note *(a)*.

(3) 3 ♗b5+!? ♗d7 4 ♗c4 ♗g4 5 f3 ♗c8!⩲

(b) 4 ... g6±; 4 ... c6±.

(c) 6 ... ♘d5 7 ♛b3!±; 6 ... ♗xf3 7 ♛xf3 ♘d5 8 ♛b3!±.

(d) 8 ... b6 9 ♘c3 bxc5?! (9 ... ♗e7±) 10 d5! ♗d6 (10 ... e5 11 d6! △ 12 ♛d5) 11 dxe6 fxe6 12 h3 ♗f5 13 g4 ♗g6 14 ♗xe6+-.

(e) 5 ... ♗g4 6 h3 ♗xf3 7 ♛xf3 c6 8 ♗d2±.

(f) 8 ... e6 (8 ... ♗xc2? 9 ♘b5 △ 10 ♘d6+!) 9 d5!

(g) 2 ... e5 3 dxe5 ♘xe5 4 ♘f3 ♛f6 5 ♘xe5 ♛xe5 6 ♗d3 ♗c5 7 ♛e2 ♘f6 8 ♘c3 ♘f6 9 h3!±/± △ 10 ♗d2, 11 0-0-0.

(h) 4 ... ♘b8 5 ♗c4 ♘f6 6 ♗f4±.

(i) 1 ... a6!? 2 d4 b5 3 ♘f3 ♗b7 4 ♗d3 ♘f6 5 ♛e2 e6± Karpov - Miles, European Team Ch, Skara 1980.

(j) 3 ♗d3 e6±; 3 ♗d3 f5?! 4 exf5!? ♗xg2 5 ♛h5+ g6 6 fxg6 ♗g7! 7 gxh7+ ♔f8 8 ♘e2! ♗xh1 9 ♘f4 ♘f6 10 ♘g6+ ♔e8 11 ♘xh8+ ♘xh5 12 ♗g6+ ♔f8 13 ♗xh5± △ 13 ... ♗xh8 14 ♗h6+ ♗g7 15 h8(♛); 3 ♘d2±.

(k) 8 0-0!? ♘xc3 9 bxc3 ♗xc3!? (9 ... ♗e7±) 10 ♖b1⩲.

QUEEN'S GAMBIT DECLINED
Semi-Tarrasch Defence

1 d4 d5 2 c4 e6 3 ♘c3 ♘f6 4 ♘f3 c5

	(1)	(2)	(3)	(4)
5	cxd5			e3
	♘xd5			♘c6
6	e4	e3	g3	a3!? (h)
	♘xc3	♘c6	♘c6	cxd4!? (i)
7	bxc3	♗d3	♗g2	exd4
	cxd4	cxd4!? (c)	♗e7	♗e7
8	cxd4	exd4	0-0	♗d3
	♗b4+ (a)	♗e7 (d)	0-0	dxc4
9	♗d2	0-0	♘xd5 (f)	♗xc4
	♗xd2+	0-0	exd5	0-0
10	♕xd2	♖e1 (e)	dxc5	0-0
	0-0		♗xc5	a6
11	♗c4±/± (b)		♕c2 (g)	♗g5 (j)

(a) 8 ... ♘c6 9 ♗c4 b5!? 10 ♗e2! ♗b4+ 11 ♗d2 ♗xd2+ (11 ... ♕a5 12 d5!) 12 ♕xd2 a6 13 a4 b4 14 d5±.

(b) 11 ... ♘c6 12 0-0 b6 13 ♖ad1 ♗b7 14 ♖fe1! ♘e7 (14 ... ♘a5 15 ♗d3 ♖c8 16 d5 exd5 17 e5!±) 15 d5!± Petrosian – Korchnoi, Il Ciocco (6) 1977.

(c) 7 ... ♗e7 8 0-0 0-0 9 ♖e1=/±; 9 ♘xd5!? ♕xd5 10 e4 ♕h5=/±.

(d) 8 ... ♗b4 9 ♕c2 (9 ♗d2 0-0 10 0-0 ♗e7 11 a3 ♗f6 12 ♕c2 h6 13 ♗e3∞ Sveshnikov – Speelman, Moscow 1985) 9 ... ♗a5!∞.

(e) (1) 10 ... ♘f6 11 a3 b6 12 ♗c2 ♗b7 13 ♕d3 g6!±; 13 ... ♖c8?! 14 d5! exd5 15 ♗g5 g6 16 ♖xe7!±.
   (2) 10 ... ♗f6 11 ♗e4 ♘ce7±.

(f) 9 e4!?:
   (1) 9 ... ♘xc3 10 bxc3 cxd4 11 cxd4 ♗f6 12 ♗e3 b6 13 e5±.
   (2) 9 ... ♘db4!? 10 a3 (10 dxc5!?; 10 d5!?/?!) 10 ... cxd4 11 axb4 dxc3 12 bxc3 b6=:

(g) 11 ... ♗e7 12 ♗e3±; 11 ... ♗b6!? 12 ♘g5 g6 13 ♕d1!? ♗e6 14 ♘h3 ♗xh3 15 ♗xh3 ♖e8 16 ♗g2 ♕e7=.

(h) 6 cxd5 exd5 – Tarrasch col 7; 6 ... ♘xd5 – col 2.

(i) 6 ... a6=/±; 6 ... ♘e4!?

(j) 11 ... b5 12 ♗a2 ♗b7=.

QUEEN'S GAMBIT DECLINED
Tarrasch Defence

1 d4 d5 2 c4 e6 3 ♘c3 c5 4 cxd5

	(5)	(6)	(7)	Hennig-Schara (8)
4	exd5			cxd4?!
5	♘f3			♕a4+
	♘c6			♗d7
6	g3		e3	♕xd4
	♘f6 (a)		♘f6	exd5
7	♗g2		♗e2	♕xd5
	♗e7		cxd4	♘c6
8	0-0		♘xd4	♘f3
	0-0		♗d6	♘f6
9	♗g5	dxc5 (d)	0-0	♕d1!
	cxd4 (b)	♗xc5 (e)	0-0	♗c5
10	♘xd4	♗g5!	♘f3!?	e3
	h6	d4	a6	♕e7
11	♗e3	♗xf6	b3	♗e2
	♖e8	♕xf6	♖e8	g5!?
12	♖c1 (c)	♘d5 (f)	♗b2=	0-0±/± (g)

(a) 6 ... c4!? 7 ♗g2 ♗b4 8 0-0 ♘ge7 9 e4 dxe4 (9 ... 0-0 10 exd5 ♘xd5 11 ♗g5±) 10 ♘xe4 0-0 11 ♕c2 ♕d5 12 ♗e3 ♘g6 13 ♘h4 ♕b5 14 ♘xg6 hxg6 15 a3 ♗e7 16 d5!±.

(b) (1) 9 ... ♗e6 10 dxc5 ♗xc5 11 ♗xf6 ♕xf6 12 ♘xd5 ♕xb2 13 ♘c7 ♖ad8 14 ♕c1 ♕xc1 15 ♖axc1±.

(2) 9 ... c4 10 ♘e5 ♗e6 11 ♘xc6 bxc6 12 b3=/±.

(c) (1) 12 ♕b3 ♘a5 13 ♕c2 ♗g4 14 ♘f5 ♗b4!∞ (14 ... ♖c8?! 15 ♗d4 ♗c5 16 ♗xc5 ♖xc5 17 ♘e3± Karpov - Kasparov, World Ch (9) Moscow 1984).

(2) 12 ♖c1 ♗f8 13 ♘xc6 bxc6 14 ♘a4 ♗d7! 15 ♗c5 ♗xc5 16 ♘xc5 ♗f5 17 ♖e1 ♖b8= Kasparov.

(d) (1) 9 ♗e3 c4! 10 ♘e5 ♕a5=.

(2) 9 b3 ♘e4 10 ♗b2 ♗f6 11 ♘a4 ♖e8! (11 ... b5?? 12 ♘xc5 ♘xc5 13 ♖c1+-) 12 ♖c1 cxd4 13 ♘xd4 ♗xd4! △ ... ♗f5=.

(e) 9 ... d4?! 10 ♘a4 ♗f5∞/±.

(f) (1) 12 ♘e4 ♕e7 13 ♘xc5 ♕xc5=.

(2) 12 ♘d5! ♕d8 13 ♘d2 ♖e8 14 ♖c1±.

(g) 12 ... 0-0-0 13 b4!? ♗xb4 14 ♗b2±; 13 a3!?

QUEEN'S GAMBIT DECLINED
Various Unusual Lines

1 d4 d5 2 c4 e6 3 ♘c3 ♘f6

	Ragozin		Peruvian	
	(9)	*(10)*	*(11)*	*(12)*
4	♘f3			♗g5
	♗b4		♗e7	c5!?
5	cxd5	♕a4+ *(c)*	♗f4!? *(f)*	cxd5
	exd5	♘c6	0-0	cxd4 *(h)*
6	♗g5	cxd5	e3	♕xd4
	h6	exd5 *(d)*	c5	♗e7
7	♗xf6 *(a)*	♗g5	dxc5	e4
	♕xf6	h6	♘c6	♘c6
8	e3	♗xf6	cxd5 *(g)*	♕d2
	0-0	♕xf6	exd5	♘xe4 *(i)*
9	♗e2	e3	♗e2	♘xe4
	c6	0-0	♗xc5	exd5
10	0-0	♗e2 *(e)*	0-0	♗xe7
	♘d7	♗e6	♗e6	♕xe7
11	a3 =/± *(b)*	0-0±/=	♖c1±	♕xd5± *(j)*

(a) 7 ♗h4!?∞ e.g: 7 ... c5 8 e3 ♘c6 9 dxc5 g5 10 ♗g3 ♘e4 11 ♗b5 ♘xc3 12 ♗xc6+ bxc6 13 ♕d4 ♘xa2+ 14 ♘d2 ♗xd2+ 15 ♕xd2 d4! 16 ♖xa2 dxe3 17 ♕xe3+= Uhlmann - Sosonko, Hastings 1975/76.

(b) 11 ... ♗d6 12 b4=/±.

(c) 5 ♗g5!? dxc4!? (5 ... h6 6 ♗xf6 ♕xf6 7 cxd5 - col 9) 6 e4 c5 7 e5!? cxd4 8 ♕a4+ ♘c6 9 0-0-0 ♗d7 10 ♘e4 ♗e7∞.

(d) 6 ... ♘xd5 7 ♗d2 0-0 8 e3±.

(e) 10 ♗b5?! ♗g4!

(f) 5 ♗g5 h6!? 6 ♗xf6 ♗xf6 7 e4±; 5 g3!?

(g) 8 ♕c2 ♗xc5 9 a3 ♕a5 10 0-0-0 ♗d7 11 g4 ♖fc8 12 ♔b1 b5 13 cxb5 ♘e7 14 ♘d2 ♕d8 15 ♘b3 ♘e4∞ Gelfand - Beliavsky, Linares 1991.

(h) 5 ... ♕b6 6 ♗xf6 ♕xb2 7 ♖c1 gxf6 8 e3 cxd4 9 exd4 ♗b4 10 ♗b5+ ♗d7 11 ♗xd7+ ♘xd7 12 ♘e2 ♗xc3+ 13 ♖xc3±.

(i) 8 ... ♘xd5 9 ♗xe7! (9 exd5∞) 9 ... ♘dxe7 10 ♕xd8+±/±.

(j) 11 ... 0-0 12 f3 ♘b4 13 ♕c4! ♗e6 14 ♕c5 ♕xc5 15 ♘xc5 ♘c2+ 16 ♔d2 ♘xa1 17 ♘ex6 fxe6 18 ♗d3 ♖fd8 19 ♘e2± △ 19 ... ♖xd3+? 20 ♔xd3 ♖d8+ 21 ♔c3 ♖c8+ 22 ♔d2!+-.

QUEEN'S GAMBIT DECLINED
Exchange Variations

1 d4 d5 2 c4 e6 3 ♘c3

	(13)	*(14)*	*(15)*	*(16)*
3	♘f6		♗e7	
4	cxd5		cxd5	
	exd5		exd5	
5	♗g5		♗f4	
	c6		♘f6	c6
6	♕c2 *(a)*		e3	e3
	♗e7		0-0	♗f5
7	e3		♕c2	♘ge2!? *(g)*
	♘bd7		c6?! *(e)*	♘d7
8	♗d3		♗d3	♘g3
	0-0		♖e8	♗g6
9	♘f3	♘ge2	♘f3	♗e2! *(h)*
	♖e8	♖e8	♘bd7	♘f8?! *(i)*
10	0-0	g4	0-0-0	h4!
	♘f8 *(b)*	♘f8	♘f8	♗xh4
11	♖ab1 *(c)*	h3 *(d)*	h3 *(f)*	♕b3!±/± *(j)*

(a) 6 e3 ♗f5 7 ♕f3 ♗g6 8 ♗xf6 ♕xf6 9 ♕xf6 gxf6 10 ♔d2±/∞ Ivanchuk – Short, Linares 1992.

(b) 10 ... h6 11 ♗f4!±.

(c) (1) 11 ... ♘e4 12 ♗xe7 ♕xe7 13 b4±.

(2) 11 ... a5!? 12 a3 ♘e4 13 ♗xe7 ♕xe7 14 b4 ♗f5!? 15 ♗xe4 dxe4 16 ♘e5 axb4 17 axb4 f6 18 ♘c4 ♗e6± Eising – Unzicker, East German Ch 1961.

(d) 11 ... ♔h8!? 12 0-0-0 ♘g8!? 13 ♗xe7 ♘xe7 14 ♔b1±.

(e) 7 ... c5

(f) 11 ... ♗e6 12 ♔b1 ♖c8 13 ♘g5!± Timman – Karpov, Bugojno 1978.

(g) 7 g4!? ♗e6 8 h3∞; 7 ♗d3 ♗xd3 8 ♕xd3=.

(h) 9 ♖c1?! h5 10 ♗d3 h4! 11 ♗xg6 (11 ♘f5 ♗xf5 12 ♗xf5 g5!∓/-+) 11 ... hxg3 12 ♗d3 gxf2+ 13 ♔xf2=(?) Speelman – Geller, European Team Ch, Skara 1980.

(i) 9 ... ♘gf6 10 h4 h5 11 ♗g5 ♗d6 12 ♖h3!?± Portisch – Geller, Portoroz (Interzonal Play-off) 1973.

(j) 11 ... ♗xg3 (11 ... b6 12 ♕a4±) 12 ♗xg3 ♕b6 13 ♕a3±/±.

QUEEN'S GAMBIT DECLINED
Cambridge Springs Defence and 6 ♖c1 Tartakower

1 d4 d5 2 c4 e6 3 ♘c3 ♘f6 4 ♗g5

	Cambridge Springs		Tartakower	
	(17)	*(18)*	*(19)*	*(20)*
4	♘bd7		♗e7	
5	e3 *(a)*		e3	
	c6		0-0	
6	♘f3		♖c1	
	♕a5		h6	
7	♘d2	cxd5!?	♗h4	
	♗b4	♘xd5	b6 *(f)*	
8	♕c2	♕d2	♗xf6	cxd5
	0-0	♘7b6 *(d)*	♗xf6	♘xd5
9	♗e2	♗d3	cxd5	♘xd5
	dxc4 *(b)*	♘xc3	exd5	exd5
10	♗xf6	bxc3	g3!? *(g)*	♗xe7
	♘xf6	♘d5∞ *(e)*	♗e7	♕xe7
11	♘xc4 *(c)*		♗g2 *(h)*	♗e2 *(i)*

(a) 5 cxd5 exd5 6 e3 – cols 12-13; 6 ♘xd5?? ♘xd5 7 ♗xd8 ♗b4+ 8 ♕d2 ♗xd2+ 9 ♔xd2 ♔xd8-+.

(b) 9 ... e5 10 0-0! exd4 11 ♘b3 ♕c7 12 ♘xd4 dxc4 13 ♗xc4±; 10 ... e4 11 c5±; 10 ... ♗d6 11 ♘b3 ♕c7 12 cxd5 exd4 13 ♘xd4 ♘xd5 16 ♘xd5 ♗xh2+ 17 ♔h1 cxd5 18 g3 ♗xg3 19 fxg3±.

(c) 11 ... ♕c7 12 0-0 ♖d8 13 a3 ♗e7 14 ♖fd1 ♗d7 15 b4=/±.

(d) 8 ... ♗b4 9 ♖c1 0-0 10 e4 ♘xc3 11 bxc3 ♗a3 12 ♖b1 e5 13 ♗d3 ♖e8 14 0-0±

(e) (1) 11 0-0 ♕xc3 (11 ... ♘xc3? 12 ♖fc1 ♗b4 13 a3!+-) 12 ♕e2 ♗d6 13 ♖ac1∞.

(2) 11 ♖c1 ♘xc3 12 0-0 ♗b4 13 a3 ♕xa3 14 ♖a1 ♕b3 15 ♖fc1 ♘c2 16 ♕xa2 ♕xd3 17 d5! 0-0 18 ♖d1∞ △ 19 d6.

(f) 7 ... ♘e4 8 ♗xe7 ♕xe7 9 cxd5 ♘xc3 10 ♖xc3 exd5 11 ♗d3 c6 12 ♘e2 ♘d7 13 0-0 ♘f6 14 ♕b1±.

(g) 10 ♕f3!? ♗b7 11 ♗c4 c6 12 ♗b3 ♘d7 13 ♘ge2=.

(h) 11 ... c6 12 ♘ge2 ♘d7 13 0-0 ♘f6=.

(i) 11 ♘f3 – col 21; 11 ♗e2 c5! 12 dxc5 bxc5 13 ♕xd5 ♗b7 14 ♕xc5 ♕xc5 15 ♖xc5 ♗xg2 16 ♗f3 ♗xh1 17 ♗xh1 ♘a6 18 ♖a5 ♖ac8 19 ♖xa6 ♖c1+=.

QUEEN'S GAMBIT DECLINED
Tartakower and Lasker Variations

1 d4 d5 2 c4 e6 3 ♘c3 ♘f6 4 ♗g5 ♗e7 5 e3 0-0
6 ♘f3 h6 7 ♗h4

	Tartakower		Lasker	
	(21)	*(22)*	*(23)*	*(24)*
7	b6		♘e4	
8	cxd5	♗e2 *(d)*	♗xe7	
	♘xd5	♗b7	♕xe7	
9	♗xe7	♗xf6	cxd5	♖c1 *(g)*
	♕xe7	♗xf6	♘xc3	c6
10	♘xd5 *(a)*	cxd5	bxc3	♗d3
	exd5	exd5	exd5	♘xc3
11	♖c1	0-0 *(e)*	♕b3	♖xc3
	♗e6	♕e7	♖d8	dxc4
12	♕a4 *(b)*	♕b3	c4	♖xc4 *(h)*
	c5	c6	dxc4	♘d7
13	♕a3	♖fe1	♗xc4	♗b1
	♖c8	♗c8	♘c6	e5
14	♗e2 *(c)*	♖ac1±	♕c3± *(f)*	♕c2±

(a) 10 ♖c1 ♘f6 11 ♗e2 ♗b7 12 0-0 ♘bd7 13 ♕a4 c5=.

(b) 12 ♗d3!? c5 13 dxc5 bxc5 14 0-0 ♘d7 15 e4 dxe4 16 ♗xe4 ♖ab8 17 b3±/=.

(c) (1) 14 ♗b5 ♕b7! (14 ... a6 15 dxc5 bxc5 16 0-0± Fischer - Spassky, World Ch (6), Reykjavik 1972) 15 dxc5 bxc5 16 ♖xc5 ♖xc5 17 ♕xc5 ♘a6 18 ♗xa6 ♕xa6 19 ♕a3 ♕c4= Geller.
(2) 14 ♗e2 ♕b7 15 dxc5 bxc5 16 0-0 ♕b6=.

(d) 8 ♗d3 ♗b7 9 0-0 ♘bd7 10 ♖c1 c5 11 ♕e2 ♖c8= e.g. 12 ♖fd1 cxd4 13 ♘xd4 ♘e5=; 12 cxd5 ♘xd5 13 ♗xe7 ♘xc3 14 ♗xd8 ♘xe2+ 15 ♗xe2 ♖fxd8=.

(e) 11 b4 c6 12 0-0 ♖e8 13 ♕b3 a5 14 a3 ♘d7 15 b5 c5 16 ♘xd5 ♗xd4!!= Karpov - Short, Amsterdam 1991.

(f) 14 ... ♗g4 15 0-0 ♗xf3 16 gxf3 ♕f6 17 ♗e2 ♖d6 (17 ... ♖ac8 18 ♖ab1 b6 19 ♖fc1 ♘e7 20 ♔h1 ♖d5∓ Karpov - Yusupov, London (m) 1989) 18 ♔h1 ♖e8 19 ♖ae1 ♕h4∞.

(g) 9 ♕c2 ♘xc3 10 ♕xc3 dxc4!? 11 ♗xc4 b6 12 ♖c1 ♗b7 13 ♗e2 ♘d7 14 0-0 (14 ♕xc7?? ♖ac8-+) 14 ... c5=.

(h) 12 ♗xc4 ♘d7 13 0-0 e5 14 ♗b3! exd4 15 exd4 ♘f6 16 ♖e1 ♕d6 17 ♘e5± Karpov - Yusupov, London (m) 1989.

1 d4 d5 2 c4 e6 3 ♘c3 ♘f6 4 ♗g5 ♗e7 5 e3 0-0 (a) 6 ♘f3

	(25)	(26)	(27)	(28)
6	h6	♘bd7 (e)		
7	♗xf6	♕c2		
	♗xf6	c5		a6
8	♖c1 (b)	0-0-0!?	cxd5	cxd5
	c6	♕a5	♘xd5! (i)	exd5
9	♗d3	♔b1	♗xe7	♗d3
	♘d7	h6?! (f)	♕xe7	♖e8
10	cxd5 (c)	h4!?	♘xd5	0-0-0
	exd5!? (d)	dxc4	exd5	♘f8
11	b4	♗xc4	dxc5	h3
	a6	cxd4 (g)	♘xc5	b5
12	a4	exd4	♗e2	♔b1
	a5	♘b6	♗g4!	♗b7
13	b5±	♗b3 (h)	0-0 (j)	♘e2±/±

(a) 5 ... h6 6 ♗h4 0-0 7 ♘f3 b6; 7 ... ♘e4 - cols 21-24; 6 ♗xf6 ♗xf6 7 ♘f3 0-0 - col 25.

(b) (1) 8 ♕b3 c6 9 0-0-0!? ♘d7 10 e4 dxc4 11 ♗xc4 e5 12 d5 (12 dxe5 ♗xe5 13 ♘xe5 ♕g5+=/±) 12 ... ♘c5 13 ♕c2 ♕b6=.

(2) 8 ♕c2 c5 9 dxc5=; 9 0-0-0?! cxd4 10 exd4 ♘c6 11 h4 ♕c7 12 ♔b1 ♖d8∓.

(c) 10 0-0 dxc4 11 ♗xc4 e5 12 h3! (12 ♘e4 exd4 13 ♘xf6+ ♘xf6=) 12 ... exd4 13 exd4 ♘b6 14 ♗b3 ♗f5 15 ♖e1± Kasparov - Karpov, World Ch (22), Leningrad 1986.

(d) 10 ... cxd5 11 0-0 b6 12 e4 dxe4 13 ♗xe4 ♖b8 14 ♕e2 ♗b7 15 ♘b5 ♗a6 16 a4±.

(e) 6 ... ♘e4?!; 6 ... b6?!

(f) 9 ... cxd4 10 exd4 dxc4 11 ♗xc4 ♘b6 12 ♗b3 ♗d7∞ (Kasparov).

(g) 11 ... ♘b6? 12 ♗xf6! gxf6± (12 ... ♗xf6 13 ♘e4±) Kasparov - Marovic, Banja Luka 1979.

(h) 13 ... ♗d7 14 ♘e5 ♖ac8 15 ♖h3!± Kasparov.

(i) (1) 8 ... cxd4 9 ♘xd4 ♘xd5 10 ♗xe7 ♘xe7 11 ♗e2 ♘f6 12 0-0 ♗d7±/±.

(2) 8 ... exd5 9 ♗e2 c4 10 ♘e5 ♘xe5 11 dxe5 ♘g4 12 ♗xe7 ♕xe7 13 ♖d1 ♕xe5 14 ♖xd5 ♕c7 15 ♖d4±.

(j) 13 ... ♖ac8 14 ♖ac1 ♕f6 15 ♘d4!?±.

QUEEN'S GAMBIT DECLINED
Orthodox Defence

1 d4 d5 2 c4 e6 3 ♘c3 ♘f6 4 ♗g5 ♗e7 5 e3 0-0
6 ♘f3 ♘bd7 7 ♖c1

	(29)	(30)	(31)	(32)
7	c6			a6
8	♗d3		♕c2	c5! (h)
	dxc4		a6 [Dia]	c6
9	♗xc4		cxd5 (e)	♗d3 (i)
	♘d5		exd5	b6 (j)
10	♗xe7		♗d3	cxb6
	♕xe7 [Dia]		♖e8	c5 (k)
11	0-0	♘e4	0-0	0-0
	♘xc3	♘5f6	♘f8	c4
12	♖xc3	♘g3!?	a3	♗c2
	e5	e5 (c)	g6	♘xb6 (l)
13	dxe5 (a)	0-0	b4 (f)	♘e5
	♘xe5	exd4	♘e6	♗b7
14	♘xe5	♘f5	♗xf6	f4
	♕xe5	♕d8	♗xf6	♘fd7
15	f4 (b)	♘3xd4 (d)	a4 (g)	♕h5 (m)

(column 1)

(column 3)

(a) 13 ♕c2 exd4 14 exd4 ♘b6(!):

    (1) 15 ♖e1 ♕d8! 16 ♗b3 ♘d5 17 ♗xd5!? ♕xd5 18 ♖e5 ♕d6=;

    (2) 15 ♖e3 ♕d8! 16 ♗b3 ♘d5 17 ♖e5 f6! 18 ♗xd5+ cxd5 19 ♖e3 ♗g4=.

(b) (1) 15 ... ♕e7? 16 f5 ♕f6 17 e4±;

    (2) 15 ... ♕a5!? 16 f5 ♗xf5 17 ♕h5∞/±;

    (3) 15 ... ♕f6 16 f5 b5 17 ♗b3 b4 18 ♖c5 ♗a6 19 ♖f4 ♖ad8 20 ♕c1±;

    (4) 15 ... ♕e4(!) 16 ♗b3 (16 ♗d3?! ♕xe3+ 17 ♔h1 ♕e7∓; 16 ♕e2 ♗f5 17 ♗d3 ♕d5 18 e4 ♕d4+ 19 ♕f2! ♕xf2+ 20 ♔xf2± Hertneck - Sonntag, W. Germany 1986) 16 ... ♗f5 17 ♕h5 g6 18 ♕h6!? (18 ♕h4 ♖ad8 19 ♗c2 ♕d5 20 ♖d1 ♕a5 21 ♖xd8=) 18 ... ♖ad8 19 ♗c2 ♕d5 20 e4 ♗xe4 21 ♖h3 ♕c5+ 22 ♖f2 (22 ♔h1? ♗xg2+-+) 22 ... ♖fe8 23 ♕xh7+ ♔f8∞/=.

(c) 12 ... ♕b4+ 13 ♕d2 ♕xd2+ 14 ♔xd2 c5 15 dxc5 ♘xc5±.

(d) 15 ... ♘e5 16 ♗b3 ♗xf5 17 ♘xf5 g6!=; 17 ... ♕b6? 18 ♕d6± Alekhine - Lasker, Zurich 1934.

(e) 9 a3 h6 10 ♗h4 ♖e8 11 ♗d3 dxc4 12 ♗xc4 b5 13 ♗a2 c5=.

(f) 13 ♘a4 ♘e6 14 ♗h4 ♘g7 15 ♘c5 ♖b8 16 b4± Agdestein - C Hansen, Espoo (zt) 1989.

(g) 15 ... ♘g7 16 b5 axb5 17 axb5 ♗f5±.

(h) 8 ♗d3 dxc4 9 ♗xc4 b5 10 ♗d3 c5=; 8 cxd5 exd5 9 ♗d3 c6 10 ♕c2 - col 31; 8 a4!?±.

(i) 9 b4?! a5 10 a3 axb4 11 axb4 b6 12 ♗f4 bxc5 13 bxc5 ♖a3=.

(j) 9 ... e5 10 dxe5 ♘e8 11 ♗f4 ♘xc5 12 ♗b1∞ Vaganian - Speelman, London 1984.

(k) 10 ... ♕xb6? 11 0-0 ♕xb2 12 ♘a4 ♕b7 13 ♘e5± Hort - Portisch, Madrid 1973.

(l) 12 ... ♖b8 13 b3! ♘xb6 14 ♘e5±.

(m) 15 ... f5± Averbakh.

QUEEN'S GAMBIT DECLINED
Chigorin Defence, Albin Counter-Gambit et al

1 d4 d5 2 c4

	Chigorin Defence		Albin Counter-Gambit	
	(33)	*(34)*	*(35)*	*(36)*
2	Nc6 *(a)*		e5!?	
3	Nf3	Nc3	dxe5	
	Bg4	dxc4 *(e)*	d4	
4	cxd5	e3 *(f)*	Nf3 *(h)*	
	Bxf3	Nf6 *(g)*	Nc6	
5	dxc6 *(b)*	Bxc4	g3	
	Bxc6	e6	Bg4	
6	Nc3	Nf3	Bg2	Nbd2
	Nf6 *(c)*	Bb4	Qd7	Qd7
7	Bg5!	Qc2	0-0	Bg2
	e6	0-0	0-0-0	0-0-0
8	Qd3 *(d)*	a3±	Qb3±/± *(i)*	h3 *(j)*

(a) (1) 2 ... Nf6?! 3 cxd5 Nxd5 4 e4 (4 Nf3) 4 ... Nf6 5 Nc3 e5 6 Nf3 exd4 7 Qxd4±.

(2) 2 ... c5 (Symmetrical Defence) 3 cxd5 Nf6 4 Nf3 cxd4 5 Nxd4 Nxd5 6 e4 Nc7! 7 Nc3 e5±.

(3) 2 ... Bf5!? 3 Nf3 e6 4 Nc3 Nf6 5 Qb3 Nc6 6 c5!± (6 Qxb7? Nb4∓).

(b) 5 gxf3!? Qxd5 6 e3 e5 7 Nc3 Bb4 8 Bd2 Bxc3 9 bxc3±.

(c) 6 ... e6 7 e4 Bb4 8 f3 f5 9 Bc4!±.

(d) 8 ... Be7 9 Rd1 0-0 10 e4 b6 11 Qc2 Bb7 12 f3 Nd7 13 Be3±.

(e) 3 ... Nf6 4 Nf3 Bg4 5 cxd5 Nxd5 6 e4 Nxc3 7 bxc3 e5 8 d5 Nb8 9 Qa4+ Nd7 10 Nxe5 Qf6 11 f4!±.

(f) 4 d5 Ne5! 5 Bf4 Ng6 6 Bg3 e5!=; 4 Nf3!? Bg4 5 d5!±; 4 ... Nf6!

(g) 4 ... e5? 5 d5 Na5 6 Qa4+ c6 7 b4 b5 8 Qxa5 Qxa5 9 bxa5 b4 10 Nd1 cxd5 11 e4!+-.

(h) 4 e3? Bb4+ 5 Bd2 dxe3 6 Bxb4? (6 fxe3∓) 6 ... exf2+ 7 Ke2 fxg1(N)+!-+.

(i) 8 ... h5 9 Rd1!? Δ Nxd4∞/±.

(j) (1) 8 0-0 h5!? 9 b4 Bxb4 10 Rb1∞/±(?).

(2) 8 h3 Bf5 9 a3 f6 10 exf6 Nxf6 11 b4 Re8 (11 ... Ne4!?) 12 Bb2! Qd3 13 0-0 Bxe2 14 Qa4 Bxf1 15 Rxf1±.

QUEEN'S GAMBIT SLAV DEFENCE

1 d4 d5 2 c4 c6

	(1)	(2)	(3)	(4)
3	♘f3			♘c3
	♘f6			e6
4	cxd5		e3	e4!?
	cxd5		♗f5	dxe4
5	♘c3		♗d3 (d)	♘xe4
	♘c6		e6	♗b4+
6	♗f4		♘c3 (e)	♘d2
	♗f5	e6	♗xd3	♕xd4
7	e3	e3	♕xd3	♗xb4
	e6	♗e7	♘bd7	♕xe4+
8	♗b5	♗d3	0-0	♗e2
	♘d7 (a)	0-0	♗e7	♘a6 (g)
9	♕a4!	h3! (c)	e4	♗c3
	♕b6	♗d7	dxe4	♘e7
10	♘h4 (b)	0-0±	♘xe4 (f)	♗xg7∞/= (h)

(a) 8 ... ♗b4 9 ♘e5 ♕a5 10 ♗xc6+ bxc6 11 0-0 ♗xc3 12 bxc3 ♖c8 13 c4! 0-0 14 g4 ♗g6 15 c5 ♘e4!? 16 f3 ♘d2? (16 ... ♘f6±/±) 17 ♖f2 ♘c4 18 ♘xc4 dxc4 19 ♗d6 ♖fe8 20 e4± Botvinnik - Pomar, Amsterdam 1966.

(b) 10 ... ♗g6 11 ♘xg6 hxg6 12 e4 ♘f6 (12 ... dxe4? 13 d5!+-; 12 ... ♗b4!?) 13 exd5 exd5 14 0-0 ♗e7 15 ♖fe1 ♔f8 16 ♗xc6 ♕xc6! 17 ♕xc6 bxc6 18 ♖ac1±.

(c) 9 0-0 ♘h5 10 ♗e5 (10 ♗g3 ♘xg3=) 10 ... f5 (10 ... f6? 11 ♘g5! ♕e8 12 ♘b5!± Euwe - Landau, Dutch Ch 1939) 11 ♖c1 ♘f6 12 ♗xf6 gxf6!=/± e.g. 13 ♘h4 ♔h8 14 f4 ♖g8 15 ♖f3 ♗d7= Capablanca - Lasker, New York 1924.

(1) 5 ♕b3 ♕c7 6 ♘c3 e6 7 ♗d2 ♘bd7 8 ♖c1 ♕b6=

(2) 5 cxd5 cxd5 6 ♕b3 ♕c7 7 ♘a3 ♘c6 8 ♗d2 e6 9 ♖c1 ♘e4 10 ♗b5 ♘xd2 11 ♔xd2!? (11 ♘xd2 ♖c8=) =/±(?).

(3) 5 ♘c3 e6=.

(e) 6 ♗xf5 exf5 7 ♘c3 ♗e7=.

(f) 10 ... 0-0 11 ♗f4 ♘xe4 12 ♕xe4 ♘f6 13 ♕e2 ♕a5=/±.

(g) 8 ... ♕xg2!? 9 ♗f3 ♕g6∞; 8 ... c5!? 9 ♗xc5 ♘d7!?

(h) 10 ... ♖g8 11 ♗c3 ♘d5!? (11 ... ♕xg2 12 ♕d2!∞/±) 12 cxd5 ♕xg2 13 dxe6 ♗xe6 14 ♗f6 ♕xh1 15 ♕d6 ♖xg1+ 16 ♔d2 ♕d5+ 17 ♕xd5 ♗xd5 18 ♖xg1 ♔d7 19 ♖g7 ♖h8=.

QUEEN'S GAMBIT SLAV DEFENCE

1 d4 d5 2 c4 c6 3 Nf3 Nf6 (a) 4 Nc3 dxc4

	(5)	(6)	(7)	(8)
5	a4			e3 (j)
	Bf5		Na6 (g)	b5
6	e3	Ne5	e4	a4
	e6	e6 (d)	Bg4	b4
7	Bxc4	f3	Bxc4	Nb1
	Bb4	Bb4	e6	Ba6! (k)
8	0-0	Nxc4 (e)	Be3 (h)	Qc2
	0-0	0-0	Bb4	e6 (l)
9	Qe2	Bg5	Qd3	Bxc4
	Nbd7 (b)	h6	Bxf3	Bxc4
10	e4	Bh4	gxf3	Qxc4
	Bg6	c5	Nc7	Qd5
11	Bd3 (c)	dxc5 (f)	Rg1 (i)	Nbd2=

(a) 3 ... e6 4 Nc3 dxc4 5 a4 Bb4 6 e3 b5 7 Bd2 a5 8 axb5 Bxc3 9 Bxc3 cxb5 10 b3 Bb7 11 bxc4 b4 12 Bb2 Nf6 13 Bd3∞ (Noteboom Variation).

(b) 9 ... Ne4 10 Na2! Be7 11 Bd3 (△ 12 Qc2) 12 ... Ng5 12 Ne1! Bxd3 13 Nxd3 Na6 14 Nc3±.

(c) (1) 11 ... h6 12 Bf4 Qe7 13 Na2 Nh5 14 Be3±.

(2) 11 ... Bh5 12 e5 Nd5 13 Nxd5 cxd5 14 Qe3 Be7 15 Bd2 Nb8!? 16 a5± Averbakh - Furman, USSR Ch 1954.

(d) 6 ... Nbd7 7 Nxc4 Qc7 8 g3 e5 9 dxe5 Nxe5 10 Bf4 Nfd7 11 Bg2±.

(e) 8 e4!? Bxe4 9 fxe4 Nxe4 10 Bd2 (10 Qf3!?) 10 ... Qxd4 11 Nxe4 Qxe4+ 12 Qe2 Bxd2+ 13 Kxd2 Qd5+±.

(f) 11 ... Qxd1+ 12 Rxd1 Bc2 13 Rc1 Bh7 14 e4 Nc6 15 Be2 Bxc5 16 Bf2 Be7±.

(g) 5 ... Bg4?! 6 Ne5 Bh5 7 f3 Nfd7 8 Nxc4 e5 9 Ne4!±.

(h) 8 Bxa6?! bxa6= △ ... c5.

(i) 11 ... Nh5 (11 ... g6!?) 12 Ke2± Polugaevsky - Larsen. Riga (izt) 1979.

(j) 5 e4!?/?! b5 6 e5 Nd5 7 a4 Nxc3 8 bxc3 Be6∞/∓(?).

(k) 7 ... a5 8 Bxc4±.

(l) 7 ... b3!? 8 Qd1 e6 9 Nbd2 Bb4 10 Be2 Ne4 11 0-0 Bxd2 12 Bxd2 0-0 13 Bb4 c5 14 Bxc5 Nxc5 15 dxc5±/± Ribli - Portisch, Hungary 1978.

QUEEN'S GAMBIT SLAV DEFENCE
Anti-Meran Gambit and 5 Bg5 h6

1 d4 d5 2 c4 c6 3 Nf3 Nf6 4 Nc3 e6 5 Bg5!?

	(9)	(10)	(11)	(12)
5	dxc4			h6
6	e4			Bxf6
	b5			Qxf6
7	e5 (a)			e3
	h6			Nd7
8	Bh4			Bd3
	g5			Qd8
9	Nxg5			exf6	0-0
	hxg5	Nd5!?/?!	gxh4	Be7
10	Bxg5	Nxf7	Ne5	e4
	Nbd7	Qxh4	Qxf6 (e)	dxc4
11	exf6 (b)	Nxh8	g3 (f)	Bxc4
	Bb7	Bb4∞ (d)	Nd7	b5
12	g3∞ (c)		Qe2	Bb3 (h)
			Nxe5 (g)	

(a) 7 Qc2!?

(b) 11 g3 Qa5 12 exf6 Ba6 (12 ... b4 13 Ne4 Ba6∞) 13 a3 0-0-0 14 Bg2 Nc5 15 0-0 Nb3∞ Beliavsky – Novikov, USSR Ch 1990.

(c) (1) 12 ... Qb6 13 Bg2 0-0-0 14 0-0 Ne5 (14 ... c5!?) 15 dxe5! Rxd1 16 Raxd1 Bc5 17 Ne4 Bd4 18 Nd6+ Kc7 19 Bf4± Hollis – Baumbach, corr 1976.

(2) 12 ... c5!?∞ e.g. 13 d5 Qb6 (13 ... Bh6!?) 14 Bg2 0-0-0 15 0-0 b4 16 Na4 Qb5 17 dxe6 (17 a3 Nb8?! {17 ... exd5!∞} 18 axb4 cxb4 19 Be3 Bxd5 20 Bxd5 Rxd5 21 Qe2 Nc6 22 Rfc1± Kasparov – Timoshchenko and Kasparov – Dorfman, USSR Ch 1982) 17 ... Bxg2 18 e7 Bxf1 19 exd8(Q)+ Kxf1 20 Kxf1 Rxh2 21 Kg1= Gerusel – Capelan, Berlin 1971.

(d) 12 Qd2 c5!? 13 dxc5 Nd7 14 0-0-0∞/±(?)

(e) 10 ... Bb7? 11 Nxf7!+-.

(f) 11 a4 Bb7 12 Be2 c5 13 Bh5 Bg7! 14 Bxf7+ Ke7∞ Tukmakov – Kuijf, Wijk aan Zee II 1991.

(g) 13 dxe5 Qe7 14 Bg2 Bb7 15 0-0-0 Bg7 16 f4 0-0∞/=.

(h) 12 ... 0-0 13 Rc1 Ba6!? 14 Re1 c5 15 a4!± Geller – Dorfman, USSR (zt), Lvov 1978.

1 d4 d5 2 c4 c6 3 Nf3 Nf6 4 Nc3 e6 5 e3 Nbd7
6 Bd3 *(a)* dxc4 *(b)* 7 Bxc4 b5

	(13)	*(14)*	*(15)*	*(16)*
8	Bd3			Bb3
	a6		Bb7	b4
9	e4		0-0 *(i)*	Ne2
	c5		b4!?	Be7
10	e5	d5	Ne4	0-0
	cxd4 *(c)*	e5 *(f)*	Be7	0-0
11	Nxb5	b3	Nxf6+	Nf4
	axb5 *(d)*	c4 *(g)*	Nxf6	Bb7
12	exf6	bxc4	e4	Re1
	Qb6!	Bb4	0-0	c5
13	fxg7∞/= *(e)*	Bd2 *(h)*	e5 *(j)*	Ng5 *(k)*

(a) 6 Qc2 Bd6 7 b3 0-0 8 Be2 dxc4 9 bxc4 e5 10 0-0±.

(b) 6 ... Bd6 7 e4 dxe4 8 Nxe4 Nxe4 9 Bxe4 0-0 10 0-0±.

(c) 10 ... Ng4? 11 Bf4 cxd4 12 Ne4 Bb4+ 13 Kf1! Bb7 14 h3 Nh6 15 Bxh6 gxh6 16 a4±.

(d) 11 ... Nxe5!? 12 Nxe5 axb5 13 Qf3 Bb4+ 14 Kf1 Rb8! 15 Qg3 Qd6 16 Nf3 Qxg3 17 hxg3 Bd6 18 Bf4 Bxf4 19 gxf4 Bd7 20 Nxd4=; 13 0-0 Qd5 14 Qe2 Ba6 15 Bg5 Be7 16 f4=.

(e) 13 ... Bxg7 14 Qe2 (14 0-0 Bb7 15 Bf4 0-0 16 Re1 Bd5 17 Ne5 Nxe5 18 Bxe5 Bxe5 19 Bxg7+ Kxh7 20 Qh5+ - perpetual check) 14 ... 0-0 15 0-0:

    (1) 15 ... Nc5 16 Bxh7+ Kxh7 17 Ng5+ Kg6! 18 Qg4 f5 19 Qg3 Rf7! 20 Bf4 e5 21 Nxf7+ Kxf7 22 Bxe5 Qg6=.

    (2) 15 ... Bb7 16 Rd1 e5∞.

(f) 10 ... c4 11 dxe6 fxe6 12 Bc2 Qc7 13 0-0 Bb7 14 Qe2 Bd6 15 Ng5 Nc5 16 f4 h6 17 Nf3 Nd3 18 Bxd3 Qxd3 19 Qxd3 0-0∞ Bareev - Shirov, Hastings 1991/92.

(g) 11 ... Bd6 12 0-0 0-0 13 a4 c4 14 bxc4 b4 15 Ne2±/±.

(h) 13 ... bxc4 14 Bc2! Qa5 15 Ne2 Nxe4 16 Bxe4 c3 17 Nxc3 Bxc3 18 0-0 Bxd2 19 Nxd2=/±.

(i) 9 e4 b4 10 Na4 c5 11 e5 Nd5 12 0-0 cxd4 13 Re1±.

(j) 13 ... Nd7 14 Be4 Qb6 15 Bg5 Rfe8±/=.

(k) △ 14 Nxe6 13 ... Bd5! 14 Nxd5 exd5 15 dxc5 Nxc5 16 Bc2 Nfe4= (Tal).

QUEEN'S GAMBIT ACCEPTED

1 d4 d5 2 c4 dxc4

	(1)	(2)	(3)	(4)
3	Nf3			e4!? (j)
	Nf6		a6	e5 (k)
4	e3		e3	Nf3
	Bg4		Bg4 (g)	Bb4+
5	Bxc4 (a)		Bxc4	Bd2
	e6		e6	Bxd2+
6	h3	Qb3?! (e)	h3	Nbxd2
	Bh5	Bxf3	Bh5	exd4
7	Nc3	gxf3	Nc3	Bxc4
	Nbd7 (b)	Nbd7	Nf6	Nh6!?
8	0-0	Qxb7!?	0-0 (h)	0-0
	Bd6	c5	Nc6	0-0
9	e4	dxc5	Be2	Nb3
	e5	Bxc5	Bd6	Qe7
10	Be2 (c)	Nc3	b3 (i)	Qxd4
	0-0 (d)	0-0 ∞/∓ (f)		Nc6=

(a) △ Ne5! or Bxf7+!

(b) 7 ... Nc6? 8 Nb5!±; 7 ... a6 8 0-0 - col 3.

(c) 10 g4!? Bg6 11 dxe5 Nxe5 12 Nxe5 Bxe5 13 f3 Qd4+ 14 Qxd4 Bxd4+ 15 Kh2 Bxc3 16 bxc3 Bxe4 17 g5 Bd5! 18 Re1+ Kd7 19 Rd1 Bc6!±.

(d) 11 dxe5 Nxe5 12 Nd4! Bc5! 13 Nb3 (13 Bxh5 Bxd4 14 Nd5 c5= Hübner - Miles, Wijk aan Zee 1979) 13 ... Qxd1 14 Bxd1 Bb6 15 a4 Bxd1 16 Rxd1 a5!±.

(e) 6 Nbd2 Nbd7 7 b3 c5=.

(f) 11 f4 Nb6! 12 Be2 Nfd5 13 0-0 Qh4 14 Bf3 Rab8 15 Qa6 Nxc3 16 bxc3 f5 17 Bg2 Rf6∓.

(g) 4 ... Nf6 5 Bxc4 e6 6 0-0 c5 cols 5-7; 4 ... b5?! 5 a4 Bb7 6 b3 e6 7 bxc4 bxc4 8 Bxc4±/±.

(h) 8 g4 Bg6 9 Ne5 Nbd7 10 Nxg6 hxg6± Petrosian - Ivkov, European Team Ch, Hamburg 1965.

(i) 10 e4? Bxf3 11 Bxf3 Nxd4!; 10 b3 0-0 11 Bb2 Qe8!?±.

(j) 3 e3 Nf6 4 Bxc4 e6 5 Nf3 cols 5-7; 3 e3 e5!? 4 exc4 exd4 5 exd4 Bb4+ 6 Nc3 Nf6=/±.

(k) (1) 3 ... Nf6 4 e5 (4 Nc3 e5=) 4 ... Nd5=.
   (2) 3 ... c5 4 d5 e6 5 Bxc4±/=.

QUEEN'S GAMBIT ACCEPTED

1 d4 d5 2 c4 dxc4 3 ♘f3 ♘f6

	(5)	(6)	(7)	(8)
4	e3			♘c3!?
	e6			a6
5	♗xc4			e4
	c5			b5
6	0-0			e5
	a6			♘d5
7	♕e2		a4	a4
	b5		♘c6	c6 *(g)*
8	♗b3		♕e2	axb5
	♗b7	♘c6	cxd4 *(e)*	♘xc3
9	♖d1	♘c3! *(b)*	♖d1	bxc3
	♘bd7	♗e7 *(c)*	♗e7	cxd5
10	♘c3± *(a)*	dxc5 *(d)*	exd4 *(f)*	♘g5∞ *(h)*

(a) 10 ... ♕b8 (10 ... b4!? 11 ♘a4±; 10 ... ♕c7 11 e4 cxd4 12 ♘xd4±; 10 ... ♗d6 11 e4 cxd4 12 ♖xd4 ♗c5 13 ♖d3±):

  (1) 11 e4 cxd4 12 ♘xd4 ♗d6 13 g3 b4 14 ♘a4 0-0=.

  (2) 11 ♘e5!? ♗d6 (11 ... ♘xe5 12 dxe5 ♕xe5? – 12 ... ♘d7 13 f4±/± – 13 ♘xb5!±) 12 ♘xd7 ♘xd7 13 d5 e5±.

  (3) 11 d5!? exd5 12 ♘xd5 c4!? (12 ... ♘xd5 13 ♗xd5 ♗xd5 14 ♖xd5±) 13 ♘xf6+ ♕xf6 14 ♗c2 ♗c5 15 b3!? c3 16 ♕d3 b4 17 ♕c4 ♕a7 18 ♘e5 0-0 19 ♘d3 ♖ac8∞ Bukic.

(b) 9 ♖d1 c4 10 ♗c2 ♘b4! 11 ♘c3 ♘xc2 12 ♕xc2 ♗b7=.

(c) 9 ... ♗b7?! 10 ♖d1 ♕c7 (10 ... ♕b6 11 d5 exd5 12 ♗xd5±; 12 e4!∞/±) 11 d5 exd5 12 ♘xd5±; 12 e4(!)∞/± e.g. 12 ... d4 13 ♘d5! ♕d8 14 ♗f4 ♖c8 15 a4 c4 16 axb5 d3 17 bxc6! dxe2 18 cxb7 exd1(♕)+ 19 ♖xd1 cxb3 20 ♘c7+ ♔e7 21 ♗d6+ ♕xd6 22 bxc8(♘)+!+- Neishtadt.

(d) 10 ... ♗xc5 11 e4 b4 12 e5 bxc3 13 exf6 gxf6 14 ♕c4 ♕b6 15 ♕xc3±; 15 ♗a4!?

(e) 8 ... ♗e7 9 ♖d1 ♕c7 10 ♘c3 0-0 11 b3±.

(f) 10 ... 0-0 11 ♘c3 ♘b4 12 ♘e5 ♗d7 13 ♗f4 ♗c6 14 ♘xc6±.

(g) 7 ... ♘xc3 8 bxc3 ♕d5 9 g3 ♗f5∞ e.g: 10 ♗g2 e6 11 0-0 ♕b7 12 ♘h4 ♗e4 13 ♕g4!± (Miles).

(h) 10 ... f6 11 ♕f3 ♖a7 12 e6 ♕b6! 13 d5 fxg5 14 ♕f7+?! (14 ♗xg5 ♗xe6 15 ♗e3 ♕b7 16 ♗xa7 ♗xd5 17 ♕e3∞) 14 ... ♔d8 15 ♗xg5 ♖d7!! 16 exd7 ♘xd7∞/∓.

NIMZO-INDIAN DEFENCE

1 d4 ♘f6 2 c4 e6 3 ♘c3 ♗b4

	(1)	(2)	(3)	(4)
4	f3 (a)	♘f3	g3	
	d5	0-0?! (c)	c5	0-0
5	a3	♗g5!	♘f3 (f)	♗g2
	♗e7!? (b)	h6	cxd4 (g)	d5
6	e4	♗h4	♘xd4	♘f3
	dxe4	c5	♘e4	dxc4
7	fxe4	e3	♕d3! (h)	0-0
	e5	cxd4 (d)	♕a5	♘c6 (i)
8	d5	exd4	♘b3	♖e1
	♗c5	♕a5!?	♘xc3!	♖b8
9	♘f3	♗d3!	♗d2	a3
	♗g4	♗xc3+	♘e4!	♗e7
10	h3	bxc3	♕xe4	♕a4
	♗xf3	♕xc3+	♗xd2+	b5!?
11	♕xf3=	♔f1 (e)	♘xd2±	♘xb5 (j)

(a) (1) 4 e4? ♘xe4 5 ♕g4 ♘xc3 6 ♗d2 ♘xa2 7 ♖xa2 ♗xd2+ 8 ♔xd2 ♕f6∓.
(2) 4 ♕d3 c5 5 d5 0-0 6 ♗d2 exd5 7 cxd5 d6 8 g3 b6 9 ♗g2 ♗a6∓.
(3) 4 ♗d2 0-0 5 ♘f3 b6 6 g3 ♗b7 7 ♗g2=.
(b) 5 ... ♗xc3+ 6 bxc3 see Sämisch col 11.
(c) 4 ... c5 5 g3 - col 3; 4 ... d5 5 e3 0-0 6 ♗d3 - cols 33-48.
(d) 7 ... ♕a5? 8 ♗xf6 ♗xc3+ 9 bxc3 ♕xc3+ 10 ♘d2±.
(e) 11 ... d6 12 ♗xf6 gxf6 13 ♖b1!∞ Farago - Plachetka, Dubna 1979.
(f) 5 d5?! b5! 6 ♗g2 ♗b7∓.
(g) 5 ... ♘e4 6 ♕d3 cxd4 (6 ... d5!?) 7 ♘xd4 - the column; 6 ... d5!?; 5 ... 0-0 6 ♗g2 cxd4 7 ♘xd4 d5 8 ♕b3 ♗xc3+ 9 ♕xc3 e5 10 ♘c2 (10 ♘b3 d4 11 ♕c5 ♕e8! 12 ♗g5 ♘c6∓ Crouch-Suba, Calderdale 1990) 10 ... d4 11 ♕d2 ♘c6 12 b4∞.
(h) 7 ♕c2?! ♘xc3 8 bxc3 ♗e7∓; 7 ♕d3 ♘xc3?! 8 bxc3 ♗e7 9 ♘b5!±.
(i) 7 ... c5 8 dxc5 ♗xc5 9 ♕a4 ♘c6 10 ♕xc4±.
(j) 11 ... a6! 12 ♘c3 ♘xd4 13 ♘xd4 ♕xd4 14 ♗e3 ♕e5 15 ♕xc4 ♖xb2 16 ♗d4 ♕f5! 17 ♕xc7 ♖d2!=.

NIMZO-INDIAN DEFENCE

1 d4 ♘f6 2 c4 e6 3 ♘c3 ♗b4

	Spielmann		Leningrad	
	(5)	*(6)*	*(7)*	*(8)*
4	♕b3		♗g5	
	c5	♘c6	h6!	
5	dxc5	♘f3	♗h4	
	♘c6	d5	c5 *(f)*	
6	♘f3	a3 *(d)*	d5	
	♘e4	dxc4	d6 *(g)*	b5!?
7	♗d2	♕xc4	e3	dxe6 *(k)*
	♘xc5 *(a)*	♗d6	♗xc3+ *(h)*	fxe6
8	♕c2	♗g5	bxc3	cxb5
	f5! *(b)*	h6	e5	d5
9	a3	♗h4!?	f3 *(i)*	e3
	♗xc3	g5	♕a5	0-0
10	♗xc3	♗g3	♕c2	♗d3
	0-0 *(c)*	♗xg3 *(e)*	♘bd7 *(j)*	d4 *(l)*

(a) 7 ... ♘xd2 8 ♘xd2 f5 9 e3 0-0 10 ♗e2 ♗xc5=.

(b) 8 ... 0-0 9 a3 ♗xc3 10 ♗xc3 a5 11 g3±.

(c) 11 b4 ♘e4 12 ♗b2 d6 13 e3 e5 14 ♗e2 ♗e6=.

(d) 6 ♗g5!? h6 7 ♗xf6 ♕xf6 8 e3=.

(e) 11 hxg3 g4 12 ♘e5 ♕xd4 13 ♕xd4 ♘xd4 14 ♖d1 ♘c6=.

(f) 5 ... g5 6 ♗g3 ♘e4 7 ♕c2 ♘xg3 (7 ... d5 8 e3±) 8 hxg3 d5 9 a3 ♗xc3+ 10 ♕xc3±.

(g) 6 ... ♗xc3+ 7 bxc3 e5 8 d6!? ♘c6 9 e3! g5 10 ♗g3 ♘e4 11 ♗xe5 ♘xe5 12 ♕d5 ♕f6 13 ♕xe4 0-0∞.

(h) 7 ... g5 8 ♗g3 ♘e4 9 ♕c2 ♕f6 10 ♕xe4!? ♗xc3+ 11 ♔d1 ♗xb2 12 ♖b1 ♗d7 13 ♗d3∞ Kavalek; 10 ♖c1 exd5 11 cxd5 ♗f5 12 ♗d3 ♕g6∓ Timman – Guillermo Garcia, Orense 1976.

(i) 9 ♗d3 e4! 10 ♗c2 ♘bd7 11 f4! exf3 12 ♘xf3 ♕e7 13 0-0±/∞ Hort – Suba, Tunis (izt) 1985.

(j) 11 ♖b1!? a6 12 a4 g5 13 ♗g3 ♘b6 14 ♗d3 ♘xa4 15 ♘e2 b5 16 0-0⩲/∞ Timman – Sosonko, Wijk aan Zee 1977.

(k) 7 e3 ♗b7 8 dxe6!? fxe6 9 cxb5⩱; 7 e4!? g5 8 ♗g3 ♘xe4 9 ♗e5 (9 ♕f3!?) 9 ... 0-0 10 ♕h5 d6 11 ♗d3 ♘xc3 12 ♕xh6 ♘e4+ 13 ♔f1 dxe5 14 ♗xe4 f5 15 ♕g6+ =.

(l) 11 exd4 cxd4 12 a3 ♗a5 13 b4 dxc3 14 bxa5 ♗b7 15 ♘e2 (15 ♘f3) 15 ... ♗xg2 16 ♖g1 ♗f3 17 ♗c2 ♘bd7 18 ♕d6 ♘e5!!-+.

NIMZO-INDIAN DEFENCE
Sämisch Variation

1 d4 Nf6 2 e4 e6 3 Nc3 Bb4 4 a3 Bxc3+ 5 bxc3

	(9)	(10)	(11)	(12)
5	b6!? (a)	c5	0-0	
6	f3	f3 (c)	f3	e3
	Nc6	d5	d5 (f)	c5
7	e4	cxd5	cxd5	Bd3
	Ba6	Nxd5	exd5	Nc6
8	e5	dxc5! (d)	e3	Ne2
	Ng8	f5	Bf5 (g)	b6
9	Nh3	Qc2	Ne2	e4
	Na5	0-0	Nbd7	Ne8
10	Qa4	e4	Ng3 (h)	0-0 (i)
	h6	fxe4	Bg6	Ba6(!)
11	Bd3	fxe4	Bd3	Qa4
	Ne7	Qh4+	c5	Qc8
12	Nf4	g3	0-0	Be3
	0-0 (b)	Qf6 (e)	Re8±	Na5 (j)

(a) (1) 5 ... d6 6 f3 Nh5 7 Nh3 e5 8 Nf2 0-0 9 e4 Nc6 10 g4 Nf6∞/±/±.

(2) 5 ... Ne4!? 6 Qc2 f5 7 f3!? (7 Nh3 0-0 8 f3 Nf6=) 7 ... Qh4+ 8 g3 Nxg3 9 hxg3 Qxh1 10 Nh3∞/∓.

(b) 13 h4 d6 14 Bb1 dxe5 15 dxe5 Bxc4 (Niklasson - Adamski, Poland 1978) 16 Qc2!?∞/±/±.

(c) 6 e3 0-0 - col 12; 6 e3 b6!? 7 Ne2 Ba6!? 8 Ng3 Qc7 9 e4 cxd4 10 cxd4 Bxc4 11 Bg5 Bxf1 12 Kxf1∞/±/±.

(d) 8 Qd3 0-0 9 e4 Ne7 10 f4 b6 11 Qe3 Ba6 12 Bxa6 Nxa6 13 Nf3 cxd4 14 cxd4± Shirov - Chandler, Hastings 1991/92.

(e) 13 Bd3 Qxc3+ 14 Qxc3 Nxc3 15 Bf4 Rd8! (15 ... Bd7 16 Rc1 Na4 17 Bd6 Rc8 18 Nf3 b6 19 Ne5 Nxc5 20 Bxc5! Rxc5 21 Rxc5 bxc5 22 0-0+- Hollis - Kauranen, corr (Potter Memorial Tournament) 1976 16 Bc2 Bd7!= (Hollis).

(f) 6 ... d6 7 e4 e5 8 Bg5± ; 6 ... Ne8 7 e4 b6 8 Nh3 Ba6 9 e5!?±; 6 ... c5 7 e4 Ne8 8 Be3 d6 9 Ne2±.

(g) 8 ... Nh5 9 g3±.

(h) 10 g4? Nxg4 11 fxg4 Qh4+ 12 Kd2 Be4 13 Rg1 Nb6∓.

(i) 10 e5!? f5 11 exf6 Qxf6 12 Be3 Ba6!?=.

(j) 13 dxc5 d6 14 Ng3! dxc5 15 e5 f5 16 exf6 Nxf6=.

NIMZO-INDIAN DEFENCE
4 ♕c2

1 d4 ♘f6 2 c4 e6 3 ♘c3 ♗b4 4 ♕c2

	(13)	(14)	(15)	(16)
4	c5		d5	♘c6 (i)
5	dxc5		a3!? (f)	♘f3
	0-0 (a)		♗xc3+	d6
6	♘f3		♕xc3	♗d2
	♘c6	♘a6	♘e4	♕e7
7	♗f4	♗d2!? (d)	♕c2	a3
	♗xc5	♘xc5	♘c6!? (g)	♗xc3
8	a3	a3	e3	♗xc3
	d5	♗xc3	e5	a5
9	e3	♗xc3	cxd5	e3
	♕a5	b6	♕xd5	e5
10	♖d1	♘g5	♗c4	♗e2
	♖e8 (b)	♖e8!	♕a5+	0-0
11	♘d2	b4 (e)	b4	0-0
	e5	h6!	♘xb4	♗g4
12	♗g5	h4	♕xe4	b4
	♘d4!	hxg5	♘c2++	♖fe8
13	♕b1! (c)	bxc5∞	♔e2 (h)	dxe5±

(a) 5 ... ♘a6 6 a3 ♗xc3+ 7 ♕xc3±; 6 ... ♗xc5 7 ♗g5±.

(b) 10 ... ♗e7 11 ♘d2 e5 12 ♗g5 d4 13 ♘b3 ♕d8 14 ♗e2 h6?!± Korchnoi - Karpov, World Ch (9) 1978. 14 ... ♘g4!?: 14 ... g6!=.

(c) 13 ... ♗f5 14 ♗d3 e4 15 ♗f1!?∞/±.

(d) 8 e3 ♘xc5 9 ♗d2 b6 10 ♗e2 ♗b7 11 0-0 ♘ce4 12 ♘xe4 ♗xe4 13 ♗d3 ♗xd3 14 ♕xd3 d5 15 cxd5 ♕xd5=.

(e) 11 ♗xf6?! ♕xf6 12 ♕xh7+ ♔f8∞.

(f) 5 cxd5 exd5 6 ♗g5 h6 7 ♗xf6 (7 ♗h4 c5 8 dxc5! ♘c6 {8 ... d4 9 0-0-0} 9 e3 g5 10 ♗g3± Kasparov - Spassky, Linares 1990) 7 ... ♕xf6 8 a3 ♗xc3+ 9 ♕xc3=/±.

(g) 7 ... c5(!) 8 dxc5 ♘c6 9 e3 ♕a5+ 10 ♗d2 ♘xd2 11 ♕xd2 dxc4 12 ♗xc4 ♕xc5 13 ♖c1 ♗g5 14 f4 ♕h4+ 15 ♔f2=.

(h) 13 ... ♕e1+ 14 ♔f3 ♘xa1 15 ♗b2 0-0 16 ♔g3 h6 17 h4! (_ 18 ♔h2, 19 ♘f3) 17 ... ♕d2 18 ♘f3! ♕xb2 19 ♘g5!±.

(i) 4 ... b6? 5 e4±; 4 ... 0-0!? 5 ♗g5 d6 6 ♘f3 ♘bd7 7 e3 e5 8 ♗e2=/±; 4 ... d6!? 5 ♘f3 ♘bd7=/±.

NIMZO-INDIAN DEFENCE

1 d4 Nf6 2 c4 e6 3 Nc3 Bb4 4 e3 b6

	(17)	(18)	(19)	(20)
5	Bd3 (a)		Nge2	
	Bb7		Ba6	
6	Nf3		a3	
	Ne4 (b)	0-0	Be7	Bxc3+
7	0-0!	0-0	Nf4! (h)	Nxc3
	Bxc3	c5	d5	d5
8	bxc3	Na4! (e)	cxd5	b3
	Nxc3?! (c)	cxd4	Bxf1	0-0
9	Qc2	exd4 (f)	Kxf1 (i)	Be2
	Bxf3	Be7 (g)	Nxd5!? (j)	Nc6
10	gxf3	Re1	Ncxd5	a4
	Qg5+	d6	exd5	dxc4
11	Kh1 (d)	b4±	Qh5 (k)	bxc4 (l)

(a) 5 f3!? Nh5!? (5 ... c5) 6 Nh3 f5 7 e4 0-0 8 Bg5∞.

(b) 6 ... Bxc3+!? 7 bxc3 d6 8 0-0 0-0 9 Nd2 e5 10 e4±.

(c) 8 ... f5! 9 Ne1 0-0 10 f3 Nd6 11 Ba3 c5 12 dxc5 bxc5 13 Bxc5 Qc7 14 Ba3±.

(d) 11 ... Qh5 12 Bg1 Qxf3+ 13 Rg2 f5 14 Ba3! (14 Qxc3 Qd1+= perpetual check)14 ... Ne4 15 Rf1 Rg8 16 Be2 Qh3 17 f3 Nd6 18 d5± Keres – Spassky (m) 1965.

(e) 8 a3 Bxc3 9 bxc3 Be4 10 Be2 Nc6 11 Nd2 Bg6=; 8 Bd2 cxd4 9 exd4 d5∞ Yusupov – Ivanchuk, Brussels (8) 1991.

(f) 9 a3 Be7 10 exd4±.

(g) (1) 9 ... d5 10 c5 bxc5 11 a3 c4 12 axb4 cxd3 13 Qxd3 Ne4 14 Nc5 Qb6 15 b5 h6 (15 ... Nxc5?! 16 dxc5 Qxc5 17 Ng5!) 16 b4±.

(2) 9 ... Re8 10 a3 Bf8 11 b4 d6±; 10 Bg5!?; 10 Bf4.

(h) 7 Ng3 d5 8 cxd5 Bxf1 9 Nxf1 exd5 10 Ng3=.

(i) 9 dxe6?! Ba6 10 exf7+ Kxf7 11 e4!? (11 Qb3+ Ke8 12 Ne6 Qd7∓) 11 ... c5 12 Qb3+ c4 13 Qd1 Nc6 14 Be3 Bd6!∓.

(j) 9 ... exd5 10 g4! g5! 11 Nh5 Nxh5 12 gxh5 c6 13 Qf3 Ba6 14 e4 Nc7±.

(k) 11 ... c6 12 Ne6 g6 13 Qe5 Bf6 14 Nxd8+ Bxe5 15 Nxf7 (15 Nxc6 Nxc6 16 dxe5 Nxe5 17 Bd2± Hübner) 15 ... Kxf7 16 dxe5 Nd7 17 f4 Nc5∞ Timman – Hübner, Montreal, 1979.

(l) 11 ... Qd7 12 Nb5 Rfd8 13 Bb2 Na5 14 Qc2 c6 15 Na3±.

NIMZO-INDIAN DEFENCE

1 d4 ♘f6 2 c4 e6 3 ♘c3 ♗b4 4 e3

	(21)	(22)	(23)	(24)
4	b6		♘c6 (e)	0-0
5	♘e2		♘e2 (f)	♘e2!?
	♗a6	♗b7 (c)	d5	d5 (h)
6	♘g3	a3	a3	a3
	0-0 (a)	♗e7 (d)	♗e7	♗e7
7	e4	d5!	cxd5 (g)	cxd5 (i)
	♘c6	0-0	exd5	exd5 (j)
8	♗d3	e4	♘f4	g3
	e5	d6	♗f5	c6
9	d5! (b)	♘g3	b4	♗g2
	♗xc3+	c6	♕d7	a5
10	bxc3	♗e2±	♕b3	0-0=
	♘e7!±		♖d8=/±	

(a) 6 ... ♗xc3+ 7 bxc3 d5 8 ♕f3 (8 ♗a3!?) 8 ... 0-0 9 cxd5 ♕xd5!±/=.

(b) 9 0-0? ♘xd4!! 10 ♕a4 ♗xc3 11 bxc3 ♘e6 12 ♗a3 (12 ♕xa6 ♘c5) 12 ... ♗b7 13 ♗xf8 ♕xf8∓ Lombard - Korchnoi. Switzerland 1978.

(c) 5 ... ♘e4!? 6 ♕c2 ♗b7 7 a3 ♗xc3 8 ♘xc3 ♘xc3 9 ♕xc3 ♕h4!?±/= I Sokolov - Korchnoi, Novi Sad (ol) 1990.

(d) 6 ... ♗xc3+ 7 ♘xc3 d5 8 cxd5 exd5 9 b4 0-0 10 ♗d3 ♘bd7 11 0-0±.

(e) (1) 4 ... ♗xc3+?! 5 bxc3 d6 6 ♗d3 e5 7 e4 c5 8 ♘e2±.

(2) 4 ... d5 5 a3 ♗e7±; 5 ... ♗xc3+ 6 bxc3 c5±.

(f) 5 ♘f3 d6 6 ♗e2 e5 7 0-0 (7 d5? ♗xc3+=/∓) 7 ... ♗xc3! 8 bxc3±.

(g) 7 ♘f4?! dxc4 8 ♗xc4 e5∓; 7 ♘g3 h5!?=.

(h) 5 ... b5!?; 5 ... c5 6 a3 ♗xc3+ (6 ... cxd4?! 7 axb4±/±) 7 ♘xc3 cxd4 8 exd4 d5 9 ♗e3 (9 c5!?) 9 ... dxc4 10 ♗xc4 ♘c6 col 25.

(i) 7 ♘g3 c5=; 7 ♘f4 dxc4 8 ♗xc4 c5 9 d5 e5 10 ♘e2 ♘e8 11 ♘g3 ♘d6=.

(j) 7 ... ♘xd5 8 ♕c2 ♘d7 9 g3 ♘xc3 10 bxc3 c5 11 ♗g2 ♖b8! 12 e4 e5 13 0-0= M Gurevich - Motwani, Ostend 1991.

NIMZO-INDIAN DEFENCE

1 d4 ♘f6 2 c4 e6 3 ♘c3 ♗b4 4 e3 c5

	(25)	(26)	Hübner Variation (27)	(28)
			♗d3	
5	♘ge2!?			
	d5	cxd4	♘c6	
6	a3	exd4	♘f3 (e)	
	♗xc3+ (a)	0-0!? (c)	♗xc3+	
7	♘xc3	a3	bxc3	
	cxd4	♗e7!?	d6	
8	exd4	d5	e4	0-0 (g)
	dxc4	exd5	e5	e5
9	♗xc4	cxd5	d5	♘g5!?
	♘c6	♖e8	♘e7	♕e7
10	♗e3	g3± (d)	♘h4	♕c2
	0-0 (b)		h6 (f)	♗d7 (h)

(a) 6 ... ♗a5?! 7 dxc5 dxc4 8 ♕xd8+ ♔xd8 9 ♗d2 ♘bd7 10 ♘g3 ♘xc5 11 ♗xc4±.

(b) 11 0-0 b6 12 ♕d3 (12 ♕f3! ♗b7 13 ♗d3± Kasparov - Psakhis, La Manga (m) 1990 13 ... ♘e5? 14 ♕xb7 ♘xd3 15 ♕a6! ♘xb2 16 ♕e2± Keene) 12 ... ♗b7 13 ♖ad1! h6 14 f3±/= Korchnoi - Karpov, World Ch (3) 1978; 14 ♗f4 ♘e7 15 ♗a2 ♘ed5 16 ♗e5± Botvinnik.

(c) 6 ... d5 7 c5 ♘e4 8 ♗d2 ♘xd2 9 ♕xd2=/± Korchnoi - Karpov, World Ch (5) 1978.

(d) (1) 10 g3 ♗c5 11 ♘a4 ♗f8 12 ♗g2 d6 13 0-0 ♘bd7±.

(2) 10 h3!? ♗c5 11 b4 ♗b6 12 g4!?∞ Speelman - Cummings, London 1980.

(e) 6 ♘ge2 cxd4 7 exd4 d5 8 0-0 dxc4 9 ♗xc4=.

(f) 11 f4 ♘g6 12 ♘xg6 fxg6 13 0-0 0-0= e.g:

(1) 14 fxe5 fxe5 15 ♗e3 b6= Spassky - Fischer, World Ch (5) 1972.

(2) 14 ♕e1 ♗d7 15 ♕g3 ♕e8 16 f5 g5= Tarjan - Dzindzihashvili, Hastings 1977/78.

(3) 14 f5!?

(g) 8 ♘d2 e5 9 ♘b3 b6 10 0-0 0-0 11 ♗d2=/± Portisch - Huguet, Las Palmas 1972.

(h) 11 f4 0-0-0 12 fxe5 dxe5 13 d5 ♘a5 14 e4 h6 15 ♘f3 ♘e8=/± Trincardi - Damjanovic, Reggio Emilia 1972.

1 d4 ♘f6 2 c4 e6 3 ♘c3 ♗b4 4 e3 0-0 5 ♗d3 *(a)*

	(29)	(30)	(31)	(32)
5	c5 *(b)*		d5	
6	d5!?	♘ge2	a3	
	b5 *(c)*	d5	♗xc3+	
7	dxe6	0-0	bxc3	
	fxe6	cxd4	c5	dxc4!
8	cxb5	exd4	cxd5	♗xc4
	a6!? *(d)*	dxc4	exd5	c5
9	♘e2	♗xc4	♘e2	♘e2 *(i)*
	d5	♘bd7	b6	e5!
10	0-0	♕d3	0-0	0-0
	e5	a6	♗a6	♘c6
11	a3	a4	♗xa6 *(g)*	♗b2 *(j)*
	axb5	♘b6 *(f)*	♘xa6	♕c7 *(k)*
12	♗xb5 *(e)*		f3± *(h)*	♗a2=

(a) 5 ♘e2 col 24; 5 ♘f3 c5 6 0-0 d5 cols 35–48.

(b) 5 ... b6?! 6 ♘ge2 ♗b7 7 a3 ♗e7 (7 ... ♗xc3+?! 8 ♘xc3 ♗xg2 9 ♖g1 ♗b7 10 e4∞/±) 8 e4±/±.

(c) 6 ... h6!?

(d) 8 ... ♗b7 9 ♘f3 d5 10 0-0 ♘bd7 11 ♘e2⩲ Korchnoi – Karpov, World Ch (7) 1978.

(e) 12 ... ♗xc3 13 bxc3 ♗a6⩲/± Korchnoi – Karpov. World Ch (17) 1978.

(f) 11 ... b6?!± Petrosian – Bronstein, Tallinn 1979; 11 ... ♘b6 12 ♗b3 ♘bd5= (Petrosian).

(g) 11 f3 ♖e8 12 ♘g3 ♕c8 13 ♗xa6 ♘xa6 14 ♕d3 ♕b7 15 ♖a2± Beliavsky – Short, Linares 1990.

(h) △ ♘g3, e4 e.g. 12 ... ♘c7 13 ♘g3 ♘e6 (13 ... ♖e8!?) 14 ♗b2 ♕d7 15 e4 cxd4 16 cxd4 ♘e8± Szabo – Barcza, Hungarian Ch 1967.

(i) 9 ♘f3 ♕c7 10 ♗e2 (10 ♗d3?? cxd4 11 cxd4? ♕c3+) 10 ... b6=.

(j) 11 ♖b1 ♕c7 12 ♗a2 ♖d8 13 ♕c2 b6 14 ♘g3 exd4 15 cxd4 cxd4? 16 exd4± Speelman – Karpov, Linares 1991; 15 ... ♗a6! 16 ♖e1∞.

(k) 11 ... ♗e6 12 ♗xe6 fxe6 13 ♕b3 ♕d5 14 ♕a2 ♕xa2 15 ♖xa2= Vaganian – Ehlvest, Tallinn 1983.

NIMZO-INDIAN DEFENCE

1 d4 ♘f6 2 c4 e6 3 ♘c3 ♗b4 4 e3 0-0 5 ♗d3 d5 6 ♘f3

	(33)	(34)	(35)	(36)
6	b6 *(a)*		c5	
7	0-0		0-0	
	♗b7		dxc4	
8	cxd5	a3	♗xc4	
	exd5	♗d6 *(e)*	b6 *(g)*	cxd4
9	♘e5 *(b)*	b4	a3	exd4
	♘bd7!?	dxc4	cxd4?! *(h)*	b6
10	f4!? *(c)*	♗xc4	axb4	♗g5
	c5	a5	dxc3	♗b7
11	♕f3	b5	♕xd8	♖e1 *(j)*
	♖e8	♘bd7	♖xd8	♘bd7
12	♕h3 *(d)*	♗b2 *(f)*	bxc3 *(i)*	♖c1
				♖c8 *(k)*

(a) 6 ... ♘c6 7 0-0 a6 8 ♕e2 (8 h3!? dxc4 9 ♗xc4 ♕e8!±) 8 ... dxc4 9 ♗xc4 ♕e8 10 e4 e5±.

(b) 9 ♗d2 a6 10 ♖c1 ♗b6 11 ♘e5 c5 12 f4 ♘c6 13 ♕f3 cxd4 14 ♘xc6 ♗xc6 15 exd4 ♕d7 16 f5 ♖fe8=.

(c) 10 ♕a4 ♗d6 11 ♘xd7 ♘xd7 12 ♗b5 ♘b8!=; 12 ♗a6 ♗xa6 13 ♕xa6 c6=/±.

(d) 12 ... ♘f8 13 ♗d2 ♖c8 14 a3 ♗xc3 15 ♗xc3 c4 16 ♗c2∞.

(e) 8 ... ♗xc3 9 bxc3 dxc4 10 ♗xc4 c5 11 ♖e1 ♘bd7 12 ♗d3 ♗e4 13 ♗f1∞ Korchnoi – Hübner, Manila (izt) 1990.

(f) 12 ... e5 13 ♖e1 e4 14 ♘d2 ♕e7=/±.

(g) (1) 8 ... ♕e7 9 a3 ♗a5!? 10 ♕d3 ♘bd7 11 ♘e4 ♗b6 12 ♘xf6+ ♕xf6 13 ♗d2±.

(2) 8 ... ♗d7 9 ♕e2 ♗c6 10 ♖d1 ♕e7 11 a3 ♗xc3 12 bxc3 ♘bd7 13 a4! ♖fc8 14 ♗b3 ♕e8 15 c4 cxd4 16 exd4 △ a5±.

(h) 9 ... ♗xc3 10 bxc3 ♗b7±/=.

(i) 12 ... ♗b7 13 ♗e2 ♘c6 14 ♗b2 ♘e4 15 ♖fd1 ♖xd1+ 16 ♖xd1 ♖d8 17 ♖xd8+ ♘xd8 18 ♘d4 ♘c6 19 ♘c2!±.

(j) 11 ♖c1 ♘c6 12 a3 ♗e7 13 ♕d3 ♘d5 14 ♗xd5 exd5 15 ♗xe7 ♘xe7 16 ♖fe1± Ivanchuk – Karpov, Linares 1991.

(k) (1) 13 ♕b3!? ♕e7?! (13 ... ♗xc3±; 13 ... ♗a5! 14 ♘e5 ♘xe5 15 dxe5 ♕d4 16 exf6 ♕g4∞ Ljubojevic) 14 ♗d5!!± Browne – Ljubojevic, Tilburg 1978.

(2) 13 ♗d3 ♖e8 14 ♗h4!?=/±.

1 d4 Nf6 2 c4 e6 3 Nc3 Bb4 4 e3 0-0 5 Bd3 d5
6 Nf3 c5 7 0-0

	(37)	(38)	(39)	(40)
7	dxc4			Nc6
8	Bxc4	a3		a3
	Nbd7			dxc4 (h)
9	a3	Qe2		Bxc4
	Bxc3 (a)	b6		Ba5!? (i)
10	bxc3	d5	Rd1	Qd3
	b6	Bxc3	cxd4	a6
11	Bd3	dxe6	exd4	Rd1
	Bb7	Ne5 (d)	Bb7	b5
12	Re1	exf7+	d5 (f)	Ba2
	Ne4 (b)	Kh8	Bxc3	c4 (j)
13	Bb2	bxc3	dxe6	Qe2
	Rc8 (c)	Bg4 (e)	Bxf3 (g)	Qe8 (k)

(a) 9 ... Ba5!?; 9 ... cxd4 10 exd4 (10 Qxd4!?; 10 axb4 dxc3 11 bxc3 Qc7 12 Qb3 e5=) 10 ... Bxc3 11 bxc3 Qc7 12 Qe2 Nb6 13 Bb3 Nbd5 (13 ... Rxc3!? 14 Bg5∞) 14 c4=/±.

(b) 12 ... Be4?! 13 Bf1 Qc7 14 Nd2±/±.

(c) 14 c4 Ndf6 15 Ne5 Rc7 16 a4±.

(d) 11 ... Ba5 12 exd7 Qxd7 13 Rd1 Qg4 14 h3±.

(e) 14 e4 Qe7 15 Re1 b5 16 Bxb5 Nh5 17 Bg5 Qe6 18 Qe3 Bxf3 19 gxf3 Qxf7 20 Be2 h6 21 f4! Nxf4 22 Bxf4 Qxf4 23 Rad1!±/± Gligoric - H Olafsson, Lone Pine 1979.

(f) 12 Bd2 Bxc3 13 bxc3 Qc7 14 Bd3 Rac8 15 Rac1 Qd6=.

(g) (1) 14 gxf3 fxe6 15 bxc3 Qc7 16 Bxe6+ Kh8 17 Be3=.

(2) 14 Qxf3 Ne5! 15 exf7+ Kh8 16 Rxd8 Nxf3+ 17 gxf3 Raxd8 18 bxc3 Rd7 19 Ba3 Rfxf7 20 Bxf7 Rxf7= Portisch - Donner, Hamburg 1965.

(h) 8 ... Ba5 9 cxd5 exd5 10 dxc5 Bxc3 11 bxc3 Qa5 (11 ... Bg4!?±) 12 Qc2 Qxc5 13 a4 Re8 14 Ba3 Qa5 15 Rfb1 Qc7 16 c4±/±.

(i) 9 ... cxd4 10 axb4!? dxc3 11 bxc3 Qc7 12 Qb3 b6 13 Rd1 Bb7 14 Be2 Rfd8 15 Bb2±.

(j) 12 ... Bb7 13 dxc5 Bxc3 14 Qc2!±; 12 ... Bb6!?=.

(k) 14 e4 e5 15 d5 Nd4 16 Nxd4 exd4 17 Rxd4 Qe5 18 Be3 Ng4 19 f4 Qb8 20 Rad1 Nxe3 21 Qxe3 Bb6 22 Bb1∞.

1 d4 ♘f6 2 c4 e6 3 ♘c3 ♗b4 4 e3 0–0 5 ♕d3 d5
6 ♘f3 c5 7 0–0 ♘c6 8 a3 ♗xc3 9 bxc3

	(41)	(42)	(43)	(44)
9	♕c7		b6	dxc4
10	cxd5		cxd5	♗xc4
	exd5		exd5	♕e7!?
11	♘h4	h3 (c)	♘e5! (e)	♘e5!? (g)
	♘e7 (a)	♘e7	♕c7 (f)	♘xe5
12	a4	dxc5	♘xc6	dxe5
	♖e8	♗f5!	♕xc6	♘d7
13	♗a3	c4	f3	f4 (h)
	c4	♗xd3	a5	♘b6
14	♗c2	♕xd3	♕e2	♗d3 (i)
	♘g6	♕xc5	♗b7±	♗d7
15	♘f5 (b)	cxd5 (d)		a4∞/∓ (j)

(a) (1) 11 ... ♖e8!? 12 f3 b6 13 ♖a2 a5? (13 ... ♗b7) 14 ♖e2 ♗b7 15 ♗b2 ♖ad8 16 ♕e1! Portisch – Hort, Niksic 1978 ± (Hort).

(2) 11 ... c4 12 ♗b1 ♘e4 13 ♕c2! ♕e7 14 f3 ♕xh4 15 fxe4 ♕xe4 16 ♕xe4 dxe4 17 ♗xe4± Vaiser – Zilberstein, USSR 1978.

(b) 15 ♘xg6? hxg6 △ ... ♗f5∓; 15 ♘f5 ♘e4 16 ♗xe4 ♖xe4 17 ♘g3 ♖e8 18 ♕h5±.

(c) (1) 11 a4 ♖e8 12 ♗a3 c4 13 ♗c2 ♘e4 14 ♕e1 ♕d8 15 ♘d2?? (15 ♗xe4=) 15 ... ♘xc3 16 ♗b2 ♘xd4!–+ Brinck-Claussen – Sigurjonsson, Esbjerg 1978.

(2) 11 ♘d2!? ♖e8 12 h3 ♘e7±/=.

(d) 15 ... ♕xd5 16 ♕xd5 ♘fxd5=.

(1) 11 ♗b2 c4 12 ♗c2 ♗g4 13 ♕e1 ♗xf3 14 gxf3±.

(2) 11 ♘d2 ♗e6 12 ♗b2 c4 13 ♗c2 ♘a5 14 a4±.

(f) 11 ... ♘xe5?! 12 fxe5 ♘d7 13 f4 c4!? 14 ♗c2 ♘c5 15 a4 ♗b7 16 ♗a3±/±.

(g) 11 a4± Portisch – Miles, Tilburg 1981.

(h) 13 ♕d6!? ♕xd6 14 exd6±.

(i) 14 ♗b3!?; 14 ♗e2!?

(j) 15 ... ♖ad8! 16 ♕c2 ♗xa4 17 ♗xh7+ ♔h8 18 ♖xa4 ♘xa4 19 ♖f3 (19 ♗e4) 19 ... g6 20 ♖h3 ♔g7(∓/+–) 21 f5 exf5 22 e4 ♕xe5 23 ♗h6+ ♔f6 24 ♖c3 ♘xc3!–+ Chandler – Speelman, Brighton 1979.

1 d4 Nf6 2 c4 e6 3 Nc3 Bb4 4 e3 0-0 5 Bd3 d5
6 Nf3 c5 7 0-0 Nc6 8 a3 Bxc3 9 bxc3 dxc4 10 Bxc4 Qc7

	(45)	(46)	(47)	(48)
11	Bd3	Ba2	a4?!	Re1?!/? (h)
	e5	e5 (c)	e5	e5
12	Qc2	Qc2 (d)	Ba3	d5
	Re8	Bg4	e4	Na5!
13	Nxe5	dxe5	Nd2	d6
	Nxe5	Nxe5	b6	Qd8
14	dxe5	Ne1!	Qc2	Nxe5
	Qxe5	Qd7!? (e)	Na5	Nxc4
15	f3	f3	Be2	Nxc4
	Bd7	Be6	Re8	Be6
16	a4	c4	dxc5	Qd3?! (i)
	Bc6 (a)	b5!?	bxc5	Ng4! (j)
17	Re1	cxb5	c4	Re2
	h5 (b)	Bxa2 (f)	Bg4 (g)	Bxc4∓ (k)

(a) 16 ... Rac8 17 Re1 Red8 18 e4 Nd5 19 Bd2 Nb6 20 a5± Yusupov - Ivanchuk, Brussels (m) 1991.

(b) 18 e4 Nd5 19 Bd2 Nf4 20 Bf1 h4=.

(c) 11 ... Re8 12 Qc2 e5 13 g5!±.

(d) 12 h3 e4 13 Nh2 b6 14 c4 Rd8 15 Bb2 cxd4 16 exd4 Ne5 17 d5± Knaak - Schmittdiel, Dortmund 1990.

(e) 14 ... Rad8 15 f3 Be6 16 c4!± Portisch - Sosonko, Tilburg 1978; 14 ... c4!? 15 f3 Be6 16 e4±/±; 14 ... b5!?

(f) 18 Rxa2 Qxb5 19 Qc3! Rfe8 20 e4±/±.

(g) 18 Bd1 Bxd1 19 Rfxd1 Ng4 20 Nf1 Ne5 21 Rd5 Nd3=.

(h) (1) 11 Bb5!? a6 12 Bd3 e5 13 Qc2 Bg4 14 Nxe5 Nxe5 15 dxe5 Qxe5 16 f3 Bd7= cf. col 45.
(2) 11 Be2 Rd8 12 Qc2 e5 13 dxe5 Nxe5 14 Ne1 c4 15 e4 Bg4 16 f3 Qc5+ 17 Kh1 Be6= Taimanov.
(3) 11 Qc2 e5 12 Ba2 - col 46; 12 h3!?

(i) 16 Nb2 Ne4 17 f3 Nxd6∓.

(j) 16 ... Bxc4? 17 Qxc4 Qxd6=.

(k) 18 Qxc4 Qxd6 19 g3 Ne5 20 Qa2 Qg6! 21 e4 Rad8 22 Bf4 Nf3+ 23 Kg2 Qg4 24 h3 Nh4+ 25 Kh2 Qf3 26 Rg1 Qg2+!! 0-1 O Rodriguez - F Olafsson, Las Palmas 1978.

QUEEN'S INDIAN DEFENCE

1 d4 ♘f6 2 c4 e6 3 ♘f3 b6 4 g3 ♗b7 5 ♗g2 ♗e7
6 0-0 0-0 7 ♘c3 ♘e4

	(1)	(2)	(3)	(4)
8	♕c2		♗d2	♘xe4
	♘xc3		♗f6 *(h)*	♗xe4
9	♕xc3		♕c2 *(i)*	♘e1
	c5	♗e4 *(d)*	♘xd2	♗xg2
10	♖d1	b3 *(e)*	♕xd2	♘xg2
	d6	c5	d6	d5
11	b3	♗b2	♖ad1	♕a4
	♗f6	♘c6	g6 *(j)*	♕e8
12	♗b2	dxc5 *(f)*	e4	♕xe8
	♕e7 *(a)*	♗f6	♗g7	♖xe8
13	♕c2 *(b)*	♕d2	♕e3	cxd5
	♘c6	♗xb2	♘d7	exd5
14	e4	♕xb2	♖d2	♗e3
	g6	bxc5	♕e7	a5=
15	d5 *(c)*	♖fd1 *(g)*	♖fd1=	

(a) 12 ... ♘d7!= Andersson - Karpov, Tilburg 1983, GLC London 1984 and USSR - World Match, London 1984!!!

(b) 13 ♕d2 ♘d7 14 dxc5 ♗xb2 15 c6 ♗xc6 16 ♕xb2 ♖fd8 17 ♖d4= Ribli - Short, Skelleftea 1989.

(c) 15 ... ♘b4 16 ♗xf6 ♕xf6 17 ♕d2 exd5!? (17 ... e5 18 a3 ♘a6± Vaganian - Karpov, USSR Ch 1976) 18 exd5 ♗c8 19 a3 ♘a6 20 ♘g5!± Browne - Grefe, USA Ch 1977.

(d) (1) 9 ... d6 10 b3 ♘d7 (10 ... c5 11 ♖d1 - col 1) 11 ♗b2 ♘f6=; 10 ♕c2 f5 11 ♘e1 ♗xg2 12 ♘xg2±.

(2) 9 ... f5 10 b3 ♗f6 11 ♗b2 d6 12 ♖ad1=/±.

(e) 10 ♘e1; 10 ♖d1; 10 ♗f4.

(f) 12 ♕d2 ♗f6=.

(g) 15 ♘e5= Filip - Keres, Göteborg (izt) 1955; 15 ♖fd1= Najdorf - Keres, Budapest (ct) 1950.

(h) 8 ... f5 9 d5 ♗f6 10 ♖c1 ♘a6±; 8 ... d6 9 d5±; 8 ... d5 9 cxd5 exd5 10 ♖c1=/±.

(i) 9 ♖c1 d6 10 d5 ♘xd2 11 ♕xd2 e5 12 h4 ♘d7 13 ♗h3 g6 14 e4 ♗g7 15 h5± Epishin - Ehlvest, Terrassa 1991.

(j) 11 ... ♘d7 12 ♖fe1 g6 13 h4∞ Speelman - Anand, Novi Sad (ol) 1990.

QUEEN'S INDIAN DEFENCE

1 d4 ♘f6 2 c4 e6 3 ♘f3 b6 4 g3

	(5)	(6)	(7)	(8)
4	♗b7		♗a6	
5	♗g2		b3	♕a4 (l)
	♗e7	♗b4+	♗b4+	c5
6	0-0	♗d2	♗d2	♗g2
	0-0	♗xd2+ (e)	♗e7 (h)	♗b7
7	♘c3 (a)	♕xd2	♘c3 (i)	0-0
	d5 (b)	0-0	c6	cxd4
8	♘e5	♘c3	e4	♘xd4
	♘a6	d6 (f)	d5	♗xg2
9	♗g5 (c)	0-0	e5 (j)	♔xg2
	c5	♘e4	♘e4	♗e7
10	e3	♘xe4	♗d3 (k)	f3
	♘e4 (d)	♗xe4 (g)		0-0=

(a) 7 d5!? exd5 8 ♘d4 ♘c6 9 cxd5 ♘xd4 10 ♕xd4 c5 11 ♕d3 d6∞/=; 7 ♕c2 d5 8 cxd5 ♘xd5 9 ♘c3 c5=; 7 ♖e1 d5=.

(b) 7 ... ♘a6!? 8 d5(!); 8 ♗g5 d5 - the column.

(c) 9 ♗e3 c5 10 ♖c1 ♘e4= Browne - Tal, Las Palmas 1977; 9 cxd5 exd5 10 b3=/±; 10 ♕a4 ♕e8=.

(d) 11 ♗xe7 ♕xe7 12 cxd5 exd5=/±.

(e) 6 ... ♗e7 7 0-0 ♘a6 8 ♘c3 d5=/± cf. col 5.

(f) 8 ... ♘e4 9 ♕c2 ♘xc3 10 ♘g5! ♘e4 11 ♗xe4 ♗xe4 12 ♕xe4 ♕xg5 13 ♕xa8 ♘c6 14 ♕b7 ♘xd4 Euwe - Capablanca (10) 1931 15 0-0! ♘xe2+ 16 ♔g2± Voronkov.

(g) 11 ♘h4 ♗xg2 12 ♘xg2 ♘c6!?= Tarjan - Larsen, Riga (izt) 1979; 12 ... c6=/± Browne - Hübner. Tilburg 1978.

(h) 6 ... ♗xd2+ 7 ♕xd2 c6 8 ♘c3 d5 9 e4 ♘xe4 10 ♘xe4 dxe4 11 ♘g5± Dzindzihashvili - Miles, Tilburg 1985.

(i) 7 ♗g2 c6 8 ♗c3 d5 9 ♘bd2 ♘bd7 10 0-0 0-0 11 ♖e1 c5 12 e4 dxc4 13 ♘xc4 ♗b7 14 ♕d3!± Karpov - Khalifman, Reykjavik 1991.

(j) 9 ♗d3 dxc4 10 bxc4 e5!=/∓ Sosonko - Speelman, Amsterdam (zt) 1978.

(k) 10 ... ♘xc3 (10 ... ♘xd2!?/?! Browne - Speelman, Lone Pine 1978) 11 ♗xc3 c5 12 cxd5 ♕xd5 13 ♗xa6 ♘xa6 14 dxc5 ♕e4+ 15 ♕e2 ♘xc5=/∓.

(l) 5 ♘bd2 c5=; 5 ♕c2 c5=.

QUEEN'S INDIAN DEFENCE and BOGO-INDIAN DEFENCE

1 d4 ♘f6 2 c4 e6 3 ♘f3

	(9)	(10)	(11)	Bogo-Indian (12)
3	b6			♗b4+
4	e3	♗f4	a3 *(e)*	♗d2 *(l)*
	♗b7	♗b7	♗b7 *(f)*	♕e7
5	♗d3	e3	♘c3	g3
	♗e7	♗e7 *(b)*	d5 *(g)*	0-0
6	♘c3	h3! *(c)*	cxd5 *(h)*	♗g2
	d5	0-0	♘xd5 *(i)*	♗xd2+
7	0-0	♘c3	e3	♘bxd2
	0-0	d5	♗e7 *(j)*	d6
8	b3	cxd5	♗b5+	0-0
	c5	exd5 *(d)*	c6	e5
9	♗b2	♗d3	♗d3	e4
	♘c6	c5	0-0	a5
10	♖c1 *(a)*	0-0±	0-0 *(k)*	d5=/±

(a) (1) 10 ♕e2 cxd4 11 exd4 ♘b4! 12 ♗b1 dxc4 13 bxc4 ♗xf3 14 gxf3∞/=.

(2) 10 ♖c1 cxd4 11 exd4 ♖c8 12 ♖e1 ♘b4 13 ♗f1 ♘e4 14 a3 ♘xc3 15 ♖xc3 ♘c6= Keres - Smyslov, Zurich (ct) 1953.

(b) 5 ... ♗b4+(!) 6 ♘fd2 0-0 7 ♗d3 d5 (7 ... ♗xg2!?) 8 0-0 c5= Miles - Andersson, Buenos Aires (ol) 1978.

(c) 6 ♘c3?! ♘h5=.

(d) 8 ... ♘xd5 9 ♘xd5 ♗xd5 10 ♗d3±/=.

(e) 4 ♘c3 ♗b4 5 e3 - Nimzo-Indian cols 17-18; 4 ... ♗b7 5 ♗g5 h6 6 ♗h4 g5 7 ♗g3 ♘h5 8 e3 ♘xg3 9 fxg3!? (9 hxg3=) 9 ... ♗g7 10 ♗d3∞/±/= Romanishin - Ribli, Riga (izt) 1979.

(f) 4 ... c5?! 5 d5!?±; 5 e3!±; 4 ... ♗a6!? 5 e3±:

(g) 5 ... ♗e7?! 6 d5!±/±; 5 ... ♘e4 6 ♘xe4 ♗xe4 7 ♗f4 c5 8 d5 exd5 9 cxd5 ♗e7 10 ♕b3±.

(h) 6 ♗g5 ♗e7 7 ♗xf6 ♗xf6 8 cxd5 exd5=/±.

(i) 6 ... exd5 7 g3 ♗e7 8 ♗g2 0-0 9 0-0±.

(j) 7 ... ♘d7 8 ♗d3 c5 9 e4 ♘5f6 10 ♗f4 a6 11 d5 exd5 12 ♘xd5± Portisch - Miles, Thessaloniki (ol) 1984.

(k) 10 ... ♘xc3 11 bxc3 c5 12 e4 ♘c6 13 ♗e3 ♖c8=/±.

(l) 4 ♘bd2 0-0=.

CATALAN OPENING

1 d4 ♘f6 2 c4 e6 3 g3 d5 4 ♗g2

	(1)	(2)	(3)	(4)
4	dxc4	♗e7		
5	♘f3 (a)	♘f3		
	a6!? (b)	0-0		
6	0-0	0-0		
	b5?! (c)	dxc4		♘bd7 (j)
7	♘e5	♛c2 (f)		♛c2
	♘d5	a6		c6
8	♘c3!	a4	♛xc4	♘bd2
	c6?! (d)	♗d7 (g)	b5	b6
9	♘xd5	♛xc4	♛c2	b3
	exd5	♗c6	♗b7	♗b7
10	e4!	♘c3	♗d2	♗b2
	♗e6	♘bd7	♗e4 (h)	♜c8
11	a4!	♜e1±/=	♛c1	e4
	b4		b4 (i)	c5
12	exd5±/+- (e)			exd5=

(a) 5 ♛a4+ ♘bd7 6 ♛xc4 a6 7 ♛c2 c5 8 ♘f3=.

(b) 5 ... ♗e7 6 0-0 0-0 cols 2-3; 5 ... c5 6 0-0 ♘c6 7 ♛a4 ♗d7 8 dxc5 ♗xc5 9 ♛xc4 ♗e7 10 ♘c3±.

(c) 6 ... ♘c6!?; 6 ... ♗e7 7 ♘e5!; 6 ... c5.

(d) 8 ... ♗b7?! 9 ♘xd5! ♗xd5? (9 ... exd5 10 e4∞) 10 e4 ♗b7 11 ♛h5 g6 12 ♘xg6 fxg6 13 ♛e5+- Sosonko - Schneider, Buenos Aires (ol) 1978; 8 ... ♗b4!? 9 ♘xd5 exd5 10 e4 0-0 11 a3 ♗d6 12 exd5±.

(e) 12 ... ♗xd5 13 ♛g4 h5 14 ♗xd5!! cxd5 15 ♛f5 ♜a7 16 ♜e1 ♜e7 17 ♗g5 g6 18 ♗xe7! 1-0 Sosonko - Hübner, Tilburg 1979.

(f) 7 ♘e5 ♘c6! 8 ♗xc6 bxc6 9 ♘xc6 ♛e8 10 ♘xe7+ ♛xe7 11 ♛a4 e5!∞/=; 7 ♘c3!? c5, 7 ... ♘c6!?

(g) (1) 8 ... c5 9 dxc5 ♘c6 10 ♘a3! (10 ♛xc4 e5∞) 10 ... ♗xc5 11 ♘xc4 ♛e7 12 ♘fe5!±.

(2) 8 ... ♘c6?! 9 ♛xc4 ♛d5 10 ♛d3!±.

(h) 10 ... ♘c6 11 e3 ♜a7 12 ♜c1 ♛a8 13 ♘e1 ♘b8 14 ♗a5± Timman - Short, Hilversum 1989.

(i) 11 ... ♛c8 12 ♘c3 ♗b7 △ ... c5=; 11 ... b4=/±.

(j) 9 ... ♗a6 10 ♗b2 ♜c8 11 e4 c5=.

KING'S INDIAN DEFENCE
Various Fianchetto Systems

1 d4 ♘f6 2 c4 g6 3 ♘c3 ♗g7 4 ♘f3 d6 5 g3 0-0 6 ♗g2

	Kavalek		Uhlmann	Simagin
	(1)	*(2)*	*(3)*	*(4)*
6	c6		♘c6 *(f)*	
7	0-0		0-0	
	♕a5		e5	♗g4 *(j)*
8	h3 *(a)*		d5 *(g)*	d5
	e5	♗e6	♘e7	♗xf3?! *(k)*
9	e4	d5	c5	exf3!
	exd4	cxd5	♘e8	♘a5
10	♘xd4	♘d4	cxd6	♕e2
	♕c5	♗d7	cxd6 *(h)*	c5
11	♘b3	cxd5 *(d)*	♕b3	f4
	♕b4! *(b)*	♖c8	h6	a6
12	♗a3∞ *(c)*	♗e3 *(e)*	e4 *(i)*	♗d2 *(l)*

(a) 8 e4 e5 9 h3 – the column; 8 ... ♕h5!?=: 8 d5 ♕b4 9 ♘d2 ♗d7 10 e4 a5 11 ♖e1 ♘a6 12 a3 ♕b6=.

(b) 11 ... ♕xc4? 12 ♕xd6±/±.

(c) (1) 12 ♗f4!? ♘e8 13 ♖e1 (13 c5 dxc5 14 a3 ♕c4 15 ♖c1 b6 16 ♘d5 ♕a6∞) 13 ... ♗e6 (13 ... a5!?) 14 e5!∞/± Csom – Vaganian, Buenos Aires (ol) 1978.
(2) 12 ♗e3 a5 (12 ... ♗e6!? 13 e5 dxe5 14 ♗c5 ♕xc4∞) 13 ♘d2! ♕xb2? (13 ... a4 14 a3 ♕a5∞) 14 ♘a4 ♕e5 15 c5±.

(d) 11 ♘b3!?±.

(e) 12 ♘b3!? ♕d8 13 e4±; 12 ♗e3 ♘a6 13 ♕d2 ♘c5 14 ♖fb1! ♘a4 15 b4 ♕d8 16 ♘xa4 ♗xa4 17 b5!±.

(f) 6 ... ♗g4 7 ♕b3! △ 7 ... ♕c8 8 ♘e5! dxe5 (8 ... c6±) 9 ♗xb7 ♕f5 10 dxe5+-; 6 ... ♗f5 7 ♕b3! ♕c8 8 ♘h4 ♘c6 9 ♘xf5 10 ♕xb7 ♘xd4 11 0-0±.

(g) 8 dxe5 ♘xe5 9 ♘xe5 dxe5 10 ♕xd8 ♖xd8 11 ♗g5 ♖d4!=

(h) 10 ... ♘xd6!? (±) 11 e4 c6?! 12 dxc6 ♘xc6 13 ♗g5!±/±.

(i) 12 ... f5 13 exf5 gxf5 14 ♘d2 ♘g6 15 ♘c4 ♖f7 16 a4 ♗f8 17 ♗d2± Vaganian – Stein, USSR Ch 1970.

(j) 7 ... ♗f5 'Lesser Simagin' 8 d5 ♘a5 9 ♘d2 c6 10 dxc6!? (10 e4; 10 h3) 10 ... bxc6 11 e4 ♗g4 12 ♕c2 ♖c8 13 b4±.

(k) 8 ... ♘a5 9 ♘d2 c5 10 h3 ♗d7 11 ♕c2±.

(l) 12 ... ♖b8 13 ♖ab1 ♕c7 14 b3 ♖fe8 15 ♗h3!±

1 d4 ♘f6 2 c4 g6 3 ♘c3 ♗g7 4 ♘f3 d6 5 g3 0-0
6 ♗g2 ♘c6 7 0-0 a6

	(5)	(6)	(7)	(8)
8	h3		d5	
	♖b8 *(a)*		♘a5	
9	♗e3	e4	♘d2	
	b5	b5 *(d)*	c5	
10	♘d2 *(b)*	e5!? *(e)*	♕c2	
	♗d7	dxe5	♖b8 *(g)*	
11	♖c1	dxe5	b3	
	e5	♕xd1	b5	
12	dxe5	♖xd1	♗b2	
	♘xe5	♘d7	e6	♗h6! *(i)*
13	b3	e6	♖ab1	f4
	♖e8 *(c)*	fxe6 *(f)*	♖e8 *(h)*	bxc4 *(j)*

(a) 8 ... e5 9 d5 ♘e7 10 e4± cf. col 3.

(b) 10 cxb5 axb5 11 ♖c1 ♘a5 12 b3 b4 13 ♘b1!? (13 ♘a4=) 13 ... ♗a6 14 ♖e1 c6=.

(c) 14 ♘d5 bxc4 15 ♘xf6+ ♗xf6 16 ♘xc4 ♘xc4=.

(d) 9 ... e5 10 ♗e3 exd4 11 ♘xd4 ♗d7 12 ♘xc6 ♗xc6 13 ♕c2±; 9 ... ♘d7 10 ♗e3 ♘a5 11 b3 b5 12 cxb5 axb5 13 ♕d2 c6 14 ♗h6!? b4 15 ♗xg7 ♔xg7 16 ♘e2 ♘f6=.

(e) 10 cxb5 axb5 11 ♖e1 e6=.

(f) 14 cxb5 axb5 15 ♗f4!? (15 ♘g5 ♘g4 16 ♗e3 c5!∞; 15 ♗e3 ♘b6 16 ♘d4 ♘xd4 17 ♗xd4 ♗xd4 18 ♖xd4 c5=) 15 ... b4 16 ♘a4 ♘b6 17 ♘xb6 ♖xb6 18 ♗xc7 ♖b7 19 ♗f4 ♗xb2=.

(g) 10 ... e5 (10 ... e6 11 dxe6!?; 11 b3±) 11 dxe6!? (11 a3±) 11 ... ♗xe6 12 b3 d5 13 cxd5 ♘xd5 14 ♗b2 ♘c6 15 ♘xd5 ♗xd5 16 ♗xg7 ♔xg7 17 ♕b2+ ♔g8 18 ♘e4!±.

(h) 14 e4 ♗d7 15 ♖fe1 bxc4 16 bxc4 ♘g4 17 ♘d1±.

(i) 12 ... bxc4 13 bxc4 ♗h6 14 ♘cb1 e5 15 ♗c3 ♗d7 16 ♘a3 ♖b4!? 17 ♗xb4 cxb4 18 ♘ab1 ♕c7±/∞ Timman - Kasparov, Tilburg 1981; 12 ... e5 13 ♖ae1 (13 dxe6 - col 7) 13 ... ♘h5 14 ♘d1 ♗h6 15 e3 ♗f6 16 ♘e4 bxc4 17 bxc4 ♕b6 18 ♗a3±.

(j) 14 bxc4 e5 15 ♖ae1 (15 dxe6!?) 15 ... exf4 16 gxf4 ♘h5 17 e3 ♗g7 18 ♘d1 ♗f5 19 ♗e4 (19 e4?! ♖xb2!) 19 ... ♗xb2 20 ♘xb2 ♖xb2!!∞/∓ Kasparov.

KING'S INDIAN DEFENCE
Panno Variation contd and Yugoslav Variation

1 d4 ♘f6 2 c4 g6 3 ♘c3 ♗g7 4 ♘f3 d6 5 g3 0-0 6 ♗g2

	Panno		Yugoslav	
	(9)	*(10)*	*(11)*	*(12)*
6	♘c6	c5		
7	0-0	0-0		d5
	a6	♘c6		♘a6 *(i)*
8	b3!? *(a)*	dxc5 *(c)*		0-0
	♖b8	dxc5		♘c7
9	♗b2	♗f4	♗e3	a4
	b5	♘h5 *(d)*	♕a5 *(g)*	♖b8
10	cxb5	♗e3 *(e)*	♕d2	♗f4!?
	axb5	♘d4	♗f5	a6
11	♖c1	♕d2	♘d5	a5
	♘a5	♗g4	♕d8	b5
12	♕c2± *(b)*	♖ad1 *(f)*	♘h4 *(h)*	axb6±

(a) (1) 8 e4?! ♗g4 9 ♗e3 ♘d7=

(2) 8 ♘d5!? ♗g4! 9 ♘e3! ♗xf3 10 ♗xf3 ♘d7 11 d5 ♘d4 12 ♗g2 c5= Timman – Portisch, Montreal 1979.

(b) 12 ... ♗b7 13 ♖fd1 ♕d7? (13 ... ♕e8) 14 e4 b4 15 e5! bxc3 16 ♗xc3± Romanishin – Grünfeld, Riga (izt) 1979.

(c) 8 d5 ♘a5 9 ♘d2 a6 10 ♕c2 cols 7-8.

(d) (1) 9 ... ♘d4 10 ♗e5 ♘c6 11 ♕xd8 ♖xd8 12 ♗c7 ♖d7 13 ♗f4 ♘d4 14 ♖fd1 ♘h5 15 ♗d2 ♖d8 16 ♘xd4 cxd4 17 ♘d5 e6 18 ♘e7+ ♔h8 19 ♖ac1± Gligoric – Vukcevic, Yugoslav Ch 1958.

(2) 9 ... ♗e6 10 ♘e5 ♘h5 11 ♘xc6 bxc6 12 ♗e3 ♕xd1 13 ♖fxd1 ♖ab8 14 ♖d2 ♖xb2! 15 ♖xb2 ♗xc3∞/±.

(e) 10 ♗g5!?±/= Larsen – Bouaziz, Riga (izt) 1979 (Rd. 14).

(f) 12 ... ♗xf3 13 exf3!? e6 (13 ... ♕d7) 14 ♘e4 b6 15 b4± Larsen – Ribli (izt) 1979 (Rd. 4 cf. note *[e]*).

(g) 9 ... ♗e6=/± △ 10 ♗xc5 ♕a5=.

(h) 12 ... ♗g4 13 h3 ♗d7 14 ♗c3 e5 15 e3 ♖e8 16 ♘xf6+ (16 ♘f3!?) 16 ... ♗xf6 17 ♘f3= Smejkal – Gligoric, Hastings, 1968/69.

(i) 7 ... e5!? 8 dxe6 ♗xe6 9 ♘g5 ♗xc4 10 ♗xb7 ♘bd7 11 ♗xa8 ♕xa8 12 0-0 d5 ∞.

KING'S INDIAN DEFENCE
Classical Fianchetto

1 d4 ♘f6 2 c4 g6 3 ♘c3 ♗g7 4 ♘f3 d6 5 g3 0-0
6 ♗g2 ♘bd7 7 0-0 e5 8 e4 *(a)* c6 9 h3 *(b)*

	(13)	(14)	(15)	(16)
9	♖e8		♕b6 *(h)*	
10	♖e1	♗e3	♖e1 *(i)*	
	a5	exd4	♖e8	exd4
11	♕c2 *(c)*	♘xd4	d5	♘xd4
	exd4	♘c5	♘c5	♖e8
12	♘xd4	♕c2	♖b1	♖e2!
	♘c5	♕e7	a5	♘g4?!
13	♗e3	♖fe1	♗e3	♖d2
	a4	♗d7 *(f)*	♕c7	♘ge5
14	♖ad1	f3	♘d2	b3
	♘fd7 *(d)*	a6	♗d7	♘c5
15	♖e2	♗f2	♗f1	♖c2!
	♕a5	b5	♖ab8	a5
16	♖ed2 *(e)*	cxb5 *(g)*	a3 *(j)*	♗e3±/±

(a) 8 e3 ♖e8 9 b3 c6 10 ♕c2 (10 ♗b2!? e4!) 10 ... exd4!? 11 ♘xd4 a5 12 ♗b2 ♘c5=.

(b) 9 ♕c2 ♖e8 10 ♖d1 ♕e7! 11 b3 exd4 12 ♘xd4 ♘c5 13 f3 a5 14 ♖b1 ♘fd7 15 ♘ce2 ♘e5 16 ♗f4 ♕c7=.

(c) 11 ♖b1 exd4 12 ♘xd4 ♘c5 13 ♗f4 a4 14 ♕d2 ♘h5 15 ♗e3 ♕c7 16 b4 axb3 17 axb3±.

(d) 14 ... ♕a5 15 ♗f4 ♗f8±.

(e) 16 ... ♕b4 17 ♘b1 ♘b6 18 ♘a3±.

(f) 13 ... ♘fxe4? (13 ... ♘cxe4?? 14 ♗f4+-) 14 ♘xe4 ♘xe4 15 ♗xe4 ♕xe4 16 ♗d2!±.

(g) 16 ... axb5 17 a3 ♘e6 18 f4 ♘xd4 19 ♗xd4 c5 20 ♗xf6 ♕xf6 21 e5 dxe5 22 ♗xa8 ♖xa8⩲.

(h) (1) 9 ... ♕a5!? 10 ♗e3 exd4 (10 ... ♘b6 11 ♘d2±) 11 ♘xd4 ♘b6 12 ♘b3 ♕b4 13 e5! ♘fd7 14 a3 ♕xc4 15 exd6±;
(2) 9 ... a6?! 10 ♖e1 b5!? 11 c5! dxc5 12 ♘xe5±.

(i) 10 c5 dxc5 11 dxe5 ♘e8 12 ♘a4 ♕a6 13 ♗f4 ♘c7 14 ♕c2 ♘e6 15 ♖fd1 ♖e8 16 ♖d6 ♕a5 17 ♖ad1 ♘b6 18 ♘xb6 axb6⩱ Yusupov – Kasparov, Linares 1990.

(j) 16 ... cxd5 17 cxd5 b5 18 b4 ♘d3! 19 ♗xd3 ♕xc3 20 ♖b3 ♕c7 21 bxa5± Najdorf – Tal, Belgrade 1970.

KING'S INDIAN DEFENCE

1 d4 ♘f6 2 c4 g6 3 ♘c3 ♗g7

	(17)	(18)	(19)	(20)
4	♘f3		e4	
	d6		d6 (f)	
5	♗g5	e3 (d)	g3	h3 (h)
	0-0 (a)	0-0	0-0	0-0!?
6	e3	♗e2	♗g2	♗g5
	♗f5!? (b)	♘bd7	e5	h6
7	♗e2	0-0	♘ge2	♗e3
	♘e4	e5	♘c6	e5
8	♘xe4	b3	d5	d5
	♗xe4	♘e8 (e)	♘d4! (g)	♘bd7
9	0-0=/± (c)			♗d3 (i)

(a) 5 ... h6 6 ♗h4 g5 7 ♗g3 ♘h5 8 e3 e6 9 ♗e2 ♘d7 10 ♘d2 ♘xg3 11 hxg3=.

(b) 6 ... c5! 7 ♗e2 ♕a5 8 ♕d2 ♗g4 9 0-0 ♘bd7 10 h3 ♗xf3 11 ♗xf3(±/=) 11 ... ♖ac8 12 ♗xb7!? cxd4 13 exd4 ♖xc4=.

(c) 9 ... b6?!±/± Hartston - Biyiasas, Hastings 1978/79; 9 ... h6 △ 10 ... g5, 11 ... ♗g6±.

(d) 5 ♗f4 0-0 6 h3 ♘bd7 7 e3 c6 8 ♗e2 ♕e8 9 0-0 e5 10 ♗h2 ♕e7=.

(e) 9 ♗a3!? (9 ♗b2 exd4 10 ♘xd4 ♘c5=) 9 ... exd4 10 ♘xd4 ♘c5 11 ♕c2 ♘fe4 12 ♘xe4 ♘xe4 13 ♗b2 a5=.

(f) 4 ... 0-0 5 e5!? ♘e8 6 f4 d6 7 ♗e3 dxe5 8 dxe5 ♕xd1+ 9 ♖xd1=; 4 ... 0-0 5 ♘f3 / 5 ♗e2, 5 ... d6 etc; 4 ... 0-0 5 ♗e3! d6 6 f3 - Sämisch; 5 f3 c5!? 6 dxc5 b6!?∞.

(g) (1) 9 ♘xd4? exd4 10 ♘e2 (10 ♕xd4?? ♘xe4) 10 ... ♖e8 11 f3 c5 12 dxc6 bxc6 13 ♘xd4 ♕b6⩱/∓.
   (2) 9 0-0 c5! 10 dxc6 bxc6 11 ♘xd4 exd4 12 ♘e2 ♗g4 13 f3 ♗e6 14 ♘xd4 ♗xc4 15 ♖e1 ♕b6=.

(h) (1) 5 ♘ge2 0-0 6 ♘g3 c5! 7 d5 e6 8 ♗d3 exd5 9 cxd5 - Modern Benoni cols 13-14.
   (2) 5 ♗d3 0-0!? 6 ♘ge2 e5 7 d5 ♘h5 8 0-0 f5 9 exf5 gxf5 10 f4 ♘d7=.
   (3) 5 ♗g5 h6 6 ♗h4 c5 7 d5 0-0 8 ♗d3 e6 9 ♘ge2 exd5 10 exd5=; 10 cxd5=.

(i) 9 ... ♘c5 10 ♗c2 a5 (10 ... ♘h5!?) 11 ♕d2 ♔h7 12 g4± Suba - Botterill, Hastings 1978/79.

KING'S INDIAN DEFENCE
Four Pawns Attack

1 d4 ♘f6 2 c4 g6 3 ♘c3 ♗g7 4 e4 d6 5 f4 0-0 6 ♘f3 c5 (a)

	(21)	(22)	(23)	(24)
7	d5			♗e2 (i)
	e6			cxd4
8	♗e2			♘xd4
	exd5			♘c6
9	cxd5		exd5	♗e3
	♖e8 (b)		♘h5 (f)	♘g4
10	e5!?	♘d2	0-0	♗xg4
	dxe5	♘a6 (e)	♗xc3	♗xd4
11	fxe5	0-0	bxc3	♗xd4
	♘g4	♘c7	f5 (g)	♗xg4
12	♗g5	a4	♘g5	♕d2
	♕b6 (c)	a6	♘g7	♘xd4
13	0-0∞ (d)	♗f3=/±	♗f3 (h)	♕xd4=

(a) 6 ... e5!? 7 dxe5 dxe5 8 ♕xd8 ♖xd8 9 ♘xe5 ♖e8 10 ♗d3 ♘xe4 11 ♗xe4 f6 12 ♘d5 ♘a6 13 ♘xf6+ ♗xf6 14 0-0 c6!± Boleslavsky; 6 ... c6?!; 6 ... ♘a6!? △ ... e5.

(b) 9 ... b5 10 e5! dxe5 11 fxe5 ♘g4 12 ♗g5±; 9 ... ♗g4 10 0-0 ♘bd7 11 ♘d2!? (11 a4 ♖e8 12 h3=) 11 ... ♗xe2 12 ♕xe2 ♖e8 13 ♕f3 ♕e7 14 a4 c4 15 ♔h1 ♘c5 16 e5 dxe5 17 fxe5 ♕xe5∞/=/∓ Peev - Tseshkovsky, Albena 1977.

(c) 12 ... f6 13 exf6 ♗xf6 14 ♕d2 ♗f5=.

(d) (1) 13 ... ♘xe5 14 ♘xe5!? ♗xe5 15 ♗c4∞.

(2) 13 ... ♘xe5 14 d6 c4+ 15 ♔h1 ♘d3 16 ♗xd3 cxd3 17 ♕xd3±.

(3) 13 ... ♗f5!? 14 d6 ♕xb2 15 ♘d5 ♘xe5 16 ♘e7+ ♖xe7 17 dxe7 ♘bc6=.

(e) 10 ... a6 11 a4 ♘bd7±; 10 ... ♘g4!? 11 ♗xg4 ♕h4+ 12 g3 ♕xg4 13 ♕xg4 ♗xg4 14 ♘b5!? (14 ♔f2 a6 15 a4±) 14 ... ♘a6 15 h3 ♖xe4+! 16 ♘xe4 ♗f3 17 0-0 ♗xe4∞.

(f) 9 ... ♖e8 10 0-0 ♘g4 11 h3 ♘e3 12 ♗xe3 ♖xe3 13 ♕d2±.

(g) 11 ... ♘g7 12 f5! ♗xf5 13 ♗f4∞∓.

(h) 13 ... ♘d7 14 ♖e1 ♘f6 15 ♖b1 ♖e8 16 ♖xe8+ ♕xe8 17 ♖b2 ♗d7!= Forintos - Gligoric, Ljubliana 1969.

(i) 7 dxc5 ♕a5 8 ♗d3 ♕xc5 9 ♕e2 ♘c6 10 ♗e3 ♕h5!? 11 h3 ♘g4 12 ♗d2 (12 ♗g1!?) 12 ... ♘d4 13 ♕f1 ♘xf3+ 14 ♕xf3 ♗d4∞.

KING'S INDIAN DEFENCE
Averbakh

1 d4 ♘f6 2 c4 g6 3 ♘c3 ♗g7 4 e4 d6 5 ♗e2 0-0 6 ♗g5

	(25)	(26)	(27)	(28)
6	c5			h6 (e)
7	d5			♗e3
	h6		e6?!	e5 (f)
8	♗f4	♗e3	♕d2!	d5
	e6 (a)	e6	exd5	♘bd7
9	dxe6	♕d2	exd5	♕d2 (g)
	♗xe6	exd5	♖e8	h5
10	♗xd6	exd5	♘f3	f3
	♖e8	♔h7	♗g4	♘e8
11	♘f3	h3	0-0	g4
	♘c6	♖e8	♘bd7	f5
12	0-0 (b)	♗d3 (c)	h3 (d)	gxf5 (h)

(a) 8 ... e5 9 dxe6 – the column; 9 ... a6 10 a4 ♕a5 11 ♗d2!±.

(b) (1) 12 ... ♘d4 13 e5 ♘d7 14 ♘xd4 cxd4 15 ♕xd4 (15 ♘b5∞) 15 ... ♘xe5= Bareev – Akopian, Moscow 1989.

(2) 12 ... ♕a5 13 ♘d2 ♖ed8 14 ♗f4! (Uhlmann; 14 ♘b3 ♕b6 15 ♘a4 ♕b4 16 ♘bxc5 ♗xc4!∞/∓ Alburt – Kasparov, USSR Ch 1978) 14 ... ♘d4 15 ♘d5! ♘xd5 16 cxd5±/± Uhlmann – Peev, Bucharest 1979.

(c) 12 ... ♘a6 13 ♘f3 ♘b4 14 ♗b1 ♗f5! 15 a3 (15 ♗xf5? gxf5 16 a3 f4∓; 16 0-0 ♘e4±) 15 ... ♗xb1 16 ♖xb1 ♘a6=.

(d) 12 ... ♗xf3 13 ♗xf3± Yusupov – Zapata, St. John 1988.

(e) (1) 6 ... e5?? 7 dxe5 dxe5 8 ♕xd8+-.

(2) 6 ... ♘bd7 7 ♕d2 (7 ♕c2) 7 ... c5 8 d5 b5!= Hort – Westerinen, Helsinki 1979.

(3) 6 ... c6! 7 ♘f3±; 7 f4!?

(4) 6 ... ♘a6 7 h4!? h6 8 ♗e3 e5 9 d5 ♘c5 10 ♕c2 c6 11 h5 g5 12 f3 a5 13 g4 ♗d7 14 ♘h3 a4∞ Bareev – Kasparov, Linares 1992.

(f) 7 ... c5 8 d5 – col 26; 7 ... c5 8 e5!±.

(g) 9 g4 ♘c5 10 f3 a5 11 h4 h5∞/=.

(h) 12 ... gxf5 13 exf5 ♘b6 14 ♗g5 ♕d7 15 ♘h3± Seirawan – Nunn, Lucerne (ol) 1982.

1 d4 Nf6 2 c4 g6 3 Nc3 Bg7 4 e4 d6 5 f3

	(29)	(30)	(31)	(32)
5	c6 *(a)*	0-0		
6	Be3	Bg5!?	Be3	
	a6	c5	c6!?	b6 *(g)*
7	c5 *(b)*	d5	Bd3 *(e)*	Bd3
	b5	e6 *(c)*	a6	Bb7 *(h)*
8	cxd6	Qd2	Nge2	Nge2 *(i)*
	exd6	exd5	b5	c5
9	Bd3	cxd5	0-0	d5
	0-0	Re8	Nbd7	e6
10	Nge2	Bd3	Qd2	0-0
	Nbd7	h6	bxc4	exd5 *(j)*
11	0-0±	Be3 *(d)*	Bxc4 *(f)*	

(a) 5 ... c5 6 dxc5 dxc5 7 Qxd8+ Kxd8 8 Be3±; 5 ... e5 6 dxe5!?±; 6 Nge2; 6 d5.

(b) 7 a4? a5=; 7 Qd2 b5 8 0-0-0 Qa5 9 Kb1 Nbd7 10 Bh6 Bxh6! 11 Qxh6 Bb7 12 Qd2 0-0-0=; 7 Bd3 b5 8 e5 Nfd7 9 f4 0-0 10 Nf3±.

(c) 7 ... Nbd7 8 Nh3!±.

(d) 11 Bxh6? Nxe4! △ ... Qh4+; 11 Be3 Nbd7 12 Nge2=/±.

(e) 7 Qd2 a6 8 0-0-0 b5 9 Bh6 Qa5=.

(f) 11 ... Nb6 12 Bb3 a5 13 Na4±.

(g) 6 ... Nbd7 7 Qd2 c5 8 d5 Ne5 9 Bg5 (9 h3? Nh5 10 Bf2 f5 11 exf5 Rxf5!! 12 g4 Rxf3 13 gxh5 Qf8∓ Beliavsky - Nunn, Wijk aan Zee 1985) 9 ... a6 10 f4±.

(h) (1) 7 ... c5? 8 e5! Ne8 9 Be4±.

(2) 7 ... a6 8 Nge2 c5 9 e5 Nfd7 (9 ... Ne8 10 Be4 Ra7 11 dxc5 bxc5 12 Bxc5 Rd7 13 Be3 Bb7 14 Bxb7 Rxb7 15 b3±) 10 exd6 cxd4 11 dxe7 Qxe7 12 Nd5 Qd6= Beliavsky - Hellers, Thessaloniki (ol) 1988.

(i) 8 Nh3 c5 9 d5±.

(j) (1) 11 cxd5 Ba6 12 Bxa6 Nxa6 13 Qd3 Nc7 14 a4 Nd7 15 f4±.

(2) 11 exd5 Nbd7 12 Bg5 h6 13 Bh4 Ne5 14 f4 Nxd3 15 Qxd3=/±.

KING'S INDIAN DEFENCE
Sämisch

1 d4 ♘f6 2 c4 g6 3 ♘c3 ♗g7 4 e4 d6 5 f3 0–0 6 ♗e3

	Panno		Orthodox	
	(33)	*(34)*	*(35)*	*(36)*
6	♘c6		e5	
7	♘ge2		♘ge2	d5
	a6		c6	c6 *(i)*
8	♕d2		♕d2	♗d3 *(j)*
	♖b8		exd4	cxd5 *(k)*
9	h4!	♘c1 *(b)*	♘xd4 *(f)*	cxd5
	h5	e5	d5	♘e8(!)
10	0–0–0	d5 *(c)*	cxd5 *(g)*	♕d2
	b5	♘d4	cxd5	f5
11	♗h6	♘b3 *(d)*	e5	♘ge2
	e5	♘xb3	♘e8	♘d7
12	♗xg7 *(a)*	axb3 *(e)*	f4 *(h)*	exf5 *(l)*

(a) 12 ... ♔xg7 13 d5 ♘a5 14 ♘g3 b4 15 ♘b1 ♖b6 16 ♕g5 ♘b7 17 ♘d2=.

(b) 9 g4!?; 9 ♖d1.

(c) 10 ♘b3 exd4 11 ♘xd4 ♘xd4 12 ♗xd4 ♗e6 13 ♗e2 c6 14 0–0 b5=.

(d) 11 ♘1e2(!) ♘xe2 12 ♗xe2±; 11 ... c5!? 12 dxc6 ♘xc6±.

(e) 12 ... c5 13 g4!? (13 b4!?; 13 ♗d2) 13 ... h5 14 h3 ♘h7 15 gxh5 ♕h4+ 16 ♔f2 ♕xf2+ 17 ♔xf2 gxh5=.

(f) 9 ♗xd4!?

(g) 10 exd5 cxd5 11 ♗e2 dxc4=.

(h) 12 ... f6 13 ♗b5! fxe5 14 fxe5 ♗xe5 15 ♘f3 ♗g7 16 0–0 ♘c6= Pachman – Gligoric, Oberhausen 1961.

(i) 7 ... ♘h5 8 ♕d2 f5 9 0–0–0 ♘d7± e.g. 10 ♗d3 ♘c5 11 ♗c2 a6 12 ♘ge2 b5 13 b4 ♘d7 Timman – Kasparov, Linares 1992.

(j) 8 ♕d2 cxd5 9 cxd5 ♘a6; 9 ... a6=/±.

(k) 8 ... b5 9 ♘ge2±.

(l) 12 ... gxf5 13 0–0 ♔h8 14 ♖ac1 ♘df6=/± Polugaevsky – Geller, Petropolis (izt) 1973.

1 d4 ♘f6 2 c4 g6 3 ♘c3 ♗g7 4 e4 d6 5 ♘f3 0-0 6 ♗e2

	(37)	(38)	Gligoric (39)	Petrosian (40)
6	♗g4	e5 (b)		
7	♗e3	dxe5	♗e3	d5
	♘fd7	dxe5	♘bd7 (d)	♘bd7
8	♘g1	♕xd8	0-0	♗g5
	♗xe2	♖xd8	c6	h6
9	♘gxe2	♗g5	♕c2	♗h4
	e5	♖e8	♘g4 (e)	g5!?
10	0-0	♘d5	♗g5	♗g3
	a5	♘xd5	f6	♘h5
11	♕d2 (a)	cxd5 (c)	♗h4=/±	h4∞ (f)

(a) ± Kasparov - Vukic, Banja Luka 1979.

(b) (1) 6 ... c5 7 0-0 ♘c6 (7 ... cxd4 8 ♘xd4 - Sicilian Maroczy Bind!) 8 d5 ♘a5 9 a3 b6 10 b4 ♘b7 11 ♖b1±.

(2) 6 ... ♘bd7 7 0-0 e5 - cols 42-44.

(c) 11 ... c6 12 ♗c4=/±.

(d) 7 ... ♘g4 8 ♗g5 f6 9 ♗c1=/±; 7 ... ♕e7=/±; 7 ... ♘c6 8 dxe5 dxe5 9 ♕xd8 ♖xd8 10 ♘d5±; 7 ... exd4 8 ♘xd4 ♖e8 9 f3 c6 10 ♕d2 d5 11 exd5 cxd5 12 0-0 ♘c6 13 c5 ♖xe3!! 14 ♕xe3 ♕f8!!∞ Karpov - Kasparov, World Ch (11), New York 1990 and Gelfand - Kasparov, Linares 1992.

(e) 9 ... ♕e7 10 ♖fe1 exd4 11 ♗xd4 ♘c5 12 ♘d2 ♖e8 13 ♖ad1 h5 14 h3 ♗h6= Pinter - Tal, Taxco (izt) 1985.

(f) (1) 11 ... g4(!) 12 ♘d2 ♘xg3 13 fxg3 h5∞/± Yusupov - Correa, Mendoza 1985.

(2) 11 ... ♘f4 12 hxg5 hxg5 13 ♕c2±.

(3) 11 ... ♘xg3 12 fxg3 gxh4 13 ♘xh4 ♕g5 14 ♗g4 ♘c5 15 ♗xc8 ♕xg3+ (15 ... ♖axc8 16 ♘f5±) 16 ♔f1 ♖axc8 17 ♘f5 ♕f4+ 18 ♕f3± Balashov - Penrose, Hastings 1966/67.

KING'S INDIAN DEFENCE

1 d4 ♘f6 2 c4 g6 3 ♘c3 ♗g7 4 e4 d6 5 ♘f3 0–0 6 ♗e2 e5

Petrosian contd

	(41)	*(42)*	*(43)*	*(44)*
7	d5 *(a)*	0–0		
	a5	♘bd7		
8	♗g5	d5	♖e1	
	h6	♘c5	c6	
9	♗h4	♕c2	♗f1	
	♘a6	a5	a5	
10	♘d2	♗g5	♖b1!	♖e8 *(h)*
	♕e8	h6	exd4	
11	0–0	♗e3	♘xd4	d5
	♗d7	♘fd7 *(d)*	♖e8	♘c5!? *(i)*
12	b3 *(b)*	♘d2	♗f4! *(f)*	b3
	♘h7	f5	♘c5	♗d7
13	f3 *(c)*	exf5 *(e)*	f3 *(g)*	dxc6!± *(j)*

(a) 7 ... ♘a6 8 ♗g5±; 7 ... c5!? 8 ♗g5 h6 9 ♗h4±.

(b) 12 a3 ♘h7 13 b3 f5!? 14 exf5 gxf5 15 ♗h5 ♕c8 16 ♗e7 ♖e8 17 ♗xe8 ♕xe8 18 ♗h4 e4 19 ♕c2 ♕h5⩲ Yusupov – Kasparov, Barcelona 1989.

(c) 13 ... h5 14 a3 ♗h6 15 ♗f2 ♕e7= Petrosian – Stein, USSR 1967.

(d) 11 ... ♘e8; 11 ... ♘h5; 11 ... ♘g4?! 12 ♗xc5 dxc5 13 h3 ♘f6 14 ♘xe5 ♘xd5 15 cxd5! ♗xe5 16 f4 ♗d4+ 17 ♔h2!±/±; 11 ... b6 12 ♘d2 ♗g4 13 f3 ♗d7 14 b3 ♘h5∞ Keene – Torre, Manila 1979.

(e) 13 ... gxf5 14 f4± Plaskett – Nunn, England 1982.

(f) 12 f3 d5! 13 cxd5 cxd5 14 ♘db5!? dxe4 15 ♘d6 exf3 16 ♘xe8 ♗g4!∞ Polugaevsky – Kochiev, USSR Ch 1978.

(g) 13 ... d5 14 cxd5 ♘xd5! 15 exd5 ♖xe1 16 ♕xe1 ♗xd4+ 17 ♗e3 ♗xe3+ 18 ♕xe3±/± Tal – Grigorian, USSR Ch 1977.

(h) 10 ... ♕b6 11 d5 c5±; 11 h3 exd4 12 ♘xd4 ♘g4 13 hxg4 ♗xd4 14 ♗e3 ♗xe3 15 ♖xe3±.

(i) 11 ... c5 12 a3±.

(j) 13 ... ♗xc6±; 13 ... bxc6? 14 ♕xd6 ♘fxe4 15 ♖xe4! ♘xe4 16 ♘xe4 ♗f5 17 ♘fd2!± Farago – Vogt, Kecskemet 1977.

KING'S INDIAN DEFENCE
Classical

**1 d4 ♘f6 2 c4 g6 3 ♘c3 ♗g7 4 e4 d6 5 ♘f3 0-0
6 ♗e2 e5 7 0-0 ♘c6 8 d5 (a) ♘e7**

	(45)	(46)	(47)	(48)
9	♘e1		♘d2	b4
	♘d7		c5 (f)	♘h5
10	♘d3 (b)		♖b1 (g)	c5!? (i)
	f5		♘e8	♘f4
11	♗d2		b4	♗xf4
	♘f6	fxe4 (e)	b6	exf4
12	f3	♘xe4	a4	♖c1
	f4	♘f6	f5	h6!
13	c5	♗f3	a3	♘d2
	g5	♘f5	♔h8	g5
14	♖c1 (c)	♘xf6+	♕a4	♘c4
	♘g6	♕xf6	♗d7	♘g6!=/∓ (j)
15	cxd6	♗e4	♕a3	
	cxd6	♗d7	♘g8	
16	♘b5 (d)	♖e1±	♗d1=	

(a) 8 ♗e3 ♘g4 9 ♗g5 f6=.

(b) 10 f3 f5 11 g4!? (Benko Attack) 11 ... ♘f6 12 ♘g2 c6!=;
10 ♗e3 f5 11 f3 f4 12 ♗f2 g5 13 b4 ♘f6 14 c5 ♘g6 15 cxd6
cxd6 16 ♖c1 ♖f7 17 a4 ♗f8 △ ... ♖g7∞ Piket - Kasparov,
Tilburg 1989.

(c) 14 cxd6 cxd6 15 ♘f2 h5 16 h3 ♘g6± Karpov - van der
Wiel, Brussels 1987.

(d) 16 ... ♖f7 17 ♕c2 ♘e8 18 a4 h5 19 ♘f2 ♗f8! 20 h3 ♖g7
21 ♕b3 ♘h4= Ftacnik - Zsu Polgar, Trencianske Teplice
1985.

(e) 11 ... c5!? 12 f4 exf4 13 ♗xf4 ♗xc3 14 bxc3 fxe4 15 ♘e1
♘f6 16 g4!± Ftacnik - Egmond, Amsterdam (2) 1977.

(f) 9 ... ♗h6!?; 9 ... a5.

(g) 10 dxc6 bxc6 11 b4=/±.

(h) 9 ♗d2 ♘h5 10 g3 f5 11 exf5 ♘xf5 12 ♘e4 (12 g4? ♘g4
13 gxh5 ♘xe2+ 14 ♕xe2 ♗g4+-) 12 ... ♘f6 13 ♗g5 h6 14 ♗xf6
♗xf6=.

(i) 10 g3 f5 11 ♘g5 ♘f6 12 f3 f4!=

(j) △ 15 cxd6 cxd6 16 ♘b5 a6! 17 ♘bxd6 b5∓.

GRÜNFELD DEFENCE
Systems with Bg5 or Bf4

1 d4 Nf6 2 c4 g6 3 Nc3 d5

	(1)	(2)	(3)	(4)
4	Bg5	Bf4	Nf3 *(g)*	
	Be4	Bg7	Bg7	
5	Bh4	e3	Bg5	Bf4
	Nxc3 *(a)*	0-0!?	Ne4	0-0
6	bxc3	cxd5!?	cxd5	e3 *(k)*
	Bg7	Nxd5	Nxg5	c5 *(l)*
7	e3	Nxd5	Nxg5	dxc5
	c5	Qxd5	e6	Qa5
8	cxd5	Bxc7	Nf3 *(h)*	Qa4 *(m)*
	Qxd5	Na6 *(d)*	exd5	Qxc5
9	Qf3	Bxa6	e3 *(i)*	Qb5
	Qd8 *(b)*	Qxg2 *(e)*	0-0	Qxb5
10	Bb5+ *(c)*	Qf3 *(f)*	b4 *(j)*	Nxb5 *(n)*

(a) 5 ... c5 6 cxd5 Nxc3 7 bxc3 Qxd5 8 e3 cxd4 9 Qxd4 Qxd4 10 cxd4 e6! 11 Rb1 Be7=.

(b) 9 ... Qxf3?! 10 Nxf3 Nc6 11 Rb1±; 9 ... Qd7.

(c) 10 ... Nd7 11 Ne2 cxd4 12 exd4 0-0=.

(d) 8 ... Nc6?! 9 Ne2 Bg4 10 f3 Rac8 (10 ... Bxf3?±) 11 Nc3 Qe6 12 Bf4 Nxd4∞/± 12 ... Bxd4 13 fxg4 g5 14 Bxg5 Rfd8 15 Qc1!

(e) 9 ... bxa6?!

(f) 10 ... Qxf3 11 Nxf3 bxa6 12 Rc1 Bb7 13 Ke2 f6=.

(g) (1) 4 Qb3 dxc4 5 Qxc4 Bg7 6 Nf3 - cols 9-12; 5 ... Be6!? 6 Qb5+ Bd7 7 Qb3 Nc6 8 Nf3 Bg7 9 e4 0-0 10 h3 Rb8 11 Be3 b5∞.

(2) 4 e3 Bg7 5 Nf3 - cols 5-8; 5 Bd2!?

(h) 8 Qd2 exd5 9 Qe3+ Kf8 10 Qf4 Nf6 11 h4 h6=; 8 Nh3!? exd5 9 Nf4 0-0 10 g3 Re8 11 Bg2 Nc6 12 0-0 Nxd4±.

(i) 9 b4 Qd6! 10 a3 0-0 11 e3 c6 12 Be2 Bf5 13 0-0 Nd7= Seirawan - Kasparov, Dubai (ol) 1986.

(j) 10 ... c6 11 Be2±/=.

(k) 6 Rc1 c5 7 dxc5 Be6 8 Nd4 Nc6 9 Nxe6 fxe6=.

(l) 6 ... c6 7 Qb3; 7 Rc1=/±.

(m) 8 Rc1 dxc4 9 Bxc4 Qxc5±.

(n) 10 ... Na6 11 Rd1 Be6 12 Nfd4 Bd7=.

GRÜNFELD DEFENCE

1 d4 ♘f6 2 c4 g6 3 ♘c3 d5 4 ♘f3 ♗g7 5 e3 0-0

	(5)	(6)	(7)	(8)
6	♗d2	b4	♗e2	♕b3 (i)
	c5 (a)	b6	c5 (e)	c6
7	dxc5	♕b3	dxc5 (f)	♗d2
	♘a6	c5 (c)	♕a5	e6
8	cxd5	bxc5	cxd5	♗d3
	♘xc5	bxc5	♘xd5	b6
9	♗c4	cxd5	♕xd5	0-0
	a6	♘a6	♗xc3+	♗b7
10	a4	♗d2	♗d2 (g)	e4
	♗f5	♖b8	♖d8	c5
11	0-0	♕a4	♕xd8+	cxd5
	♖c8 (b)	♘b4 (d)	♕xd8 (h)	cxd4 (j)

(a) 6 ... c6±; 6 ... e6±.

(b) 12 ♕e2 ♘fe4! 13 ♘xe4 ♗xe4 14 ♗b4 ♗xd5 15 ♖fd1 ♕b6 16 ♗xc5 ♗xc4= Gulko – Navarovsky, USSR 1971.

(c) 7 ... c6 8 cxd5 cxd5 9 b5!± Miles – Ribli, Tilburg 1978; 7 ... ♗b7.

(d) 12 ♖c1 ♗d7 13 ♕d1!=; 13 ♕xa7? cxd4 14 ♘xd4 ♖a8 15 ♕c5 ♘xa2 16 ♘xa2 ♖xa2∓.

(e) 6 ... dxc4 7 ♗xc4 c5 8 d5± ; 6 ... c6±.

(f) 7 0-0 cxd4 8 exd4 ♘c6 9 h3 b6 10 ♘e5 ♗b7= Marjanovic – Smejkal, Marseilles 1986.

(g) 10 bxc3!? ♕xc3+ 11 ♕d2 ♕xa1 12 0-0 ♕g7! 13 ♗b2 f6∞ Lputian – Gavrikov, USSR Ch 1985.

(h) 12 ♗xc3=.

(i) (1) 6 ♗d3 c5=; 6 ... c6=.

   (2) 6 cxd5 ♘xd5 7 ♗c4 ♘b6 (7 ... ♘xc3=) 8 ♗b3 c5 9 0-0 cxd4 10 ♘xd4 ♘c6!=.

(j) 12 ♘xd4 exd5 13 exd5 ♘bd7 (13 ... ♘xd5 14 ♗e4 ♗xd4=/±) 14 ♗g5 ♘c5 15 ♕c2 ♗xd5 16 ♖ad1= (Smyslov).

GRÜNFELD DEFENCE
Smyslov Variation et al

1 d4 ♘f6 2 c4 g6 3 ♘c3 d5 4 ♘f3 ♗g7 5 ♕b3 dxc4 6 ♕xc4 0-0 7 e4

	Smyslov		Prins	
	(9)	*(10)*	*(11)*	*(12)*
7	♗g4		a6	♘a6 *(j)*
8	♗e3		♕b3 *(g)*	♗e2
	♘fd7		b5	c5
9	♕b3 *(c)*		e5	d5
	♘b6		♘fd7 *(h)*	e6
10	♖d1		♗e3	0-0
	♘c6	e6!	♘b6	exd5
11	d5	♗e2 *(e)*	♘d3	exd5
	♘e5	♘c6	♗e6	♗f5
12	♗e2	♘g1!?	♕c2	♖d1
	♘xf3+	♗xe2	♘c6	♖e8
13	gxf3	♘gxe2	a3	d6
	♗h5!	♕e7	♘a5	h6
14	♖g1 *(d)*	0-0 *(f)*	0-0 *(i)*	♗f4 *(k)*

(a) 5 ♕a4+ ♗d7 6 ♕b3 dxc4 7 ♕xc4 0-0 8 e4 ♗g4 – cols 9–10; 5 ... c6?! 6 cxd5 ♘xd5 7 e4±.

(b) 5 ... c6 6 cxd5!? cxd5 7 ♗g5±; 6 e3± – col 8.

(c) 9 0-0-0!?; 9 ♖d1 ♘c6 10 ♗e2 ♘b6 11 ♕c5 ♕d6 12 e5!± Karpov – Kasparov, World Ch (17), Leningrad 1986.

(d) (1) 14 ... ♕b8? 15 f4! ♗xe2 16 ♘xe2 c6 17 dxc6 bxc6 18 h4 ♖d8 19 ♖xd8+ ♕xd8 20 h5±.

(2) 14 ... ♕d7 15 ♖g3 c6 16 dxc6±; 15 ... ♔h8!? 16 ♘b5 f5 17 ♗d4 fxe4 18 ♗xg7+ ♔xg7 19 ♘d4 exf3 Sosonko – Timman, Amsterdam 1975.

(e) 11 ♗b5 ♗xf3! 12 gxf3 ♕h4 13 ♘e2 a6 14 ♗d3 ♘c6∓.

(f) =/± Kuligowski – Smejkal, Warsaw (zt) 1979.

(g) 8 ♗e2 b5 9 ♕b3 c5 10 dxc5 ♘bd7 11 e5 ♘xc5 12 ♕b4 ♘fd7 13 0-0 a5 14 ♕h4 ♗b7=.

(h) 9 ... ♗e6?! 10 exf6 ♗xb3 11 fxg7 ♔xg7 12 axb3±/±.

(i) 14 ... f5 15 exf6 exf6±/=.

(j) 7 ... c6 8 ♕b3 e5 9 dxe5 ♘g4 10 ♗e2 ♕b6 11 0-0±.

(k) 14 ... ♘d7∞ Karpov – Kasparov, World Ch (21), Seville 1987.

GRÜNFELD DEFENCE
Exchange Variation

**1 d4 Nf6 2 c4 g6 3 Nc3 d5 4 cxd5 Nxd5 5 e4 Nxc3
6 bxc3 Bg7 7 Bc4 0-0 8 Ne2**

	(13)	(14)	(15)	(16)
8	c5			Nc6
9	0-0			0-0
	Nc6			b6
10	Be3			Be3
	cxd4 (a)	Qc7		Bb7 (i)
11	cxd4	Rc1		Rc1
	Bg4	Rd8		Qd6
12	f3	Qd2	f4 (e)	f4
	Na5	Qa5	Bg4 (f)	e6
13	Bd3 (b)	Rfd1	f5	f5
	Be6	Bg4!?	gxf5	Na5
14	d5!?	Qb2!?	Bxf7+?! (g)	Bd3
	Bxa1	Qb6	Kxf7	exf5
15	Qxa1	Qxb6	Qb3+	exf5
	f6∞ (c)	axb6 (d)	e6 (h)	Qc6 (j)

(a) 10 ... Bg4 11 f3 Na5 12 Bxf7+ (Seville Variation) 12 ...
Rxf7 13 fxg4 Rxf1+ 14 Kxf1 Qd6 15 e5 Qd5 16 Bf2 Rd8 17
Qc2 Qc4= Novikov - Lhagvasuren, Belgograd 1991.

(b) 13 Bxf7+=; 13 Bd5 Bd7=; 13 Rc1 Nxc4 14 Rxc4 Bd7 15
Qb3 Qa5=.

(c) (1) 16 Bh6 Re8 17 Kh1!? Rc8 18 Qd4 Bd7 19 Qxa7∞.

(2) 16 Qb1!?

(3) 16 Rb1 Bd7 17 Bh6 Rf7 18 e5 fxe5 19 Qxe5 b5!? (19
... Qb8=) 20 Bd2! (20 Be3 Qb8=) 20 ... Rc8 (20 ... Nb7 21
Bc3 Rf6 22 Ng3∞) 21 Bc3 Rxc3 22 Nxc3±.

(d) 16 f3 Be6 17 d5 Ne5 18 Bb3 Bd7=.

(e) 12 Qe1 Qa5=; 12 h3.

(f) 12 ... e6 13 f5 exf5 14 Bg5 Rf8∞/=.

(g) 14 h3 Bxe2 15 Qxe2 cxd4 16 cxd4 Qb6=; 14 exf5!?

(h) 16 Nf4 Qd7 17 exf5 Na5 18 Qxe6+ Qxe6 19 Nxe6 cxd4!
20 Nxd8+ Rxd8 21 cxd4 Nc6∓.

(i) 10 ... Na5 11 Bd3 c5 12 Rc1 Bb7=/∞.

(j) 16 Rf2 Nc4=.

GRÜNFELD DEFENCE
Exchange Variation

1 d4 Nf6 2 c4 g6 3 Nc3 d5 4 cxd5 (a) Nxd5 5 e4 Nxc3
6 bxc3 Bg7

	(17)	(18)	(19)	(20)
7	Bc4		Nf3 (f)	
	0-0		c5	
8	Ne2		Bb5+	Be3
	Qd7 (b)		Nc6 (g)	0-0
9	0-0		0-0	Rc1
	b6		cxd4 (h)	Qa5
10	e5!?	Be3 (d)	cxd4	Qd2
	Bb7	Bb7	0-0	e6
11	Nf4	f3	Be3	d5!?
	e6	Nc6	Bg4	exd5
12	Qg4	Bb5	Bxc6	exd5
	c5	e6	bxc6	Re8
13	Be3	Rb1	Rc1	Be2
	Nc6	Rad8	Qa5	Bf5
14	Rad1 (c)	Bg5 (e)	Qd2 (i)	0-0 (j)

(a) 4 Nf3 Bg7 5 cxd5 Nxd5 6 e4 Nxc3 7 bxc3 cols 19–20.

(b) 8 ... b6?! 9 h4!; 8 ... Qd7 9 h4? Qg4!

(c) 14 ... cxd4 15 cxd4 Ne7! 16 d5!? Qc8 17 dxe6! Qxc4 18 Rd7 Bc8! 19 Rxe7 Bxe6= (Hort).

(d) 10 f4!? Bb7 11 Qd3 Nc6 12 f5 Na5 13 Bb3∞/±; 13 Ba6!?

(e) ± Hort – Gulko, Polanica Zdroj 1977.

(f) 7 Be3 c5 8 Qd2 Qa5 9 Rb1 cxd4 10 cxd4 Qxd2+ 11 Kxd2 0-0 12 Nf3 Rd8 13 Bd3 Nc6 14 d5 Na5 15 Ke2 b6 16 Bg5 f5 17 Bxe7 fxe4 18 Bxe4 Ba6+= Speelman – Short, London (m) 1991.

(g) 8 ... Bd7 9 Bxd7+ Qxd7 10 0-0 cxd4 11 cxd4 Nc6 12 Be3 0-0 13 d5!±; 9 Be2 0-0 (9 ... Bg4!? 10 Qb3!?∞) 10 0-0 Bg4 11 Be3 cxd4 12 cxd4 Nc6 13 d5! Nb4 14 Qd4!±/±.

(h) (1) 9 ... Qa5 10 Qb3 0-0 11 Bxc6 bxc6 12 Qa3± Larsen – Hort, BBC Master Game Final 1978.
(2) 9 ... 0-0 10 d5 Na5 11 Be3!±.

(i) 14 ... Qxd2 15 Nxd2=.

(j) 14 ... Nd7 15 h3 Nb6 16 g4 Bd7 17 c4= Karpov – Kasparov, World Ch (13), Lyons 1990.

GRÜNFELD DEFENCE
Neo-Grunfeld and 3 f3

1 d4 ♘f6 2 c4 g6

	(21)	(22)	(23)	(24)
3	g3			f3!?
	d5			d5 (i)
4	♗g2			cxd5
	♗g7 (a)			♘xd5
5	cxd5	♘f3		e4
	♘xd5	0-0		♘b6
6	e4	cxd5 (e)		♘c3
	♘b4! (b)	♘xd5		♗g7
7	d5	0-0		♗e3
	c6	♘b6!	c5	0-0!
8	♘e2 (c)	♘c3	dxc5!	f4!?
	cxd5	♘c6	♘a6	♘c6
9	exd5	d5 (f)	♘g5	d5
	♗f5	♘a5	♘db4	♘a5
10	0-0! (d)	e4 (g)	♘c3 (h)	♗d4 (j)

(a) 4 ... dxc4 5 ♕a4+ ♗d7 6 ♕xc4 ♗c6=.

(b) 6 ... ♘b6 7 ♘e2 =/±.

(c) 8 a3 ♘a5 9 ♘c3 cxd5 10 ♗e3 d4 11 axb4 ♕d8=.

(d) (1) 10 0-0! 0-0 11 ♘bc3 ♘8a6 12 ♘f4 ♘c5 13 ♗e3 ♘xd3 14 ♘xd3 ♗xd3 15 ♖e1 ♗a6=.

(2) 10 ♕a4+? ♘8c6 11 ♘bc3 ♘c2+ 12 ♔f1 0-0 13 dxc6 b5 14 c7 ♕xc7 15 ♗f4 e5∓.

(e) 6 0-0 c6 7 cxd5 cxd5 8 ♘c3 ♘e4! 9 ♘e5! ♘xc3 10 bxc3 ♘c6 11 ♘xc6=; 6 ... dxc4 7 ♘a3 ♘c6 8 ♘xc4 ♗e6 9 b3 a5 10 ♗b2 a4=/±.

(f) 9 e3 ♖e8 10 ♖e1 e5 11 d5 ♘a5 12 e4 c6 13 ♗g5 f6 14 ♗e3 ♘ac4!?=/∞ Karpov - Kasparov, Amsterdam 1988.

(g) 10 ... c6=/± e.g. 11 ♘d4 cxd5 12 exd5 e5!=; 11 ♗f4; 11 h3!? cxd5 12 exd5 ♗xc3∞.

(h) 10 ... ♕xd1 11 ♖xd1 ♘xc5±.

(i) 3 ... ♗g7 4 e4 d6 5 ♘c3 - King's Indian Defence, Sämisch Variation cols 29-36.

(j) 10 ... ♗g4! 11 ♕d3 (11 ♘f3 ♗xf3 12 gxf3 e5 13 fxe5 ♘ac4∓) 11 ... e5 12 fxe5 ♘ac4 13 ♕g3 ♕g5? Gheorghiu - Jansa, Warsaw (zt) 1979; 13 ... ♗h5∞.

MODERN BENONI
Fianchetto Variation

**1 d4 Nf6 2 c4 c5 3 d5 e6 4 Nc3 exd5 5 cxd5 d6
6 Nf3 g6 7 g3 Bg7 8 Bg2 0-0 9 0-0**

	(1)	(2)	(3)	(4)
9	Nbd7 (a)	Re8		Qe7 (i)
10	Nd2	h3	Bf4!? (f)	Nd2
	a6	Ne4	a6	Nbd7
11	a4	Nxe4	a4	Nc4!? (j)
	Re8	Rxe4	Ne4	Ne5
12	h3	Bg5	Nxe4	Nxe5
	Rb8 (b)	Qc7	Rxe4	Qxe5
13	Nc4	Nd2	Nd2	a4
	Ne5	Re8	Rb4	a6
14	Na3	Bf4 (d)	Ne4	Bf4
	Nh5	Nd7	h6	Qe7
15	e4	Nc4	Bd2 (g)	Qd2±
	Rf8! (c)	Ne5 (e)	Rxb2 (h)	

(a) 9 ... a6 10 a4 Nbd7 11 Bf4 Qe7 12 h3 Rb8 13 e4 b5 14 axb5 axb5 15 Re1± Razuvaev - Psakhis, Irkutsk 1986.

(b) 12 ... Nh5 13 Kh2 f5 14 f4 Ndf6 15 e4∞/±.

(c) (1) 15 ... f5? 16 exf5 Bxf5 17 g4 Bxg4 18 hxg4 Qh4 19 gxh5 Rf8! (19 ... Ng4 20 Bf4 Be5 21 Qf3 Rf8 22 Qg3+-) 20 h6 Bh8 21 Nc4! Ng4 22 Qxg4 Qxg4 23 Nxd6± Kovacevic - Nemet, Karlovac 1979.

(2) 15 ... Rf8! 16 Kh2 Korchnoi - Kasparov, Lucerne (ol) 1982 16 ... Bd7 17 f4 b5!∞.

(d) 14 Ne4?! Rxe4 15 Bxe4 Bxh3 16 Bg2 Bxg2 17 Kxg2=/∓ Kuzmin - Tal, Riga (izt) 1979 (Rd. 4).

(e) 16 Nxe5 Bxe5 17 Bxe5 Rxe5 18 e4± Kuzmin - Bouaziz, Riga (izt) 1979 (Rd. 11).

(f) 10 Nd2 Nbd7 - col 1; 10 ... Na6; 10 ... b6.

(g) 15 Ra2! Bh3!∞ Adorjan - I Armas, W Germany 1990.

(h) 16 Qc1 Rxd2 17 Qxd2 f5 18 Nc3 Qa5 19 Rac1∞.

(i) 9 ... Na6 10 Nd2 Nc7 11 Nc4 Nfe8 12 a4 b6 13 Qc2 Na6 14 b3 Nb4 15 Qd2 a6 16 Bb2± Adorjan - Speelman, Lucerne 1989.

(j) 11 h3!? Nh5 12 Kh2 f5 13 f4±; 11 ... b6!?

1 d4 Nf6 2 c4 c5 3 d5 e6 4 Nc3 exd5 5 cxd5 d6 6 Nf3 g6

Knight's Tour

	(5)	(6)	(7)	(8)
7	Nd2 / Bg7		Bg5 / h6! (f)	Bf4 / a6 (g)
8	Nc4 / 0-0		Bh4 / g5	a4 (h) / Bg7
9	Bg5 / h6 (a)	Bf4 / Ne8 (c)	Bg3 / Nh5	e4 (i) / 0-0
10	Bf4 / b6	Qd2 (d) / b6	e3 / Nxg3	Be2 / Bg4
11	Bxd6 / Re8	e3 / Ba6	hxg3 / Bg7	h3 / Bxf3
12	Bg3 / Ne4	a4 / f5	Bd3 / Nd7	Bxf3 / Qc7
13	Nxe4 / Rxe4 (b)	Be2 / Qf6 (e)	Qc2= / Qe7=	0-0 / Nbd7= (j)

(a) 9 ... Qe7 10 e3 Nbd7 11 Be2 Ne5 12 Nxe5 Qxe5 13 Bf4 Qe7= Gulko - Wahls, Groningen 1990.

(b) 14 e3 b5 15 Nd2 Rb4 16 b3 c4!∞/= Chandler - Denman, Brighton 1980; 16 ... Bxa1? 17 Qxa1± Petrosian - Nunn, Hastings 1977/78.

(c) 9 ... b6!? 10 Bxd6 Re8 11 Bg3 Ne4 12 Nxe4 Rxe4 13 e3 b5 14 Nd6 Rb4 15 Be2! Bxb2 16 Rb1∞/± cf. col 6.

(d) 10 e3? g5! 11 Bg5 f5∓.

(e) 14 Bg3 Bxc4 15 Bxc4 a6 16 0-0 Nd7 17 f4 Nc7= Osnos - Forintos, Leningrad - Budapest 1962.

(f) 7 ... Bg7 8 Nd2 h6 9 Bh4 g5 10 Bg3 Nh5 11 Qa4+ Kf8=; 8 e3 h6 (8 ... 0-0 9 Nd2±) 9 Bh4 g5 10 Bg3 Nh5.

(g) 7 ... Bg7 8 Qa4+! Bd7 9 Qb3 Qc7 (9 ... b5!?∞) 10 e4±/=.

(h) 8 Nd2!? b5 9 a4 Nh5 10 Be3 b4 11 Nce4 Nd7= A Petrosian - Guseinov, USSR 1991.

(i) 9 e3=.

(j) Vaganian - Tal, USSR Ch 1971.

MODERN BENONI

1 d4 ♘f6 2 c4 c5 3 d5 e6 4 ♘c3 exd5 5 cxd5 d6 6 e4 g6

	(9)	(10)	(11)	(12)
7	f4		♘f3	
	♗g7		♗g7	
8	e5!?	♗b5+ (c)	♗g5	
	♘fd7!	♘fd7! (d)	h6	
9	♘b5	a4 (e)	♗h4	
	dxe5	0-0	g5?!	a6!
10	♘d6+	♘f3	♗g3	♘d2!? (i)
	♔e7!	♘a6	♘h5	b5
11	♘xc8+	0-0	♗b5+	♗e2 (j)
	♕xc8	♘c7	♔f8	0-0
12	♘f3 (a)	♗d3	e5!	♕c2
	♖e8	a6	♘xg3 (g)	♘bd7
13	♗c4∞ (b)	♘d2 (f)	fxg3! (h)	a4 (k)

(a) 12 d6+ ♔f8 13 ♘f3 ♘c6 14 ♗e2 h6 15 fxe5 ♘dxe5∓.

(b) (1) 13 fxe5 ♘xe5 14 ♗b5 ♘bd7 15 ♘xe5 ♔f8! 16 0-0∞/= e.g. 16 ... ♖xe5 17 ♗f4 c4 18 ♕d4 ♖f5 19 ♕xc4 ♕xc4 20 ♗xc4=.

(2) 13 ♗c4!? ♔f8 14 0-0 e4 15 ♘g5 h6 16 ♘h3!∞/∓; 16 ♘xf7?! ♗d4+ 17 ♔h1 ♔xf7 18 f5 ♘f6 19 fxg6+ ♔g7∓ Gigerl – Grünfeld, Groningen 1974/75.

(c) 8 ♘f3 0-0 9 ♗e2 – King's Indian Defence cols 21-22.

(d) 8 ... ♘bd7? 9 e5 dxe5 10 fxe5 ♘h5 11 e6 fxe6 12 dxe6 0-0 13 ♘f3! ♖xf3 14 ♕xf3 ♗xc3+ 15 bxc3 ♘e5 16 ♕e4±.

(e) 9 a4; 9 ♗e2!?; 9 ♗d3 0-0 10 ♘f3 ♘a6 11 0-0 ♘c7=.

(f) 13 ... ♘f6 14 h3 ♖b8 15 a5 ♖e8!∞ Lukacs – Sö Maus, Budapest 1990.

(g) 12 ... g4 13 ♗h4!

(h) 13 ... dxe5 14 0-0 a6 15 ♗e2∞/±.

(i) 10 a4=.

(j) 11 a4 b4 12 ♘cb1 0-0 13 ♗d3 ♖e8 14 0-0 ♕c7 15 ♕c2 ♘bd7 16 ♘c4 b3!∓ Veresov – Suetin, Bielorussian Ch 1961.

(k) 13 ... b4 14 ♘d1 ♖e8 15 0-0∞/= Taimanov – Boleslavsky, USSR Team Ch 1960.

Penrose – Tal Variation and Main Line

1 d4 ♘f6 2 c4 c5 3 d5 e6 4 ♘c3 exd5 5 cxd5 d6 6 e4 g6

Penrose – Tal Variation

	(13)	(14)	(15)	(16)
7	♗d3 (a)		♘f3	
	♗g7		♗g7	
8	♘ge2		♗e2	
	0-0		0-0	
9	0-0		0-0 (g)	
	a6	b6 (e)	♘a6 (h)	a6
10	a4	h3 (f)	♗f4	a4
	♕c7	♗a6	♘c7	♗g4
11	h3 (b)	♗g5	a4	♗f4! (j)
	♘bd7	h6	b6	♗xf3
12	f4	♗h4	♘d2	♗xf3
	♖b8 (c)	♗xd3	♖e8	♖e8
13	♘g3	♕xd3	♖e1	♖e1
	c4 (d)	♘bd7=	♗a6 (i)	♕c7 (k)

(a) 7 f3 ♗g7 8 ♗g5 h6 9 ♗e3±/=; 7 ♗f4 ♗g7 (7 ... a6) 8 ♗b5+ ♗d7 9 ♗e2 ♕e7 10 ♘f3 0-0=.

(b) 11 b3!? ♘bd7 12 ♔h1 ♖e8 13 f3 ♖b8 14 a5 b5 15 axb6 ♖xb6 16 ♗d2 ♘e5 17 ♗c2 c4 18 ♗e3 ♖b4 19 ♘a2 ♖b8 20 b4±.

(c) 12 ... ♖e8? 13 ♘g3 c4 14 ♗c2 ♘c5 15 ♕f3 ♘fd7 16 ♗e3 b5 17 axb5 ♖b8 18 ♕f2! axb5 19 e5 dxe5 20 f5!± Penrose – Tal, Leipzig (ol) 1960.

(d) 14 ♗c2 b5 15 axb5 axb5 16 ♗e3 b4 17 ♖a7 ♕d8 18 ♘a4 ♖b5 19 b3 c3= Bertok – Portisch, Stockholm (izt) 1962.

(e) 9 ... ♘a6?! 10 h3 (10 ♗g5) 10 ... ♘c7 11 a4 b6 12 ♗g5 h6 13 ♗h4 ♕e8 14 f4 ♗a6 15 ♔h1±.

(f) 10 ♘g3 ♗g4!?∞ Flear – Velimirovic, Zenica 1987.

(g) 9 ♘d2 avoids cols 16-17; 9 ... ♖e8 10 0-0 cols 19-20.

(h) 9 ... b6 10 ♗g5 h6 11 ♗h4 ♗a6 (11 ... g5!? 12 ♗g3 ♘h5±) 12 ♘d2±; 9 ... ♘bd7 10 ♘d2 ♖e8 col 20; 9 ... ♗g4 10 ♗f4 a6 11 a4 cols 16-17.

(i) 14 ♗xa6 ♘xa6 15 ♘c4 ♗f8±/±.

(j) 11 h3?! ♗xf3 12 ♗xf3 ♘bd7=; 11 ♘d2; 11 ♗g5.

(k) 14 e5!? (14 ♕c2±/=) 14 ... dxe5 15 d6 ♕d7 16 ♖xe5 ♖xe5 17 ♗xe5 ♘c6 18 ♗xf6 ♗xf6 19 ♘e4±.

MODERN BENONI
Main Line

**1 d4 Nf6 2 c4 c5 3 d5 e6 4 Nc3 exd5 5 cxd5 d6
6 e4 g6 7 Nf3 Bg7 8 Be2 0-0 9 0-0**

	(17)	(18)	(19)	(20)
9	a6	Re8		
10	a4	Qc2	Nd2	
	Bg4	Na6	Na6	Nbd7 (f)
11	Bf4	Re1!? (b)	f3!	Qc2 (g)
	Re8	Bg4	Nc7	Ne5 (h)
12	Nd2	Bf4	a4	b3 (i)
	Bxe2	c4!	b6	Nh5!?/?! (j)
13	Qxe2	Bxc4	Kh1 (d)	Bxh5
	Nh5	Bxf3	Rb8	gxh5
14	Be3	gxf3	Nc4	Bb2
	Nd7	Nh5	Ba6	Nd7
15	g4!? (a)	Bg3	Bg5	Rae1
	Nhf6	Be5	h6	Qh4 (k)
16	h3±	Bf1 (c)	Ne3 (e)	

(a) 15 a5 Qc7 16 h4 Nhf6 17 f3±.

(b) 11 Bf4 Nb4 12 Qb1 Nh5! (12 ... Nxe4!!? 13 Nxe4 Bf5 14 Nfd2 Nxd5 15 Bg3! Bg6 16 Bb5±; 15 Bxd6? Nf6 16 Bf3 Nxe4∓ Averbakh – Tal, USSR Ch 1958) 13 Bg5 f6 14 Be3 f5 15 a3 fxe4 16 Ng5 Nd3=.

(c) ∞/∓ Nemet – Rogulj, Karlovac 1979.

(d) 13 Nc4 Ba6 14 Bg5±.

(e) 16 ... Bxc4 17 Bxc4 a6 18 Qd3 Qc8 19 Bf4!±/±.

(f) 10 ... a6 11 a4 Nbd7 12 Qc2 Ne5 13 Ra3±.

(g) 11 Re1 Ne5 12 a4 a6 13 h3 g5 14 Nf1∞ Ivanchuk – De Firmian, Biel 1989.

(h) 11 ... Nh5?! 12 Bxh5 gxh5 13 Nd1! (13 Nc4 Ne5 14 Ne3 Qh4= Spassky – Fischer, World Ch (3) 1972) 13 ... Ne5 14 a4± Gligoric – Kavalek, Skopje (ol) 1972.

(i) 12 a4 g5 13 Ra3 g4 14 Nd1 Nh5 15 g3 Qf6 16 Ne3 Nf3+ 17 Bxf3 gxf3 18 Nf5 Bxf5 19 exf5± Nunn.

(j) 12 ... g5(!)±/= Korchnoi – Mecking (m) 1974.

(k) 16 Nd1±; 16 f4? Bg4 17 Nf3 Bd4+ 18 Kh1 Nf2+ 19 Rxf2 Qxf2 20 Qc1 Bh3!∓ Polugaevsky – Nunn, European Team Ch, Skara 1980.

BENKO GAMBIT

1 d4 ♞f6 2 c4 c5 3 d5 b5

	(1)	(2)	(3)	(4)
4	cxb5			
	a6			
5	♞c3!?	e3 *(a)*	bxa6	
	axb5	g6	♗xa6	
6	e4	♞c3	♞c3	
	b4	♗g7	d6	
7	♞b5	♞f3	♞f3	
	d6	0–0	g6	
8	♗f4	♗e2!? *(b)*	g3	
	g5!	d6 *(c)*	♗g7	
9	♗e3	0–0	♗g2	♗h3
	♞xe4∞/=	e6 *(d)*	♞bd7 *(e)*	♞bd7 *(f)*

(a) (1) 5 f3!? e6 6 e4 exd5 7 e5 ♛e7 8 ♛e2 ♞g8 9 ♞c3 ♗b7 10 ♞h3 c4 11 ♗e3!± Dlugy – Alburt, USA Ch 1991.

(2) 5 b6 d6 6 ♞c3 ♞bd7 7 a4 ♛xb6?! 8 a5 ♛c7 9 e4 g6 10 f4!± Shirov – Hauchard, Paris 1990.

(b) 8 a4 e6?! 9 e4 ♗b7=; 9 d6!?; 9 bxa6?! ♞xa6 10 ♗c4 ♞b4=/∓ Reinhardt – Szmetan, Argentina 1977; 8 ... d6 9 ♗e2=; 9 ♖a3!?

(c) 8 ... axb5 9 ♗xb5 ♛a5; 9 ... e6.

(d) 10 e4 exd5 11 ♞xd5 ♞xe4 12 ♖e1∞/± Speelman – Fedorowicz, Brighton 1979.

(e) 10 0–0 0–0 11 ♛c2 ♛b6 12 ♖b1 ♖fb8 13 b3 ♞e8 14 ♞d2 ♛a5 15 ♗b2± Korchnoi – Quinteros, Leningrad (izt) 1973; 11 ... ♛a5 12 ♗d2 (12 ♖d1 ♞g4 13 ♗d2 ♖fb8 14 b3 ♛b6 15 h3 ♞ge5 16 ♞xe5 ♞xe5∞ van der Sterren – Adams, Ter Apel 1992) 12 ... ♖fb8 13 h3 ♞e8 14 ♖fc1 ♞c7 15 b3 c4 16 ♖ab1 cxb3 17 axb3 ♞b5 18 ♞xb5 ♛xb5 19 ♛e4± Donner – Browne, Wijk aan Zee 1975.

(f) 10 0–0 0–0 11 ♛c2 ♗c4 13 ♖d1 ♖a7 13 e4 ♛a8∞ Furman – Geller, USSR 1975.

BENONI

1 d4 ♘f6 2 c4 c5 3 d5

	Benko Gambit		Czech Benoni	
	(5)	(6)	(7)	(8)
3	b5		e5 (e)	
4	cxb5	a4!? (b)	♘c3	
	a6	bxc4	d6	
5	bxa6	♘c3	e4	
	♗xa6	e6	♗e7	
6	♘c3	e4	♘f3	♗d3
	d6	exd5	0-0	0-0
7	e4	e5!? (c)	♗e2	♘ge2
	♗xf1	d4	♘e8	♘e8
8	♔xf1	exf6	0-0	♘g3
	g6	d5!	♘d7	a6
9	g3	♗xc4!	a3	h4
	♗g7	dxc4	g6	g6±
10	♔g2 (a)	♕f3 (d)	♗h6±	

(a) 10 ... 0-0 11 ♘f3 ♘bd7 12 ♖e1∞/± e.g.

(1) 12 ... ♕b6 13 ♖e2 ♖fb8 14 h3 ♘e8 15 ♗f4 ♕a6 16 ♖c1 ♘c7 17 e5∞/±.

(2) 12 ... ♘g4 13 ♖e2 ♕a5 14 ♗g5 ♖fe8 15 ♖c1±.

(3) 12 ... ♕a5 13 ♖e1 ♖fb8 14 e5 dxe5 15 ♘xe5 ♘xe5 16 ♖xe5 ♖a7 17 ♕e2 ♖bb7 18 g4 ♘e8 19 ♖e3 ♘d6 20 a4 c4 21 ♖f3 ♗xc3 22 bxc3 ♕xd5 23 ♗h6 ♕e4 24 ♕xe4 ♘xe4 25 ♖f4 ♘d6 26 ♖d4 ♖b3 ½–½ Spassky – Ivanchuk, Linares 1990.

(b) 4 ♘c3 b4=; 4 ♘f3; 4 f3!?; 4 ♘d2 bxc4 5 e4 ♕a5!?

(c) 7 exd5=.

(d) 10 ... dxc3 11 ♕xa8∞/=/∓ Keene – Borik, EEC Team Ch, Berlin 1980.

(e) 3 ... e6 4 ♘f3 b5!? (4 ... exd5 5 cxd5 d6 6 ♘c3 g6 – Modern Benoni) Blumenfeld Counter-Gambit:

(1) 5 dxe6 fxe6 6 cxb5 d5∞.

(2) 5 e4!?∞.

(3) 5 ♗f4!? exd5 6 cxd5 ♕a5+ 7 ♗d2 ♕b6∞.

(4) 5 ♗g5(!) exd5 6 cxd5 d6 7 e4 a6 8 a4!?±/± e.g. 8 ... ♗e7 9 ♗xf6 ♗xf6 10 axb5 ♗xb2 11 ♖a2 ♗f6 12 ♘bd2± Vaganian – Grigorian, USSR Ch 1971; 6 ... h6 7 ♗xf6 ♕xf6 8 ♕c2 d6 9 e4 a6 10 a4 b4 11 ♘fd2 ♗e7 12 ♘c4±.

1 d4 Various

1 d4

	Veresov (1)	Trompowsky (2)	Budapest (3)	(4)
1	d5	♘f6		
2	♘c3 (a)	♗g5 [Dia]	c4	d6 (l)
	♘f6	♘e4 (f)	e5!?	
3	♗g5	♗h4	dxe5 [Dia]	♘c3
	♘bd7 (b)	g5	♘g4 (i)	♗f5!?
4	♘f3 (c)	f3	♘f3 (j)	f3
	h6	gxh4	♗c5	e5
5	♗h4	fxe4	e3	e4
	e6	c5	♘c6	exd4
6	e4!? (d)	e3	♗e2	♕xd4
	g5	♕b6!? (g)	♘gxe5	♘c6
7	♗g3	♘f3	0-0	♕d1
	♘xe4	♕xb2	0-0	♗e6
8	♘xe4 (e)	♘d2 (h)	♘xe5 (k)	♗d3±

(column 2)

(column 3)

1 d4 (continued)

(a) (1) 2 e4!? Blackmar – Diemer Gambit 2 ... dxe4 3 Nc3
Nf6 4 f3 exf3 5 Nxf3 Bg4 6 h3 Bh5∞/∓; 6 ... Bxf3!? 7 Qxf3
c6 8 Be3∞/=/∓.

　　(2) 2 Nf3 Nf6 3 e3 Colle System (3 c4 Queen's Gambit) 3 ... e6 4 Bd3 c5 5 c3 (5 b3) 5 ... Nc6 6 Nbd2 Bd6 7 0-0
0-0 8 dxc5 Bxc5 9 e4 Qc7! 10 Qe2 Bd6 11 Re1 Ng4 12 h3
Nge5 13 Nxe5 Nxe5=; 3 ... g6 4 Bd3 Bg7 5 0-0 0-0 6 Nbd2
c6 (6 ... Bf5!?=) 7 e4 dxe4 8 Nxe4 Nxe4 9 Bxe4 Bg4=.

(b) 3 ... Bf5 4 Bxf6 exf6 5 e3=/±.

(c) (1) 4 f3 c6!? 5 e4 dxe4 6 fxe4 e5 7 dxe5 Qa5 8 Bxf6
gxf6 9 e6 fxe6 10 Bc4 Ba3!!-+.

　　(2) 4 Qd3!? △ 4 e4=.

(d) 6 Qd3=; 6 e3=.

(e) 8 ... dxe4 9 Nd2 Qd7∞ e.g. 10 h4!? Bxd4 11 c3 Bg7∞.

(f) 2 ... g6?! 3 Bxf6±; 2 ... e6 3 e4 h6 4 Bxf6 Qxf6 5 Nf3±
d6 6 Nc3 c6 7 Qd2 e5 8 0-0-0 Be7 9 Kb1 Nd7 10 h4 exd4 11
Nxd4 Ne5 12 f4 Ng4 13 h5 Bd8 14 Ndb5 cxb5 15 Bxb5+ Bd7
16 Bxd7+ Kxd7 17 Qe2 Qxf4 18 Rhf1 Qg5 19 Rf5 Qh4 20
Qb5+ Kc8 21 Rxf7 Be7 22 Nd5 1-0 Hodgson – Zsu Polgar,
Haifa 1989; 2 ... c5 3 d5 Qb6 4 Nc3 Qxb2 5 Bd2∞; 3 ... Ne4;
3 Bxf6; 2 ... c6!? 3 Bxf6 exf6 4 c4±/=.

(g) 6 ... Bh6 7 Kf2=/±; 6 ... e6.

(h) 8 ... Qc3 9 Bd3∞

(i) 3 ... Ne4 4 Nf3 Nc6 5 Nbd2 Nc5 6 a3±/±.

(j) 4 e4 Nxe4 5 f4±/∞; 4 Bf4.

(k) 8 ... Nxe5 9 Nc3 Re8 10 Kh1 a5 11 f4 Nc6 12 Bd3 d6 13
Qh5 h6 14 Rf3 Nb4 15 Be4 c6 16 Rg3 Qf6 17 Bd2 Na6 18 a3
Kf8 19 Bd3 Ba7 20 Ne2 Nc5 21 Bc3 Qxc3 22 Nxc3 Nxd3 23
Rf1 Bxe3 24 Qe2 Nxf4 25 Qd1 1-0 Spassky – Illescas, Li-
nares 1990.

(l) 5 d5 e4 6 g4 Nxg4 7 fxg4 Qh4+ 8 Kd2 e3+ =.

1 d4 f5

Fluid (1)	Stonewall (2)	Leningrad (3)	Staunton Gambit (4)
2 c4			e4!? (i)
♘f6			fxe4
3 g3			♘c3
e6		g6	♘f6
4 ♗g2		♗g2	♗g5 (j)
♗e7		♗g7	♘c6
5 ♘f3 (a)		♘f3 (f)	d5
0-0		0-0	♘e5
6 0-0		0-0	♕d4
d6	d5 (d)	d6	♘f7
7 ♘c3	b3 (e)	♘c3	♗xf6 (k)
♕e8 (b)	c6	c6 (g)	exf6
8 b3 (c)	♗a3	d5	♘xe4
a5	♘bd7	e5	♗e7
9 ♗b2±	♗xe7=/±	dxe6 (h)	0-0-0=

(a) 5 ♘h3 0-0 6 0-0 d6 7 ♘c3 ♕e8 8 ♘f4 g5 9 ♘d3 ♕g6 10 f4 h6 11 d5±/± Karpov - Short, Linares 1992.

(b) 7 ... c6; 7 ... a5.

(c) (1) 8 ♖e1 ♕g6 9 e4 dxe4 10 ♘xe4 ♘xe4 11 ♖xe4 ♘c6 (11 ... ♕xe4? 12 ♘h4!) 12 ♖e1 e5 13 dxe5 ♗g4 14 exd6 ♗xd6∞.
    (2) 8 ♕c2 ♕h5 9 b3 (9 e4!?) 9 ... a5 10 ♗b2 ♘a6±.

(d) 6 ... c6 △ 7 b3 d6!; △ 7 ♘c3 d5.

(e) 7 ♘c3 c6 8 b3 a5 9 ♗b2=/±.

(f) 5 ♘h3 0-0 6 ♘c3 d6 7 d5 c6 8 ♘f4 ♕e8=/±.

(g) 7 ... ♘c6 8 d5 ♘a5 (8 ... ♘e5 9 ♘xe5 dxe5±) 9 ♘d2 c5 10 a3 ♗d7 11 ♕c2±.

(h) 9 ... ♗xe6 10 ♕d3±.

(i) (1) 2 ♗g5 g6 3 ♘c3 ♗g7 4 e4 dxe4 5 ♘xe4 d5 6 ♘c3 ♘f6=/±.
    (2) 2 ♘c3 ♘f6 (2 ... g6!? 3 e4 dxe4 4 ♘xe4 d5 5 ♘g5!?±) 3 ♗g5 d5!=. (1 d4 e6 2 c4 f5 avoids col 4).

(j) 4 f3 d5 (4 ... e3) 5 fxe4 dxe4 6 ♗g5 ♗f5 7 ♗c4 ♘c6 8 ♘ge2 ♕d7 9 0-0 e6 10 ♕e1 0-0-0=; 4 ... exf3 5 ♘xf3 g6 6 ♗f4∞.

(k) 7 h4 c6 8 0-0-0 ♕b6 9 ♗xf6 gxf6 10 ♕xe4 ♕xf2!∓.

1 c4

	(1)	(2)	(3)	(4)
1	♘f6 (a)		g6	c5
2	♘c3		e4! (e)	♘c3
	e6		e5 (f)	♘c6
3	e4		d4	g3
	c5	d5	♘f6	g6
4	e5	e5	♘f3	♗g2
	♘g8	d4 (c)	♗b4+	♗g7
5	d4 (b)	exf6	♗d2	a3 (j)
	cxd4	dxc3	♗xd2+	a6!?
6	♕xd4	bxc3	♕xd2!? (g)	♖b1
	♘c6	♕xf6	♘xe4	♖b8
7	♕e4	d4	♕e3 (h)	b4
	d6	c5	f5!	cxb4
8	♘f3±	♘f3 (d)	dxe5 (i)	axb4 (k)

(a) 1 ... e6 2 ♘c3 d5 3 d4 – Queen's Gambit Declined.

(b) 5 ♘f3!? ♘c6 6 d4 cxd4 7 ♘xd4 ♘xe5 8 ♘db5 a6 9 ♘d6+ ♗xd6 10 ♕xd6 f6 11 ♗e3 ♘e7 12 ♗b6 ♘f5 13 ♕c5 d6 14 ♕a5 ♕d7 15 f4⩲ Kasparov – Beliavsky, Linares 1991.

(c) 4 ... ♘e4?! 5 ♘xe4 dxe4 6 ♕g4 ♗d7 (6 ... ♘c6 7 ♕xe4±) 7 ♕xe4 ♗c6 8 ♕e3 ♘a6 9 d4 ♘b4 10 ♔d2!± Seirawan – Timman, Wijk aan Zee 1980.

(d) 8 ... h6 9 ♗d3±; 8 ... cxd4 9 ♗g5±.

(e) 2 ♘c3 c5 3 g3 – col 4; 3 ♘f3 ♗g7 △ 4 d4 cxd4 5 ♘xd4 ♗g7 6 e3=; 6 ♘c2?! ♗xc3+.

(f) 2 ... ♗g7 3 d4 d6 4 ♘c3 ♘f6 – King's Indian Defence.

(g) 6 ♘bxd2=/±.

(h) 7 ♕h6!?/?! exd4 8 ♗d3 ♘c5 9 0-0! d6!∞/∓ Kuligowski- Adorjan, Warsaw (zt) 1979.

(i) 8 ... ♕e7 9 ♘c3 ♘xc3! 10 ♕xc3 ♘a6 11 ♗e2 ♕b4? (11 ... b6!=) 12 ♕xb4 ♘xb4 13 0-0 ♘c6 14 c5!±/± Speelman – Hartston, Hastings 1978/79.

(j) 5 e3 e6 6 ♘ge2 ♘ge7 7 0-0 0-0 8 d4 cxd4 9 ♘xd4 ♘xd4 10 exd4 d5 11 cxd5 ♘xd5=; 5 e5 h5!? △ ... ♘h6-h5; 5 e3 ♘h6; 5 ♘f3; 5 d3 △ ♕d2, b3, ♗b2.

(k) 8 ... b5 9 c5!? (9 cxb5 axb5 10 ♘e4!?) 9 ... a5 10 ♗a3 axb4 11 ♗xb4 ♘xb4 12 ♖xb4 ♗xc3! 13 bxc3=.

ENGLISH OPENING

1 c4

	(5)	(6)	(7)	(8)
1	c5	b6!?	e5	
2	♘f3 (a)	d4	♘c3	
	♘f6	e6 (e)	♘f6 (g)	
3	♘c3 (b)	e4	♘f3 (h)	
	♘c6 (c)	♗b7	♘c6 (i)	
4	d4!?	♘c3	g3	e3 (m)
	cxd4	♗b4	♗b4 (j)	♗b4
5	♘xd4	f3 (f)	♘d5	♕c2
	e6	f5!?	e4 (k)	0-0!? (n)
6	g3	exf5	♘h4	♘d5
	♕b6	♘h6∞	♗c5	♖e8
7	♘b3		♗g2	♕f5!? (o)
	♗b4 (d)		d6 (l)	

(a) 2 b3!?; 2 g3 etc.

(b) 3 d4 cxd4 4 ♘xd4 ♘c6 (4 … e6; 4 … e5!? 5 ♘b5 d5 6 cxd5 ♗c5⩱) 5 ♘c3 e6 – the column.

(c) 3 … e6 4 d4 cxd4 5 ♘xd4 ♘c6 the column; 4 g3 d5 5 cxd5 exd5 6 d4 – QGD Tarrasch; 3 … e6 4 g3 b6 – 'Hedgehog' e.g. 5 ♗g2 ♗b7 6 0-0 ♗e7 7 d4 cxd4 8 ♕xd4=.

(d) (1) 7 … ♗b4(!) 8 ♗g2 ♕a6 9 ♘d2 ♗xc3 10 bxc3 0-0 11 0-0 d5= Korchnoi – Spassky (m) 1977/78.
(2) 7 … ♘e5!? 8 e4 ♗b4 9 ♕e2∞/±.

(e) 2 … ♗b7 3 d5 e6 4 a3±/±(?).

(f) 5 ♗d3 f5 6 exf5!?/?! ♗xg2∞ Browne – Miles, Tilburg 1978.

(g) 2 … d6!? △ 3 ♘f3 f5; 3 g3(!) ♘f6±; 3 … ♗e6 4 ♘f3±.

(h) 3 g3 ♗b4 (3 … c6!?) 4 ♗g2 0-0 5 ♘f3 ♖e8 6 0-0 e4=; 3 g3 d5!? 4 cxd5 ♘xd5 5 ♗g2 ♘b6±.

(i) 3 … e4?! 4 ♘g5 b5 5 d3! exd3 6 cxb5±.

(j) 4 … ♘d4 5 ♗g2 (5 ♘xe5?! ♕e7) 5 … ♘xf3+ 6 ♗xf3 ♗c5±.

(k) 5 … ♗c5.

(l) 8 0-0 ♗e6 9 ♘xf6+ ♕xf6 10 ♗xe4 ♗xc4 11 ♕a4!±/±.

(m) 4 d3; 4 d4 exd4 5 ♘xd4 ♗b4 6 ♗g5 h6 7 ♗h4 ♗xc3+ 8 bxc3 d6=.

(n) 5 … ♗xc3! 6 ♕xc3 (6 bxc3!?±) 6 … ♕e7=.

(o) 7 ♗d3 g6=; 7 ♕f5!? d6 8 ♘xf6+ gxf6 9 ♕h5∞/±.

1 ♘f3

	Reti		KIA	
	(1)	(2)	(3)	(4)
1	d5			♘f6 (h)
2	c4		g3 (e)	g3
	d4	c6 (c)	c5	g6
3	e3 (a)	b3	♗g2	♗g2
	♘c6	♘f6	♘c6	♗g7
4	exd4	♗b2	0-0 (f)	0-0
	♘xd4	♗f5	e6	0-0
5	♘xd4	g3	d3	c4
	♕xd4	e6	♘f6	d6
6	♘c3	♗g2	♘bd2	♘c3 (i)
	e5	h6	♗e7	e5!?
7	d3	0-0	e4	d3
	♘e7!	♗e7	0-0	♘c6
8	♕e2	d3	♖e1	♖b1= (j)
	♗d7 (b)	♘bd7 (d)	b5 (g)	

(a) 3 b4!?; 3 g3 c5 4 ♗g2 ♘c6 5 d3 e5= Benoni Reversed; 3 d3 △ 3 ... c5 4 e3!± Modern Benoni Reversed; 3 ... ♘c6 4 g3=.

(b) 9 ♗e3 ♕d6 10 0-0-0 0-0-0= Bagirov - A Mikhalchisin, USSR Ch 1978.

(c) 2 ... e6 3 g3 ♘f6 4 ♗g2 ♗e7 5 0-0 0-0 6 d4 Catalan cols 2-4; 2 ... e6 3 d4 QGD; 2 ... dxc4 3 e3 QGA; 3 ♘a3!?

(d) 9 ♘bd2 0-0 10 a3 a5 11 ♕c2= Botvinnik - Smyslov, World Ch (12) 1958.

(e) 2 b3; 2 d4 QGD; etc.

(f) 4 d4 e6 - Catalan.

(g) 9 e5 ♘d7 10 ♘f1 b4=.

(h) 1 ... c5 2 e4 - Sicilian Defence; 2 g3; 2 b3; 1 ... f5 2 e4?!; 2 d4 - Dutch Defence; 1 ... ♘c6!?; 1 ... d6 etc.

(i) 7 d4 - King's Indian Defence.

(j) e.g: 8 ... ♘h5 9 b4 f5 10 b5 ♘e7; 8 ... ♘d4!?=.

UNUSUAL OPENINGS

	Bird's Opening (1)	(2)	Larsen (3)	Sokolsky (4)
1	f4		b3	b4 *(j)*
	e5!?	d5 *(d)*	e5 *(f)*	d5 *(k)*
2	fxe5 *(a)*	♘f3	♗b2	♗b2
	d6	♘f6	♘c6	♘f6
3	exd6	e3	e3	e3
	♗xd6	g6	d5!? *(g)*	e6
4	♘f3	♗e2	♗b5	a3
	♘f6 *(b)*	♗g7	♗d6	a5
5	d4	0-0	♘f3 *(h)*	b5
	♘g4	0-0	f6	c5
6	♕d3	d3	c4 *(i)*	f4!?
	c5∞ *(c)*	c5= *(e)*		b6 *(l)*

(a) 2 e4 King's Gambit; column is From's Gambit.

(b) 4 ... g5!? 5 d4 g4 6 ♘e5 ♗xe5 7 dxe5 ♕xd1+ 8 ♔xd1= .

(c) e.g. 7 ♕e4+ ♗e6 8 ♘g5 ♗xh2 9 ♘xe6 ♕h4+ 10 ♔d2 fxe6 11 ♖xh2 ♕g5+ 12 e3 ♘xh2 13 ♕xe6+∞ Gigas – Farre. corr 1961-2.

(d) 1 ... ♘f6; 1 ... g6; 1 ... b6 etc.

(e) Dutch Reversed.

(f) 1 ... d5; 1 ... b6 2 ♗b2 ♗b7=.

(g) 3 ... ♘f6 4 ♗b5 d6=; 4 ... ♗d6!?=.

(h) 5 f4 f6∞.

(i) 6 d4=; 6 c4 a6! 7 cxd5 axb5 8 dxc6=.

(j) 1 g3 d5 2 ♘f3 Reti col 3; 2 ♗g2=; 1 a3, 1 c3, 1 ♘c3 1 ... g6= etc.

(k) 1 ... c6 2 ♗b2?! ♕b6!; 2 c4; 1 ... e5 2 ♗b2 f6!?; 2 ... d6=: 2 ... ♗xb4!? 3 ♗xe5 ♘f6=; 1 ... a5.

(l) 7 ♘f3 ♘bd7∞/=/∓ Ljubojevic – Matanovic, Yugoslavia 1969.